A ROYAL CONFLICT

Katherine Hudson

A ROYAL CONFLICT

Sir John Conroy

and the

Young Victoria

A John Curtis Book
Hodder & Stoughton
LONDON SYDNEY AUCKLAND

British Library Cataloguing in Publication Data

Hudson, Katherine
Royal Conflict: Sir John Conroy and the
Young Victoria
I. Title
941.081092

ISBN 0-340-60749-1

Photoset by Hewer Text Composition Services, Edinburgh
Printed in Great Britain by Mackays of Chatham plc

TO MY PARENTS

LIST OF CONTENTS

LIST OF ILLUSTRATIONS

Baron Stockmar, after Partridge (photo: *The Mansell Collection*).

Sir John Conroy (1836) by A. Tidey (*National Portrait Gallery*).

The Duke of Wellington c. 1846. From the daguerrotype by Antoine Claudet (photo: *The Mansell Collection*).

John Conry (1704–69) by Robert Hunter (photo: *Christies Images*).

Sir John Conroy, marble bust. Artist unknown. (*The Earl of Rosse, Birr Castle, Ireland*).

Sir John Conroy c. 1850 (photo: *Balliol College, Oxford*).

Victoria and Albert by Sir Edwin Landseer (*Royal Collection Enterprises*).

Illustrations in the text

Book plate of the Conroy Arms (*Balliol College, Oxford*).

Kensington Palace as it appeared in 1831, from an engraving (photo: *The Mansell Collection*).

Lady Flora Hastings by Princess Victoria (*Royal Collection Enterprises*).

Miss Victoire Conroy 'from nature' by Princess Victoria. December 1836, Claremont (*Royal Collection Enterprises*).

Arborfield Hall c. 1842. Lithograph from the drawing by J. McNevin (*Reading Central Library*).

Endpapers

Sir John Conroy silhouette by Princess Victoria; Queen Victoria silhouette (*Royal Collection Enterprises*).

ACKNOWLEDGEMENTS

My thanks are due first to Her Majesty the Queen for the gracious permission to use material from the Royal Archives at Windsor Castle. In this connection I am especially grateful to Sheila de Bellaigue, Registrar of the Royal Archives, for her patient help and meticulous attention to the text.

I am indebted to Balliol College, Oxford, for permission to use The Conroy Papers, and to the Librarian, Dr Penelope Bulloch, and her colleague Alan Tadiello, for their help while I was working on them. Especially, I must thank Dr John Jones, Dean and Archivist of Balliol College, without whose enthusiasm, interest and support, this book could not have been written.

Others who have assisted me have been legion: I thank them all unreservedly. However, I would particularly like to acknowledge the help of Captain Sir John Hanmer (who made available important family documents) and the Earl of Rosse, of Birr Castle, Ireland. I have been fortunate to have had Douglas Matthews to prepare the Index, and Jean Warren typed out the greater part of the manuscript on to her word-processor. I am extremely grateful to them both.

Finally, I must thank Elizabeth Longford for her invaluable help and criticism, and for so generously providing the Foreword to this book.

Katherine Hudson

John Conry of Mulconry
1628 – 72

Charles
1657 – 90
(Killed at Battle
of the Boyne)

John Ponsonby=
1759 – 97

JOHN = Elizabeth Fisher   George   Llewellin = Claudine
CONROY   1788–1805 1790–1825   Palmer
1786–1854

Augustus   George
b.1822   b.1824

Augustus Ayshford = 'Emily'
b.1852   c.1868
                    mar.dis.?

Edward=Alicia Parsons   Elizabeth Jane   Arthur
1809–69   1811–55   1813–17
       John
       1845–1900

= Florence Fitzgerald

Ferfeassa = Cicily Aylmer
1661–1746

John = Elizabeth Foulke
1704–69

Margaret Wilson   Elizabeth   Catherine

William   Laetitia   Deanne Josias
b.1794   b.1796   1798–1828
young   d.young

ere Valentine
b.1858

tephen Rowley Henry   Victoire Maria = Wyndham
1815–41   George   Louisa   Edward Hanmer
               1817–90   1819–66

                                    Edward
                                    b.1843

xiii

George III ⚊ Charlotte Sophia
1738–1820 | Mecklenburg-Strelitz
'Farmer George' | 1744–1818

George IV ⚊ Caroline of   Frederick ⚊ Frederika,   King William IV
1762–1830 | Brunswick   Duke of   Princess of   1765–1837
'Uncle King' | 1768–1821   York   Prussia   the 'Sailor King'
1763–1827   1767–1840

Charlotte ⚊ Leopold of
1796–1817   Saxe-Coburg-Saalfeld
'Dear Uncle'
1790–1865
later King of the Belgians   VICTORIA
1819–1901

Ernest,   Augustus,   Adolphus, ⚊ Augusta,
Duke of Cumber-   Duke of Sussex   Duke of   Princess of
land and King of   1773–1843   Cambridge   Hesse-Cass
Hanover, 1771–1851   1774–1850   1797–1889
the 'Wicked Uncle'

George,   George,
King of Hanover, the 'Blind King'   Duke of Cambridge
1819–78   1819–1904

Francis Frederick of Saxe-Saalfeld-Coburg
1750–1806

Ernest I	Sophia	Ferdinand	Leopold I,
1784–1844	1778–1835	1785–1851	King of the Belgians

delaide, | Charlotte = Frederick, | Edward, = Victoire, | Augusta Elizabeth
rincess of | 1766–1828 | King of | Duke of | Princess | 1768–1840 1770–1840
Saxe – | | Württem- | Kent | of Saxe –
leiningen | | berg | 1767–1820 | Coburg
'92–1849 | | | | 1786–1861

ALBERT
1819–61

Mary = William, | Sophia | Octavius | Alfred | Amelia
76–1857 Duke of | 1777–1848 | 1779–83 | 1780–2 | 1785–1810
Gloucester
'Silly Billy'
1776–1834

'All Sir John's invention and Princess Sophia's fearful falseness.'

– *Queen Victoria*

FOREWORD

Biography would be a poor thing without its minor characters. They can make the narrative either more acceptable and human or more bizarre and strange, all necessary factors. And sometimes it is the minor characters who turn out, however unwittingly, to have taken the major decisions. Lord Stamfordham was Private Secretary to two monarchs, Victoria and George V. He played a key role in the constitutional disputes of the early twentieth century, and 'christened a dynasty' in 1917 by suggesting the name 'Windsor' for the Royal House. Yet no biography of Stamfordham exists. Similarly, no book about Sir John Conroy, who passionately desired to be Queen Victoria's Private Secretary and radically affected her early years, has existed until now, 140 years after his death.

This absorbing study of the man whom Victoria called a 'monster and demon incarnate', is valuable for a number of reasons. It brings new facts to one of the most curious passages in Victorian royal history. It fills definite gaps. It is notably fair-minded. And in the telling, the story is stylish; switching where appropriate from the trenchant to elegance, and moving from sub-plot to sub-plot without ever losing pace and suspense.

I must not give away too much of the main plot. Enough to say that the chief new fact presented by Katherine Hudson involves Conroy's monster delusion: a delusion that dominated him from the beginning of his royal service to the end of his life. When Conroy passed into the Duchess of Kent's service after the Duke's early death, he believed himself to be, so to speak, Princess Victoria's 'Big Brother'. And not unlike the villain of *1984*, the 'Big Brother' of 1819 onward was to have the makings of a tyrant.

From this initial delusion was to spring the tragi-comedy of Sir John's extraordinary career. The inappropriate familiarity that Princess Victoria so often noticed in Sir John's posture toward herself and her widowed mother, the Duchess of Kent, was not due to Conroy's being the Duchess's lover but to his fancying that his wife and children enjoyed what might be called 'a special relationship'. In the author's fascinating, thorough and convincing detective work, she shows that the legend was still intact in the mind and imagination of Conroy's grandson as late as 1868.

Conroy himself was of Irish descent, from the O'Mulconrys of Elphin, Roscommon. The author rightly traces this descent in some detail. It accounted for his Irish charm and also his blarney. His father had once acted the part of Falstaff in Dublin and the author aptly remarks that the son showed touches of both Malvolio and Falstaff – the latter especially in his bitter sense of royal ingratitude.

His grandfather's friendship with the famous Whig family of Ponsonby made it almost inevitable that Sir John should be a Whig also. Thus some of Victoria's useful liberal upbringing she owed to the Irish 'demon'.

Katherine Hudson shows further skill in linking the *mores* of the period with the misjudgements of her characters. Within Princess Victoria's claustrophobic little court at Kensington Palace there was too high a sense of drama; as the author says, 'too many visits to the melodramas at Drury Lane', all stimulating the Gothic atmosphere; 'these children of the eighteenth and early nineteenth century lived on the edge of emotion. In fact they spent a great deal of their time in tears.' The demon 'J.C.' himself would often shed sentimental tears when he spoke of the little Princess. There were too many Frankensteins still about, with their monsters.

As for Conroy's more material services to Victoria, we are shown their positive side as well as their limitations with even-handed justice. 'The Conroy family', writes Katherine Hudson, 'were totally unsuitable for the Duchess and Princess Victoria (far more unsuitable indeed than anyone then could ever have guessed), but nevertheless it was they who were to create a home at Kensington and a family environment for Princess Victoria.' Admittedly it was Conroy who kept the Duchess and her daughter away from their natural family – at the Court of George IV and William IV. It is probable that Victoria's two 'wicked uncles' would have provided their niece with a happier childhood and youth than the Conroys did. However, no one could argue that Victoria's character would have been strengthened by an upbringing among the royal mistresses and 'bâtards' who graced the early-nineteenth-century Court. Paradoxically, her sufferings under Conroy's regime were to account in large part for the steel in a character that had gone through the fire well before she had to meet the challenges of her long reign.

Victoria's detested 'Kensington System', as Conroy's plan for her upbringing and education was called, is handled with the same fairness and instinct for fresh facts. Though Conroy was a first-class organiser, 'he had neither depth nor subtlety' but was tactless and insensitive with people despite his charm. Indeed, his very skills in organisation made his deluded aims and ambitions more dangerous than they would have been in the hands of a bungler. At the same time there was one particular aspect or offshoot of his 'system' that was to pay Victoria high dividends.

Every so often Victoria would emerge from Kensington for one of Conroy's superbly organised and sensibly devised 'Royal Progresses', by which she would be presented to an enthusiastic nation as the hope of the future. The King of England may have loathed these challenges to his authority. The King of the Belgians may have pitied his niece Victoria as a 'little white slavey', while Conroy was supposedly saving her from becoming Uncle Leopold's 'tool'; Victoria herself may sometimes have been tortured by fatigue or illness; she was nonetheless seeing England and Wales in a unique manner, and they were seeing her. If Conroy had had his way there would have been an Irish tour as well. He wrote: 'It would have been well to have left no stone unturned to draw the countries together . . .'

Today, when royal 'walkabouts' are an accepted feature of a Monarchy that is both accessible and popular, the invention of the young Victoria's royal tours cannot be despised. No wonder the University of Oxford presented Sir John Conroy with an honorary doctorate of Civil Law, as the author vividly describes in the Prologue to her story – the climax of Conroy's doomed race for power and glory. After that it was virtually downhill all the way.

One Kensington character – and dupe of Conroy – who supported the 'system' along with Conroy's ambitions, was Princess Sophia. Katherine Hudson's researches have added much to the already known outlines of Sophia's financial relations with Conroy. Daughter of George III, Princess Sophia was Victoria's unmarried (but not maiden) aunt. There is no evidence that Conroy seduced her, as General Garth had done in the past, though Victoria may have thought he did, besides seducing the tragic Lady Flora Hastings. Perhaps Conroy had deceived himself into believing that the landed estates he bought with secret royal largesse were rightly being used to support the peerage he expected for himself and his family. At any rate, what no one knew at the time was that Conroy had received from HRH vast sums of her huge fortune.

Conroy's services to the Duchess of Kent, Victoria's German mother, included in her own words, 'to make me quite English'. He did not succeed with Victoria's other close German influence: her Governess Fräulein, afterwards Baroness, Lehzen. In a chapter entitled, 'Snakes in the Grass', we are shown the almost inevitable clash between Lehzen and Conroy, though ultimately the Demon had no chance against the Snake. The Demon's allies were two simple-minded women, the Duchess and Lady Conroy; whereas the Snake was to serve and be served by a young woman of considerable shrewdness and remarkable resolution. Chief among Lehzen's services to the unmarried Victoria was the courageous backing she gave at a key incident in 1835. Very ill with a high fever, the sixteen-year-old Princess was bullied and urged in vain by Conroy to sign a document creating him her Private Secretary as soon as she became Queen. A peerage of course would have followed.

Katherine Hudson rightly does her best for her anti-hero, Conroy, and thus his arch-enemy Lehzen comes out marginally worse than she does, say, in my biography of the Queen, *Victoria R.I.* But she is not unfair to Lehzen; and indeed Prince Albert would have agreed with her judgement.

With the success of a libel action brought by Conroy against *The Times,* followed by the disgraceful Lady Flora Hastings affair – a disgrace to Lord Melbourne and Lehzen if not the young Queen – Conroy seemed to become for a few months the victim rather than the villain of royal events. But his effect on the Duchess of Kent, though diminishing, was still enough to justify Queen Victoria's advisers in their view that he must somehow be removed from the country. To put it bleakly, the Queen and her mother, long at loggerheads, would never be reconciled as long as Sir John was around. The Queen had called him a monster. Perhaps it was the atmosphere of the time, as described by the author, that made her so fond of such words. If Sir John had been in politics she would no doubt have blamed him for driving the Tories into insulting her beloved Consort, Prince Albert. As it was, they took over the 'monster' role. 'You Monsters!'

Conroy's claim to bring an English or at least Irish peerage into his family was left on hold. It was the trusty Duke of Wellington who finally provided a '*pont d'or*' over which Sir John and his family could pass honourably to a new life abroad. Actually it was to be a bridge of sighs rather than of gold, many of the sighs coming from the Duchess of Kent as well as the Conroys. For the author points out perceptively that the Duchess loved Conroy. He did not love her, his love being reserved for his family.

The tale of the Conroy family's exile abroad is a fascinating addition to our knowledge of British travellers' experiences at that date, particularly with a consumptive dear one to be nursed; in this case Sir John's son Stephen. Sir John's best points emerged in his care for Stephen, whose illness is named by Katherine Hudson 'the turning point in Conroy's life'.

When the Conroys eventually settled at Arborfield Hall in Berkshire, in 1842, Sir John is pictured as sometimes peacefully fishing in English streams instead of always for royal favours. Incidentally, his wife Elizabeth Fisher came from an up-and-coming family known as the 'Loaves and Fishers', though Elizabeth did not possess the gifts to help her husband on his way up – or down. Sir John also owned two profitable lead mines in Wales and was to live as something of a contented patriarch surrounded by his wife, old mother, daughter Victoire and son Edward and his wife Alicia (until she left him) and their child.

But not quite contented. As soon as an Irish peerage became vacant, the Queen's 'promise' that Conroy should get it was again to disturb the peace both of the Court and Berkshire countryside. With devastating clarity but always objectively, the story shows how Conroy's claim to become 'Viscount Elphin' (Hudson amusingly uses the word 'leprechaun') had involved the consciences and prejudices of the Queen, Prince Consort, his secretary and three Prime Ministers. In the end it was Prince Albert who put his foot down. 'For the defeated Viscount Elphin', writes the author, 'there was no further appeal . . . The sense of injustice however was to remain beyond the grave.'

The phrase 'beyond the grave' has come to stand for Balliol College, Oxford. Among its archives the author discovered most of the compelling and sometimes surprising new material that gives so much *élan* to her story. If Sir John Conroy himself lacked 'depth and subtlety' his biography undoubtedly possesses both. Between 1975–77 Katherine Hudson and John Jones were listing the various Conroy Papers, of which the first were received by Balliol College around 1900. *The Conroy Papers: A Guide*, the work of Jones and Hudson, was published in 1987 by the College. And now this excellent, full-scale study comes as the final result of so much careful preservation, research and hard work. I am delighted to welcome it and to be associated with it, if only through the medium of this Foreword.

Katherine Hudson has writing in her blood. Derek Hudson, her father, is the author of a book I much enjoyed on Kensington Palace. In *A Royal Conflict* his daughter has opened up many hitherto hidden aspects of the royal saga. After a successful battle the Duke of Wellington used to say that 'The Finger of Providence' was upon him. Katherine Hudson has shown that something of the same kind happened to the young Victoria. For despite the anguish of her battles with Conroy, she not only benefited from some of his constructive and original ideas but also learnt endurance and finally compassion. It is good to know that nearly thirty years after Conroy's death in 1854, the Queen was paying a pension to his daughter-in-law.

Royal conflict, as so often before and since, is seen to dissolve in royal humanity.

Elizabeth Longford

AUTHOR'S NOTE

So as to retain authenticity and historical immediacy, all manuscript material used in this book has been quoted exactly, with no correction of spelling, punctuation or sense.

PROLOGUE

On the morning of the 8th November 1832 a remarkable
procession made its way through the City of Oxford. The
decorated streets echoed to 'the plaudits of assembled
thousands' for the people of Oxford were awaiting the
occasion with much curiosity, and the local papers had been
fueling their enthusiasm for some while:

> Let cheerful notes of loyal love,
>   [wrote one Poetess,]
> Breathe through each classic shade,
> And joy on bounding footsteps move
> To greet the Royal Maid.
>
> VICTORIA comes – our Britain's hope,
> To view the ancient Towers,
> And Sylvan walks that vainly boast
> Of equal blooming flowers.[1]

The blooming flower herself was very impressed (it took
quite a lot to impress her as a matter of fact) and noted
carefully in her Journal that '. . . We were most _warmly_ and
enthusiastically received. They hurrayed and applauded us
immensely for there were all the students there; all in their
gowns and caps.'[2]

The little assembly, of which the thirteen-year-old Princess
Victoria was a part, consisted of her mother, the Duchess of

Kent, Baroness Lehzen, her Governess, their ladies-in-waiting, including Lady Conroy, and last but not least, her mother's Equerry – and man of the hour – Sir John Conroy. They were met at the Divinity School by the Vice-Chancellor, Dr Rowley, and other Heads of Colleges, who escorted them through the cheering throng into the Sheldonian Theatre.

It was a very impressive gathering. The organ played with 'melodious tones' and the Sheldonian itself was filled to capacity with the incumbents of Academe, who with 'loud and long continued cheering welcomed the fair visitors which they acknowledged most affably'.

With the Duchess and her daughter at his right hand the Vice-Chancellor stood to give his Address: he alluded briefly 'to the demonstration of loyalty' that had followed their recent tour of England, tendering his own 'tribute of dutiful respect'. The Duchess replied, as Victoria dryly observed, 'as usual', in tones adapted by Sir John to meet the needs of the occasion.

'Your loyalty . . .' she concluded with deference to King William IV 'and recollection of the favour you have enjoyed under the paternal sway of his House, could not fail, I was sure, to lead you to receive his Niece with all the disposition you evince . . . It is my object to ensure, by all the means in my power, her being so educated as to meet the just expectation of all classes in this great and free country.'[3]

Amidst the resulting applause Dr Joseph Phillimore, Regius Professor of Civil Law, arose, and in an impressive Latin speech presented Sir John Conroy to the eminent gathering: 'Most illustrious Mr Vice-Chancellor and you Learned Proctors!' he announced. 'I present to you Sir John Conroy – a most gallant gentleman Knight of the Guelphic Order: Sir John is descended from an old family in Ireland and at an early age entered the army and where he applied himself closely to the study of military tactics – in this profession he was much esteemed and was placed in the Household of that Illustrious Prince whom a premature death snatched from his country thirteen years ago.

'Thus having been received into His Household and

family, and certain duties being entrusted to his charge, he performed the important trust with singular prudence (which is a great talent) and also with much industry. Can you wonder that he who had gained the esteem of the Husband, should also have pleased His surviving Consort!

'He is here' – (perhaps we may imagine a grand gesture) – 'He who has up to the present time remained in the same situation and who has fulfilled the same duty towards Our illustrious guest . . .' At this point Dr Phillimore launched into a tribute to the Duchess of Kent and her devoted care of the Princess ('To this, she is wont to apply herself – To this, are the powers of her mind and heart steadfastly directed . . .') and finally, redirecting his energies to Sir John himself, he proposed '. . . a gentleman as much commended to your notice by his eminent qualities as by the strict confidence he enjoys with our Princesses and whom I propose – that he be admitted to the Honorary degree of Doctor of Civil Law.'[4]

'After that was over', noted our reporter with an evident sigh of relief, 'we returned through Divinity College and proceeded in our carriages to the council chamber where Mama received an address there from the Corporation of Oxford, and Sir John the Freedom of the City of Oxford.'[5]

This very curious, indeed spectacular episode – which received considerable national publicity – is interesting to us for a number of reasons. Above all, it demonstrates how popular the Duchess of Kent and her Equerry Sir John Conroy were in the eyes of the people of England, and how no less a body than Oxford University had set the seal of approval on their education of Princess Victoria; it shows too, in this year 1832, the importance of the Princess as a figurehead of unity and continuity in a time of great political upheaval; and it reveals how well-known and accepted was Sir John's personal relationship with the Duchess and the Princess. Perhaps most importantly, however, it introduces us to the chief protagonists of our story. It is hard to believe, whilst this rosy glow is yet surrounding them, that in five short years the shrewd little observer in the Sheldonian

Theatre would have brought about Sir John's ruin, and this seemingly successful and contented ménage would be divided by bitterness and hatred. Yet, even now a power struggle was slowly developing, the existence of which Victoria was not unaware: did she see the irony in Dr Phillimore's oration? Probably not, irony was never to be her strong point. But Baroness Lehzen, whose jealousy of Sir John was already strong, must have found the occasion something of an ordeal.

And what of Sir John himself? Indeed, we may ask ourselves, who was this man presented in 1832 as a knight in shining armour, and now all but forgotten to us except as the 'evil genius' of the Duchess of Kent? It has to be said that apart from the brief details of Conroy's career outlined by Dr Phillimore, very little else was known, even in his own time, of Sir John's background. The Duchess herself when questioned years later by Conroy's successor did not know the simplest details of his property and early life. Certainly Conroy's Irish inheritance was never appreciated by the German-dominated household over which he presided: 'Remember he is an Englishman' was a common warning of the Duchess and Prince Leiningen,[6] and even the worldly family adviser, Baron Stockmar. 'Remember he is an Irishman' would have been much more to the point.

These Irish antecedents were of enormous importance to Conroy, and indeed the mainspring of his life. Sir John claimed to be Chief of the Conroy clan, and the Conroys themselves held a considerable romantic attachment to their unusual history. In addition, the origins of Conroy's wife – Elizabeth Fisher – were so mysterious as to acquire an influence all of their own. The secret fantasies embodied in the person of this tall, dark-haired, simple woman were indeed formidable.

It is in The Conroy Papers* that these unexplored areas of Sir John's life are revealed, and it is helpful to be armed with the insights they bring as we do battle with Conroy's controversial reputation. This reputation – of fraud, immor-

* See Appendix, The Conroy Papers

ality and overbearing ambition – is one the present author has endeavoured to view dispassionately. It was hinted by a personal friend of Sir John (a rather more balanced and detached individual) that, at one stage of his career, Conroy was not quite sane. Suffice to say that Sir John was not mad, nor was he without very real talents, but he was deluded, and more importantly, a misfit; much of his tragedy was to stem from a desperate attempt to gain supremacy in a world to which he and his family were not suited. Such futile ambitions are of course not only pathetic but absurd, but unfortunately not enough people realised this at the time. Indeed, anyone might have been excused some degree of self-importance after such enthusiastic confirmation of their abilities as Oxford exhibited in 1832.

Sir John then was pursued by dreams that he attempted (and not without some success) to make real, not only for his own sake but for that of his family. Here we will find as much an account of Conroy's own children – Edward, Stephen, Jane and Victoire (Queen Victoria's only playmates), of his grandson John and of the mysterious 'Emily' – as of those crucial years when he found himself in control of Victoria's life and that of her mother, the Duchess of Kent. There will be no apology for allowing the Conroys to take the stage alongside their more illustrious contemporaries; this is their story, and it is one of the strangest episodes of English history that this man and his family ever held such a position alongside the heir to the throne.

1

SNAKES IN THE GRASS

The village of Kensington, in the early nineteenth century, consisted of a cluster of houses and shops grouped around the little parish church of St Mary Abbots. Southwards stretched the fields and market gardens of Brompton – whilst, to the north, making its way over Campden Hill, past Dutch-gabled houses set among old-walled gardens and fruit trees, Church Lane ran down to the turnpike at Notting Hill. The carriages rolled along the road from London under the walls of Kensington Gardens – and indeed, if Kensington came so close to the city that a schoolboy might walk twice-daily there and back – yet still it was a country place, and its people country-dwellers.

A little to the east of the village, on a slope of the hill, stood Kensington Palace – the red brick walls of its façade glowing in the sunshine, as children flew their kites in the Broad Walk and their parents took the air.

Kensington had long been a royal home. Here had come the shy and sensitive William of Orange, for whom Sir Christopher Wren transformed the original country house into a royal residence. Here, too, had lived Queen Anne and George I – and it was at Kensington that the vital and amusing Princess Charlotte, only daughter of the Prince Regent, lived with her mother, the Princess Caroline. Charlotte's happy yet fateful marriage to Prince Leopold of Saxe Coburg Saalfeld opened the way to the throne for the young Princess Victoria, and it was in 1820 that the widowed Duchess of Kent and her baby daughter had found shelter within the walls of Kensington Palace. It was a Palace that felt like a home. The sun shone warmly through the bedrooms and sitting rooms, and at evening slanted across the courtyard to lighten the magnificent King's staircase. Yet here too the wind howled around the chimneys – setting the wind-clock in the King's Gallery swinging wildly – and the inhabitants found it necessary to close the shutters at night against the damp from the Round Pond . . .

As the carriages from Oxford arrive home at Kensington Palace in 1832, it is tempting to feel that we are embarking not so much on a tragedy, as upon a rather sad and exaggerated story about ordinary, ill-assorted people attempting an impossible task. A storm in a teacup one might say, except that the teacup assumes monumental proportions, as if it had taken a dose of Alice's 'Eat Me'. Indeed, finally Princess Victoria, like Alice herself, was to feel so surrounded by lunacy that she scattered her tormentors to the four winds ('You're nothing but a pack of cards!'). That that in itself was to prove a mistake was only to be expected.

Within the confines of Kensington Palace the dramatis personae are gathering. Fräulein Lehzen and the King's

Kensington Palace as it appeared in 1831, from an engraving.

sister, Princess Sophia; the Duchess, Victoria and Conroy. Each is to have a high sense of theatricality (drawn from the atmosphere of the time, and too many visits to the melodramas at Drury Lane); and each too will bring a proper sense of their own importance to the action of the plot.

For these children of the eighteenth and early nineteenth century lived on the edge of emotion. In fact they spent a great deal of their time in tears. Conroy's eyes would fill with tears as he spoke of Princess Victoria – and with evident satisfaction he in turn brought tears to the eyes of the King of the Belgians. Lord Melbourne wept frequently; and Lord Goderich – that Prime Minister of a day – cried practically all the time. Within this highly-charged atmosphere Kensington came to be a microcosm of the outside world – with its spying, plots and brawls; its rhetoric and high ideals – all of which fed upon itself in the stifling life that Victoria's half-sister Feodora was to call the 'years of imprisonment'.

Captain Conroy himself was an improbable candidate for stardom. Certainly he was good-looking with a swash-buckling swagger; he had an engaging way with women – 'How do you do my dear lady, pretty well I hope?' was a characteristic sally[1] – but he was in fact so unqualified for his position that it is difficult to put a finger on the extra ingredients that had enabled such ordinary talents to go so far.

However, in old age Victoria conceded that Sir John was 'very plausible' and her future Prime Minister, Lord Melbourne, allowed that he was audacious and had plenty of assumption ('So much is carried in the world by assumption'). Indeed, when we discover that Conroy's father's portrayal of Falstaff had been the hit of Fishamble Street, Dublin (and his grandfather such a raconteur that he actually obtained his job as Collector of Cork through telling stories to the Lord Lieutenant of Ireland)[2], we will appreciate that the role of Majordomo would have presented few problems for their descendant. Certainly, in the heavy Germanic dullness that was to pervade what Victoria called 'the poor old Palace', Conroy's Irish charm and vivid presence must have livened things up considerably.

9

It has been supposed that in 1819 Conroy decided (as if overnight) to make the Duchess of Kent his career. Yet this is misleading. Following the death of the Duke of Kent, Conroy had worked in a part-time capacity for the Duchess, receiving (and here the Duchess's advisers, her brother Prince Leopold and Baron Stockmar, had made a great mistake) no payment whatsoever and retaining his army position until 1822. From 1824 he remained with the Duchess on half-pay from the army and worked for the Colonial Audit Office on a salary of £1,000 a year – a task he fulfilled until 1832. It is true he was said to have been offered the Consulship of Tunis in 1823 – and he evidently felt the Duchess of Kent to be a better proposition than that – yet he nevertheless retained until 1832 a dual career that did not allow for total commitment.[3]

Much more probable, and much more in keeping with the usual workings of life, was that his relationship with the Duchess had gradually changed and developed, until around 1825 when Conroy found himself in the position to become a maker of history. Then his dramatic flair, his talent for organisation, and above all his worldly ambitions, found their outlet in the Duchess's emerging status and he strode – like a two-pence coloured toy-theatre figure – bravely on to the world's stage:

> Then in Court Martial I could really swear, [wrote Conroy,]
> My dreadful doom the Colonel did declare.
> There sit those young men too with quizzing eyes
> Upon each awkward movement fearful spies
> 'See how' (they cry) 'their long arms saw the air,
> We'll play the fool while ill they act the player'.[4]

The life created for Princess Victoria at Kensington was described by Conroy's daughter-in-law as 'a happy home at first',[5] and there is no doubt this was true. Princess Feodora, emerging into adolescence, nevertheless hated the Palace; she found it claustrophobic and boring and longed for escape – but for her little half-sister, the centre of attention, the early years at Kensington were delightful. The Conroy's youngest daughter Victoire was her chief childhood companion (riding with her on their ponies in Kensington Gardens; dressing up; making cottages out of cards – and playing with 'dissected prints'). For despite the impression of isolation the Palace gave, Victoria was not without friends, although she was not always very gracious to them: 'You must not touch those, they are mine,' she warned a child about to play with her toys (it was Lady Jane Ellice), 'and I may call you Jane, but you must not call me Victoria.' She had not inherited the easy-going friendliness of Princess Charlotte, who told the coachman's daughter that they were 'Miss Charlotte and Miss Annie'; nor the almost Olympian self-confidence and heartiness of the Hanoverians, who romped about like the Gillray cartoons they inspired – poking fun at their entire entourage. (George IV laughed so much over a joke about an ambassador that it kept him warm during a freezing winter.) There was to be no laughing at Kensington. Everyone took themselves very seriously indeed.

Conroy was the careful servant of this little family. Feodora, writing to Captain Conroy at Christmas 1825, pleaded with him to find 'Some pretty almamacks' for the Duchess – 'but not the *forget me not*'. Having also omitted to ask him the price of a writing-box for her brother, 'if you do not find it two expensif,' she confided, 'I shall beg you, to order one for me.'

'Victoire', she added, of her little half-sister, 'who sends her love to Captain *Dispery*, has just taken her lecson, and was singing God Save the King quite delightfully, I wish you had heard her.'[6]

Victoria was to be described by Mrs Arbuthnot, the friend of the Duke of Wellington, as 'civil & well-bred & *Princess-like* to the greatest degree',[7] while her two near-contemporary cousins the children of the Duke of Cumberland and the Duke of Cambridge, who had their full inheritance of Hanoverian boisterousness, appalled her. Cumberland's young son (whom the Duke described as 'angelic') was so mischievous and precocious he made 'love to all the ladies'; whilst at a drawing-room he not only shouted and laughed at a roomful of judges, but seeing his Tutor in his canonicals, cried: 'What, are you come back to make a fool of yourself, too, are you?'

'What a Royal Family ours is!' sighed Mrs Arbuthnot.

Victoria did not much enjoy the company of Victoire either, whom she probably found a dull little girl; and although when older she rejoiced in the company of her mother's relatives, she seemed to turn instinctively from the children of the Royal Family to the company of her dolls. Perhaps she had already heard something of 'the Bâtards' – William IV's children by his mistress the actress Mrs Jordan – for Conroy was to uphold the nation's view of that subject and keep Victoria firmly away from them. It was no great loss, for the Princess was probably the kind of child who did not much care for other children.

Nevertheless, both Victoria's separation from her relatives and the incessant admiration everyone heaped upon her were to prove great sources of difficulty. The Duchess's Lady-in-Waiting, Baroness Späth, actually fell on her knees before her; she was indulged by Princess Charlotte's nurse Old Louis and her own nurse Mrs Brock; whilst Mrs Conroy's uncle, the Bishop of Salisbury, played with her on his hands and knees (she had previously been afraid of bishops). All in all it is not surprising that by the time she grew to be five years old Victoria, for all her natural charm and truthfulness, was becoming wilful and spoilt.

Even as an infant the Princess had been a force to be reckoned with ('Think of the baby', wrote Lady Granville, who could be spiteful, 'they say it is le Roi George in petticoats, so fat it can scarcely waddle'); and to her mother, who was nervous with Victoria, this early manifestation of obstinacy had become worrying. By nature, the Duchess was loving and caring but the enormous importance of the child she had produced had frozen her naturally warm impulses – whilst the influence of those surrounding her at Kensington, instead of helping the Duchess to remain on good terms with her daughter, actually served to pull them apart.

Too much was at stake in the person of Victoria for each and every one of them – too great the catastrophe should their own plans go awry – for any normal relationship between them to be possible.

'The passions of those, who stood between us,' the Duchess realised in later years, 'estranged my beloved Child from me.'[8]

*

Of those destined most surely to undermine the relationship between Victoria and her mother, two women – Fräulein Lehzen and Princess Sophia – were to be closely bound up with the fortunes of Conroy and the Duchess for over twenty years. Of these two, the most influential, and perhaps the most unexpected, was Princess Sophia, the favourite and once beautiful daughter of George III.

If we may carry our analogy of 'Alice' a little further, then let it be said that Princess Sophia had all the qualities of the White Queen. She was vague, well-meaning, prone to mishaps (one day absent-mindedly catching 'her cap, hand-kerchief, and dress on fire'[9] she ran, a human torch, to her maids who managed to extinguish the flames; she was left in discomfort, but apparently unperturbed). Her youth had been tragically frustrated, but passion had run sufficiently high for her to have had an illegitimate child by General Garth, her father's Equerry. The management of her son, Captain Garth, and the mystery surrounding his genesis, may well have made her vulnerable to John Conroy, and it was to him she displayed the White Queen's most endearing characteristic – the giving of 'un-birthday presents'.

When Conroy first met Princess Sophia she was nearly fifty, had lost her looks and her sight was beginning to fail. She was clearly lonely and bored and Captain Garth (a debtor and womaniser) was a constant worry: not surprisingly she had become increasingly confused, and indeed her mental stability may always have been uncertain.

At some point during the early 1820s Conroy assumed control of her affairs and became an intimate friend. In return for Conroy's attention she gave him money; money sufficient to make a place in the world for him and his offspring. Indeed, she set about to make something of Captain Conroy, as she could make nothing of Captain Garth, and on her annual treasury income of over £3,000 a year (not to mention her private fortune) this proved all too easy.

Indeed, the bank accounts for Captain Conroy that still survive in the archives of Coutts show that in 1823 his credit stood at a humble £108.10.2. By 1825 it had increased dramatically to £22,000.[10]

The Duchess of Kent's and Conroy's accounts at Coutts were 'public accounts' – used chiefly for the payment of tutors, staff, charities, and the like. Household expenditure does not feature in them, nor more personal expenses. Conroy himself banked at Cox and Co. (whose accounts do not survive) but frequent payments, chiefly to his family, were made from his Coutts account into Cox and Co. No details of the payments into either his or the Duchess's Coutts account are ever supplied, and thus it is seldom possible to know from whom any given payment is derived. Of Princess Sophia's own accounts at Drummonds Bank, records of only three years covering Conroy's period survive (1825, 1835 and 1845). In 1825 we find she gave Conroy a total of £4,726.3. and over these three separate years she was also debited for large payments to Conroy, as well as for sums of cash to which no details are attached.[11]

In 1826 the Princess bought Captain Conroy a house in Kensington (probably in Vicarage Gate) for £4,000;[12] later she purchased a property nearby and she and the Conroys were frequently in and out of each others' houses. Indeed, Conroy's home became a social centre for the entire family at Kensington Palace. Princess Victoria was often there playing with Jane and Victoire. Later, when Queen, she told her Prime Minister Lord Melbourne 'how often we used to drive there, that all my Uncles etc. were taken there, which he [Melbourne] said, must have surprised them; that Princess Sophia used to court him [Conroy] more than anyone', which surprised Lord Melbourne still more.[13]

Again, in 1826, Sophia gave Conroy Llanbrynmair, a vast estate in Wales that included farms, several mines, plantations and villages. It cost her £18,000. (Later the Princess is said to have added £10,000 more to the outlay for this enormous enterprise.)[14] Not a single member of the Royal Family knew at the time of these transactions, or even of the existence of Llanbrynmair. Miraculously, Conroy and his family kept them, and the means by which he had purchased such riches, a secret – and it was here, among the mountains of Wales, that Conroy was to indulge his dreams of patronage and power.

Such secrecy, however, was his undoing, for not only would he never be able to explain whence the money for such possessions had come – but it is almost certain that, in fact, one other person did know of Sophia's generosity: a curious character, who dodges in and out of the Conroy history like a shadow on the wall. His name was William Rea.

A search in the Royal Archives reveals that William Rea (perhaps an Irish associate of Conroy's) entered the employment of the Duchess of Kent as her Clerk of the Accounts in 1826.[15] As the Duchess's Equerry one must assume that Conroy found Rea – who had been in the army – and gave him the post. Rea had been Edward's teacher and many years later, after the death of her husband, Lady Conroy let out an impassioned plea in their defence that contains an allusion to Rea: 'He, poor man,' she wrote to her son Edward of Sir John, in 1854, 'when at Woolwich was anything but rich, & he thought then that he was acting for the best, for you & all his little children – & he, Rea, was really a good master to begin with . . .'[16]

As Clerk of the Accounts, Rea had insinuated himself firmly into the financial affairs of all at Kensington. If anyone made a financial transaction, Rea implemented it; he was deeply influential, seems to have paid most of the Household bills (he was a repeated beneficiary from Conroy's Coutts Account) and handled vast sums of money. He alone knew of Princess Sophia's transactions with Sir John, and he was, of course, in a strong position to blackmail.

There is only one person who lacked confidence in Rea –

and that woman was to be renowned for her stupidity and lack of insight – the Duchess of Kent. 'Your stupid Rea *never* understands me,' she complained to Sir John's son Edward in 1841. And later still, in deeply distressing circumstances, she confessed to Sir George Couper that she had found Rea 'rough, and gave himself such airs . . . she was afraid of him – he might be dishonest'.[7]

Perhaps Conroy was afraid of him, too.

Much has been written of the relationship between the Duchess of Kent and Sir John Conroy. In her own time there were rumours (supposedly put about by the Duke of Cumberland) that they were actually lovers. This says more for the worldly cynicism by which the court was surrounded than it says of the Duchess of Kent herself. It was easier for such men as the Duke of Wellington and Lord Melbourne to assume she had simply 'made herself over' to Conroy (as Melbourne expressed it) than to try to understand the more complex motives underlying their relationship.

Although a certain sexual attraction may well have been present between them in the early stages of their friendship (for both were still young and good-looking) they had soon settled down into a workmanlike association that was not at all loverlike. Indeed it is hard to see how the Duchess could have maintained her intimate relationship with Conroy's wife and family if such had not been the case, and in fact from the evidence of letters in his private correspondence Conroy did not have an especially high opinion of the Duchess, or of her mental powers: 'So often, so very often, I must say to myself', wrote the Duchess to Conroy on a pencilled 'slip' of paper, 'what you said so often and what hurt me, but unhappily is true, I am not fit for my place, no, I am not. – I am just an old stupid goose, always to forget that people do not feel as I do.'[18]

Clearly the Duchess was a woman who thrived on self-denigration. It was unforgivable of Conroy to bully the Duchess and undermine her self-confidence – it was disastrous that she allowed him to do so – but it was easier for her to claim she was stupid than to take responsibility for her own thinking and actions. Indeed, as will be seen, the Duchess had always been some man's little 'goose'. It was part of her femininity, of her upbringing as a woman, to maintain a yielding, helpless, trusting nature. It was, in fact, just the sort of nature she hoped for in her own daughter.

Yet it was true she was not intellectual and had no training. She was alone. Conroy was 'wonderful'. Everyone had said so. Her brother Prince Leopold, Baron Stockmar, Lord Dunfermline – all had assured her her interests could not be placed 'in abler hands or in safer hands'.[19] Indeed, even her own husband had confided her to him.

Not only did she have no other choice than Conroy, but she was not perhaps quite as stupid as she appeared and so many others believed. For the Duchess judged by instinct, and her understanding led her not only to mistrust William Rea but to put her faith, for better for worse, in Conroy. Indeed, she knew him rather better – and 'made herself over to him' perhaps rather less – than most people realised. She said herself that 'Sir John Conroy was vain, and overbearing, as She had often told him, that he had made many enemies . . .'[20]

Conroy's attitude towards the Duchess however is not easy to define. It is clear he had the highly developed Irish understanding for where his best interests lay – subsequently becoming genuinely attached to his chosen patron – and, just as he was fond of Princess Sophia (who after all knew him and his affairs very much better even than did the Duchess) so he had a certain affection for Victoria's mother, actually declaring that he would 'die for her'. (On the whole this was unlikely, but he came to believe it in later years.) Nevertheless she undoubtedly irritated him. 'The Duchess lives in a mist', he complained to his son Edward, 'and therefore she is very difficult to deal with.'[21] And indeed, far from maintaining a flirtatious stance, Conroy took up the pose of the old adviser (he liked to stress that he had not only been a Servant – but *'an Advisor'*) signing himself to the Duchess in July 1826, when he was not yet forty, as her 'old and faithful Counsellor'.[22]

That he came in his own way to have a fondness for the

little Princess Victoria however is certain. He would delight in her humble academic achievements like a father; he commented proudly when she was growing and improving in looks. He claimed to his own family that he had for her 'a care not to be equalled'.[23] He had portraits painted of her favourite dogs and gave her carefully chosen presents. That she did not respond to his attention nor to the policies and regime that he and her mother were to devise for her upbringing, lay not only in Conroy's emerging tactlessness, arrogance and temper but in the influence of one woman – the 'snake in the grass' – Fräulein Lehzen.

The Duchess and Fräulein Lehzen were on opposite sides of the same German coin. Whilst the Duchess was a blonde, gentle, domesticated woman from the south, Lehzen was dark, sharp and Prussian in character – Melbourne described her looks as 'Italian' – with a shrewd, if limited intelligence. Like many women who are not especially attractive to men, she compensated with a passionately possessive maternal instinct which she was to lavish upon her charge, the Princess Victoria. Later Victoria was to describe Lehzen as 'My Mother'; the sole support and mainstay of her life. That this terrible situation came to pass was partly the fault of Lehzen herself.

Fräulein Louise Lehzen, the youngest of nine children born to a Lutheran clergyman at Langenhagen near Hanover, had travelled to England in the winter of 1819 to be Governess to Princess Feodora. One of her sisters was already dresser to Princess Caroline, the estranged wife of the Prince Regent, and indeed the humbleness of Lehzen's connections was destined to cause a good deal of trouble. She had however been brought up with great strictness, and from her parents she had inherited very firm ideas about life. Her father and mother 'gave us the best education by their example – instruction is quite a different thing',[24] she declared, and it was indeed through this subtle difference in her handling of Victoria that she was to gain her respect and affection.

As parents themselves, the Duchess and Conroy assumed

Victoria would naturally obey and respect them; that she would correspond to their idea of the obedient child to mould as they believed best. Lehzen however had quite a different vision as to the upbringing of a future monarch: 'she could pardon *wickedness* in a Queen,' she told the Hanmer family, 'but not *weakness*.' Elizabeth I, she added, was her 'model of perfection'.[25]

Not surprisingly, the implementation of her ideas were to come into direct conflict with the Household at Kensington. If Lehzen's 'model of perfection' was Elizabeth I – and if she was to educate 'by example' – then not only would Victoria's own mother be seen as a dreadful example of 'weakness', but Lehzen herself would have to be strong, respected, selfless and independent.

Her immediate antagonists were to be Conroy and the Duchess of Kent.

*

Conroy had plans for Victoria. Indeed, both the Duchess and Sir John had glimpsed in the person of the Princess the fulfilment of their own personal ambitions. Yet for the success of their schemes Sir John was to need the compliance of the little girl who played on a yellow carpet at Kensington, and ate bread and milk from a silver bowl. Victoria however, obstinate and self-willed as she was, was to prove a serious obstacle.

Nevertheless, Conroy would choose to meet Victoria's growing opposition – the opposition, after all, of a child – head on. He was not subtle; his was a parade-ground manner; and he did not exercise kindness or charm – although he was capable of both – in his dealings with the Household. Had he treated Victoria from her earliest days with affection and respect, he would have tempered considerably the influence of Lehzen. But this was not to be. As his own power increased so he became intolerant, rude and authoritarian – and, eventually, the deficiencies in his character betrayed themselves in a critical lack of judgement and self-control.

However, it must be said that Sir John possessed as strong a vision for the future of the little Princess as Fräulein Lehzen herself. But he was to play out his ambitions on a wider field, and he did not fully understand the landscape about him. Unlike Lehzen, his plans for Victoria and himself depended entirely on the great political movement of Reform, now filling the hearts and minds of the people, that he saw sweeping the Princess before it as its figure-head. It was not to occur to him, until too late, that those very political changes would leave no place for him in their new world.

But this is not to say there was no sincerity in his desire to make of Victoria a popular and respected Queen. On the contrary, he believed passionately in this ideal, for it appealed to his romanticism and curious sense of personal destiny. But he was far from disinterested. He believed as much in the glorious future of his own family upon which his ambitions relied.

But why was this so? Indeed at the heart of all Conroy's dealings with the Royal Family there lay a puzzle. What was it, they wondered, that drove him, past all reason, to confront their authority? Why did he act with such blind and desperate indiscretion?

'*Why* he outraged & insulted *me*', exclaimed a bewildered Victoria, many years later, '. . . I *really never* cd: understand.'[26]

Princess Sophia almost certainly understood; William Rea probably realised the truth; and Conroy's sons at length would come to know. But Sir John's strange secret was to be his fatal weakness; because of it he ruled the little Court at Kensington with a rod of iron; accumulated riches with Princess Sophia's money, and defied the will of Kings.

To understand his story (sad and exaggerated though it may be) it is necessary to open up The Conroy Papers and uncover the past. (A past in which his closest friends and colleagues took little interest and appreciated even less.) It was a story that lent itself to the Gothick novel, the Byronic hero, the nineteenth-century battleground of Good and Evil. Indeed, Conroy was to rise up in Victoria's youthful imagination like some Covent Garden brigand ('one of the greatest rascals', she cried, 'who ever existed') until, at the end of her life, the Queen could still admit: 'she shudders when she thinks of him . . .'[27]

2

'A DISGRACE TO THE HONOUR'

We owe much of our knowledge of the Conroys' early history to Sir John's eldest son Edward, who spent a large part of a valetudinarious middle age collating material for a family biography: he had considerable trouble with it, and pursued a method of cutting out slips of written text and sticking them haphazardly into ledger books which does not make for easy reading. Other memoranda (he was very keen on memoranda as was his father) were written on small pieces of paper and tied up in bundles with thin pieces of string. Edward's university education made him careful as to dates, and where his facts are verifiable they are usually found to be correct. His gullibility in matters of legend however was total and indeed symptomatic of a family failing. The biographer needs to tread warily when using him as a guide. Edward's researches did not extend much beyond the eighteenth century (evidently a three-volume work was intended) which was as well considering his subject matter. Certain references to Conroy were (for example) suppressed by the Queen's advisers from the *Memoirs of Baron Stockmar*,[1] and the subject was still capable of upsetting Queen Victoria well into old age. Edward's son John (Sir John Conroy's grandson) writing after his father's death may have been aware of this: 'I should object and object in the *strongest* way to the publication of any sort of life,' he wrote in 1893, '. . . with regard to Sir John's own wishes he would not I imagine have destroyed all his papers if he had wished his life to be written – that he did burn his papers a few years before his death is certain . . .'[2]

Despite Sir John's destruction of his papers (and we have no reason to doubt this) an enormous quantity remain: the more important of these are duplicated in the Royal Archives and it is possible that some of the destroyed documents are represented there as well. What is quite certain is that the remaining Conroy Papers were kept with a deliberate eye to posterity and his grandson, given the trouble he took to preserve them, undoubtedly felt this, too.

The Conroy family then, so Edward tells us, came of Milesian stock and traced its descent from Maine, the son of Niall of the Nine Hostages, Monarch of Ireland, in AD 400. From thence the family's slow emergence from the mists of Roscommon reads like a child's history of Ireland.

The O'Mulconrys (or O'Maolconaires) were chiefs of their clan and had, according to the Irish Chronicles, the privilege 'to stand alone, with the new king, upon the sacred Mount of Carn Fraoich, and there to deliver into his hands, the white wand or sceptre, the emblem of sovereignty, to administer the usual oath or admonition to preserve the customs of the country, and finally to record the proceedings'.[3]

Sir John's own coat-of-arms evoked these Celtic origins: two Bardic supporters rested their hands upon an open book, another hand held aloft a laurel wreath. Did Conroy see such a guardianship re-enacted in his relationship with Princess Victoria? Did he in his mind's eye hold ready 'The white wand or sceptre' to deliver into her hand? As we explore the imaginative life of this strange family almost anything becomes possible.

Forty-four generations were duly recorded on the family tree (a massive roll some six-feet-long) before we find Thorna O'Mulconry who, dying in 1647 at the height of the Civil War was succeeded by his only son John, the first of the Conrys to impress with his vitality and strength of character.

The O'Mulconrys had long owned estates in or near

Elphin in Roscommon, and it was in defence of these that twenty-two-year-old John Conry[4] joined the Catholic Royalist, Lord Clanricarde, Lord Lieutenant of Ireland, in his campaign against Cromwell's invasion in 1650. Conry was to spend three years fighting as a guerrilla in the woods and hills before escaping to France – as did thousands of other Catholics before him – in September 1653.

The young man enlisted into the service of General Vicomte de Turenne, Marshal of France. There is some irony attached to this decision, for at that time Turenne was a Protestant and indeed had actually been assisted by Cromwell's troops in the Civil War of the Fronde. Turenne's mother, Elizabeth, was a daughter of William the Silent, Prince of Orange, and it may well have been through the Marshal's influence that Conry (he had altered his name from O'Mulconry so as to be understood by the French) married in 1665 Florence Fitzgerald, daughter and heir to Gerald Fitzgerald of the House of Desmond, herself of Protestant stock. They had a daughter and two sons, Charles and Ferfeassa.

Edward claims that John could have joined the Court of Louis XIV, having received a commission into the King's Bodyguard: whether or not he actually did so, we find Conry in 1672 – accompanied by his twelve-year-old son Charles – marching with the King and Turenne (now, confusingly, a Catholic convert) in the ill-fated invasion of Holland. On 12th June, during the crossing of the Rhine, the Dutch put up stiff resistance against the French army and Conry was killed at Tollhuis by a bullet shot into his raised armpit.

John's little boy Charles was adopted and educated by Vicomte de Turenne and remained with his eminent guardian until the Marshal's own death in the Battle of Sassbach in 1675. Ferfeassa, Charles's younger brother, had been under the protection of their great-uncle in Ireland since 1674; and on Charles's own home-coming in 1677 he found that a grant of the family property had been made over to him by his uncle on 10th August 1676. A further grant of land made two years later by Charles II re-established the Conry estate.[5]

Charles never married – although he had a legendary love

affair that came to nothing – and on James II's arrival in Ireland to rally support for his Catholic cause he at once joined the King's army and was killed at the Battle of the Boyne in 1690. It was said that a banshee wailed on the night before the battle, warning the family of Charles's death; and on the same day Ferfeassa brought his body home to rest in Roscommon. 'One of the most gallant spirits', claimed Edward proudly, 'of the O'Maolconaire race.'[6]

These stirring times were not to be forgotten by Ferfeassa's descendants. Sir John Conroy's children greatly enjoyed Private Theatricals – very fashionable in the nineteenth century – and one of their favourite set-pieces was a re-enactment of the Conrys' swash-buckling career. The crossing of the Rhine in a Regency drawing-room would have been an interesting experience. In fact, from this point onwards we find self-dramatisation becoming a noticeable element in the Conroy psyche: a dangerous characteristic perhaps when unsupported by humility.

At this point too there came a distinct change in direction in the family's history; for Ferfeassa, to save his property, adopted the Protestant faith. No longer identifying with the Catholic peasantry – nor with the Dissenters – we find the Conrys allying themselves to the Anglo-Irish aristocracy. Henceforth the family married Anglo-Irish or English women and their ties with their native Ireland grew less strong. But they were still Irishmen with a conscience and in Ferfeassa's only legitimate son – by his wife Cicily Aylmer – we find not only a delightful eighteenth-century personality, but a man who was to graft himself firmly to the Irish Whig party with far-reaching influence and effect.

*

The face that contemplates us from Robert Hunter's admirable portrait of John Conry is that of a kindly, humorous but thoughtful man. The impression is of a well-rounded, sympathetic personality whose deep-set eyes and prominent 'Conry' nose are immediately evident as are also the long and sensitive hands. He was to inspire lasting affection in others, and his family would benefit from the memory of his remarkable qualities for several generations to come.

John Conry was born in 1704 and nothing is known of his early childhood and education. We first encounter him living in Ann Street, Dublin, holding the important government office of the Collector of Cork. Support for this post had come from John Ponsonby, Secretary of the Revenue Board, notable Whig, and Speaker from 1756, of the Irish House of Commons. His deep friendship with Conry spoke well for both men, and it was he who commissioned the portrait by Robert Hunter which remained at Bishopscourt, the Ponsonby home, until 1838.

John Conry had a reputation for challenging his rivals with wit and panache, and those anecdotes that Edward tells of him have a distinctly eighteenth-century flavour – not to say odour. His wooing of his future bride Elizabeth Foulke (at the age of forty-three) was typically robust.

Conry had evidently delayed his marriage until the death of his father, Ferfeassa, in 1746. If he had hoped for financial gain, however, he was disappointed; Ferfeassa's estate was divided equally between John Conry and several illegitimate offspring and only a small farm at Kilclogherna came to his legitimate son. Possibly Conry's friends thought this unfair, for, the following year, the Bishop of Elphin, Dr Edward Synge, son of the Archbishop of Tuam, granted him a Bishop's Lease, payable by a fine for ever, of land said to be a portion of the ancient territory of the O'Mulconaires. The condition of this gift was that Conry should build a lodge to be near him: this was called Shankhill – but later changed to Bettyfield after his wife, Elizabeth.

Elizabeth Foulke at the time of her marriage to Conry in 1747 was eighteen years old, very beautiful and – owing to the death of an elder brother – heiress to a large fortune. Her father did not approve of Conry and gave his support to his rival, a fellow Anglo-Irishman.

At a ball in Cork, so Edward tells us in a lively account,[7] whilst dancing with John Conry, the 'stays' of Miss Foulke's dress regrettably broke emitting a suggestive noise. Amidst the hilarity that this disaster evoked Conry threw himself at

Miss Foulke's feet and begged her forgiveness for the indecency of which he was guilty.

Into this extraordinary scene (one wonders if it was permitted in the Conroy Private Theatricals) strode Conry's rival: 'Sir,' he cried, 'you shall answer for this insult to Miss Foulke, to me.'

Immediately the two repaired to an adjoining room, called for lights, and commenced a duel. This proceeded in a defensive manner until his assailant drew blood from Conry's wrist.

'This for my wrist,' cried Conry lungeing unsuccessfully.

'That for myself,' he warned, lungeing again.

'Take that for Miss Foulke.'

The third encounter succeeded in wounding his opponent and during his rival's convalescence John Conry married Miss Foulke.

The marriage was happy. The couple had two daughters, Elizabeth and Catherine, and their only son John Ponsonby – so named after his father's greatest friend – was born in 1759. All would have continued well but for a calamity that cut short Conry's life. Following an operation to remove a tumour he died in 1769 at the age of sixty-five. His wife was grief-stricken and did not long survive him, dying in 1772, leaving her children orphaned. The Collector of Cork was buried in the churchyard at Bishopscourt, County Kildare, the seat of Speaker Ponsonby. Twenty years later when Ponsonby himself was on his death-bed, he was asked where he wished to be buried: 'Take me up the hill', he is said to have replied, '& lay me by the side of my old Friend, Johnny Conry.'

In 'John Conry of Elphin' we find talents that had revived in his descendants. He was a self-made man; businesslike and shrewd and with an undeniable flair for extracting support (and even property) from influential people; but they gave because they were fond of him and he repaid them with the charm of his company. It seems likely that if the Conry family ever achieved greatness it was in this eighteenth-century Dubliner.

Conry's son, John Ponsonby, was ten years old at the death of his father in 1769, and following the death of his mother three years later was taken under the care of Dean Cramer of County Kildare. Conry was educated at Dr Darby's School and Trinity College, Dublin, which he entered at the age of sixteen, in 1775.

'A handsome, clever but idle lad', was how one old school-friend described John Ponsonby. ('His nature as a man', commented Edward), and evidently his temperament was altogether too light-hearted to follow the legal career into which his guardian had placed him. In fact Conry must have been the despair of Dean Cramer for in 1783 we find him with a company of amateur actors performing in a theatre in Fishamble Street, Dublin. Here, he excelled in a number of Shakespearian roles including the character Falstaff, for which he was famed, and which he portrayed at the youthful age of twenty-five. He was – perhaps unfortunately – the only member of his family to fulfil legitimately what was becoming an inherited trait.

Within two years, however, Conry had put away such tendencies and fallen in love with Margaret Wilson, a daughter of Francis Vernon Wilson, descendant of Cromwellian settlers from Tully, County Longford. Following a visit to her home in Conway, North Wales, Conry complained disarmingly to Margaret that 'you put to route my legal ideas at Conway and so impregnate me with Romance as will render it difficult for me to become accustomed to the ways of men. I do nothing but compare the hardness of the flags to the softness of the sod in Arcadia.'

In the same year 1785 Conry chose Arcadia, and marrying Margaret Wilson set up home in North Wales. For the first years of marriage he lived as a country-gentleman, presumably on the income from his father's estate (worth 13/6d. an acre in 1779).[8] As the only son he never inherited the Foulke fortune, since his maternal grandfather died before his birth leaving his money elsewhere. It was a year later, at Maizey Castle, in the village of Caerhun, Caernarfonshire, Conry's eldest son, John Ponsonby Conry, was born.

Maizey Castle was a useful birthplace for an ambitious

man, conjuring up as it still can a suitably baronial image of draughty halls and loyal yeomanry. Unfortunately, as with so much in the Conroy saga, the picture dissolves on closer inspection into something rather more prosaic. Maizey Castle becomes Maesycastell, an Elizabethan gentleman's house situated on the Vaynol Estate and owned by the Assheton-Smith family. John Conry was not even the tenant of Maesycastell, which lay not far from the old mountain road running from Bangor across the Penmaenmawr headland to Talycafn Ferry. However, as the family lived there for only one year they may well have obtained a short let from the existing tenant, William Roberts.[9]

John Ponsonby Conry (the name was not changed to Conroy until 1787) was baptised at Caerhun on the 21st October 1786,[10] and since this is also given as his birthdate (and was the day he himself celebrated) we must assume that, somewhat unusually, he was baptised on the day of his birth. Unlike his father however he was never to use his middle name of Ponsonby, and was generally known as 'John Conroy'.

From Maesycastell the family moved to Conway, and a year later to nearby Placara where they lived for four or five years; it was here that two of John's younger brothers – Llewellin and George – were born.

Wales at this date was opening up to the outside world – its dramatic mountain scenery appealing to what we now perceive as the Romantic Movement then overtaking Europe – and from his letters one suspects that the wild grandeur of Conway held just such an attraction for John Conry himself. It is over-fanciful perhaps to assume that grand scenery breeds grand ideas; yet it must be said that Conry's eldest son was to maintain a life-long attachment to Wales, and the fantasies of childhood are the longest and strongest of all.

With romanticism, however, came rebellion – and with rebellion, revolution. The first stirrings of France forced all men to commit themselves politically, and in Ireland the age-old grievances surfaced once more. In 1792 we find John Conry hurrying home to exercise at last his legal skills and to protect his estate from the angry peasantry. Since his father's friendship with Lord Ponsonby, the Conry family was staunchly Whig in character and John Conry himself was almost certainly a member of the Whig Club – founded by Lord Ponsonby's son George Ponsonby, future Lord Chancellor of Ireland. Known to him too would have been another great figure of the Irish political scene, the Independent Anglo-Irishman Sir Lawrence Parsons of Birr – described by the Irish revolutionary Wolfe Tone as 'one of the very *very few* honest men in the Irish House of Commons'.[11] Sir Lawrence is destined to enter the Conroy story some years hence in very different times and circumstances.

But even now history was hastening change; Wolfe Tone succeeded in persuading the French to finance an Irish Rebellion; in 1796 the French Fleet itself attempted to invade Ireland at Bantry Bay and in 1800 the Grenville Government brought in the Act of Union between Great Britain and Ireland. From this time onwards greater numbers of Protestant Irishmen – the Conroys among them – were to make their way across the sea to establish themselves in England.

In the 1790s however, we find John Conry working as Secretary of the Savings Board – for which he received the remarkable sum of £1,000 a year[12] – and also employed by the Government in various tasks during the Irish disturbances. One such took him to Roscommon where, making full use of his histrionic gifts, he endeavoured to induce the peasantry to disarm: '*The King in his Clemency* would pardon all former violent acts,' he declared from a window at French Park Mansion.

'Ah now, Mister Counsellor', exclaimed a voice in the crowd, 'We have heard in Ireland of the King, but never of Clemency, pray yer honor what may *that* be?'[13]

But sadly there was to be no clemency for John Conry: in September 1797 in Dawson Street, Dublin, he died suddenly aged thirty-eight. He left behind five small children, his sixth, Deane Josias, being born after his own death in 1798.

How important was this loss of a father to John Conroy? To grow up with only one parent (or none at all) was certainly a commonplace until the twentieth century – Conroy's own father had been left an orphan at the age of thirteen – yet one aspect of such a bereavement never changes: with the death of a father there comes to his eldest son a sense of responsibility and power. It is clear that for Conroy this assumption became an attitude which he was never able to relinquish. Indeed, in his almost monumental ambition to turn a 'good family' into a great and aristocratic one, Sir John became the victim not only of his own special position as head of a family, but also of a society governed by its aristocracy. Rank and pedigree meant power; and the powerful connection was the only connection worth having. All these attributes Conroy was to find – and find at a very early age – in the person of his wife, Elizabeth Fisher.

*

Conroy met his 'Eliza' in 1808 when he was twenty-one years old and she seventeen. Her father, Lieutenant Colonel Fisher (later Major General), had been sent by the English Government in 1797, as Commanding Royal Engineer, to oversee the defences of Ireland's coastline. Colonel Fisher set up home in Stephen Street, Dublin, where he lived for a number of years.[14]

On the death of his father, Conroy had been educated for three years at Mr Feas's school at Summer Hill, Dublin, and following special tuition with a Mr Hopkins at Portartington and a Reverend Nickolson from Trinity College, Dublin, he had passed as Cadet into the Royal Military College, Woolwich.[15] Curiously, the Royal Regiment of Artillery's *List of Officers* describes Conroy as entering the College on 9th December 1800, when he would have been fourteen years old: as his age, however is given as sixteen years ten months, it would seem some adjustment was made by the family to his actual date of birth. That Conroy's guardian – a Mr Taylor – was himself an army agent may well have been an influence in his choice of career, and in fact all but one of the Conroy boys were to enter the forces; Conroy's favourite brother Llewellin being made a Lieutenant in the Indian Army in 1805.

On his commission into 'K' troop of the Royal Horse Artillery (also in 1805) Conroy joined a new élite. The Artillery, founded by Charles, Duke of Richmond and Lennox, Master General of the Ordnance, had received its Royal Warrant in 1783 and its first engagement was in the Irish Rebellion of 1798. This prestigious force was selected entirely on merit: all the men had to be strong, of above average intelligence and over five feet eight inches in height. The duties of a member of the force were very flexible; circulating – as Conroy was to – between the Staff, Royal Artillery and Royal Horse Artillery as needed.[16] In fact Conroy came to the Royal Horse Artillery from the Royal Artillery, into which he was commissioned in 1803 as Adjutant to the Western District, Ireland. It was in 1807 that he was made aide de camp to Colonel Fisher – and some years later still before the Duchess of Kent was to compose the Royal Artillery Slow March ('The Duchess of Kent March') that was to become the symbol of Conroy's regiment.

Colonel Fisher came from an ecclesiastical family and his father, Vicar of Peterborough and Preceptor to George III, had nine sons, all of whom made their mark. They were variously known as 'the loaves and fishers' and the elder – John Fisher – was distinguished as 'the King's Fisher' since he had been made Tutor to Prince Edward, Duke of Kent, fourth son of George III. He and his nephew were fortunate in being the intimate friends of the painter John Constable – and later, as Bishop of Salisbury, he oversaw the education (artistic and otherwise) of the ebullient Princess Charlotte. She, with her delightful predilection for nick-names, christened him 'the Bish UP', 'the great U.P.'.

The Bish UP made himself useful with his own family. By his influence his younger brother, George Fisher, became aide de camp to the Duke of Kent; together in 1791, they travelled to Canada where George Fisher's brother, Benjamin, was Captain in the Royal Engineers and living in Government House, Quebec. It was here that Benjamin's only daughter, Elizabeth, was born.

Elizabeth Fisher's royal connections might have been

considered sufficient for most people; yet she was to be endowed by the Conroy family with even more interesting affiliations than those she already possessed, since she was believed by them to be (we may perhaps indulge here in capital letters) of Noble Birth. A royal connection was an excellent thing in its way, but royal blood gave the possessor almost mystical significance; and the extraordinary expansiveness with which George III's children had spread their favours allowed every sort of rumour and suspicion as to their progeny to harden into actual fact.

One of the more intriguing items in The Conroy Papers is a purple leather diary[17], belonging to Sir John Conroy's grandson, dating from 1868. One page yields a curious paragraph written in part in a schoolboy's code (relying heavily upon the Utopian alphabet of Sir Thomas More) that begins: 'Lady Conroy was the only child of General Fisher; he had married a Miss Clarke . . .' The deciphered code tells us 'she is said to have been the illigitimate [sic] daughter of Lord Harford [sic] and to have been fathered by F. Clerke a yoman [sic] . . .' 'Lady Conroy is said', continues this curious revelation, 'to be the daughter of the Duke of Kent who', it adds, 'had been sent out to Canada to keep him out of mischief.'

There can be no doubt at all that the Conroy family believed and believed with passion that this was the literal truth. Edward Conroy, in the following year 1869, made a final and dramatic deathbed confession of the whole sorry business.[18] General Fisher, Edward declared, married Miss Clarke in Norfolk in 1783 and had no children by her for eight years. Edward, Duke of Kent, future father of Queen Victoria, was supposed, on his arrival in Canada in May 1791, to have worked something of a miracle in the circumstances and Mrs Fisher is said to have produced Elizabeth in six short months, on 25th November 1791. Not surprisingly this created a sensation in Government House and George Fisher resigned the Duke's service in consequence, leaving Prince Edward to take for ever after a tender interest in the affairs of Elizabeth Fisher. 'I am myself', Edward Conroy pointed out, 'called Edward, after him by his own command, & he promised to watch over my interests, as my Godfather.'

'Sir J. was proud', Edward added, 'and considered it *indelicate* to have let Dchss know about his wife's relation to Pss Victoria. Sir J. has often expressed his idea that it was a disgrace to the honour, & as Ly C was sufficiently fond of Gen. Fisher she could never be told that it was true she was not his own child – Hence the silence always observed on this subject, of which proof remains.'[19]

It is one of the sad duties of a biographer to dismantle legend, and alas when we apply the microscope to Edward's story we discover that Elizabeth Fisher, far from being born in 1791, was baptised in Quebec on 28th November 1790 by the Reverend Philip Toosey. Her parents were given as Benjamin Fisher Esqr and Charlotte his wife.[20] Her birth-date was said by the family to be the 25th November, and since Sir John Conroy and Princess Victoria both recorded celebrating Lady Conroy's birthday on the 25th November,[21] it is probable this was her date of birth and that she was baptised three days later.

In 1790 the Duke of Kent (or Prince Edward, as he still then was) remained far away in Gibraltar meting out 'bestial severity' to the troops under his command. As a result he was sent in disgrace, with his mistress Madame de St Laurent, to Canada. They set sail from Gibraltar on the 24th June 1791 and arrived at Quebec the following August.[22] Even by Edward's feverish calculations the Duke could not have perpetrated the indiscretion that resulted in Lady Conroy.

The Duke of Kent's relationship to the Conroys was undoubtedly one of pure friendship and he himself made this clear in a letter to the Duke of Wellington in December 1818, describing Conroy as having 'been known to me for many years, from the circumstances of his being married to the Daughter of one of my oldest military friends, the late General Fisher of the Royal Engineers, and niece to the good Bishop of Salisbury, who was my preceptor'.[23]

History of course is not merely a question of establishing the truth. Indeed, the truth may become incidental to the much more important matter of what people actually believed to be true at the time. How the Conroy family came to know, let alone accept the story of Lady Conroy's supposed parentage is a mystery, but accept the story they did. Indeed, it seems likely that the Conroys were caught up – albeit unconsciously – in the atmosphere of their time; with the romantic fashion for melodrama, mystery and dreadful family secrets. The very fact that they were secret conveniently insured that the truth would never be known.

Their speculation upon 'Lord Harford', however, is less easy to refute. The Lord Hertford alluded to (pronounced 'Harford') could be identified as Algernon Seymour, Duke of Somerset and Earl of Hertford, only son of the 6th Duke of Somerset. His mother was Lady Elizabeth Percy and through her Algernon was created Earl of Northumberland in 1749. Northumberland's only son died before him and on his death in 1750 the succession passed through his daughter Elizabeth, Baroness Percy, to her husband Sir Hugh Smithson. He was created 1st Duke of Northumberland in 1750.

It is an undoubted fact that the Northumberlands play an important role in the Conroy story. The Duchess of Northumberland became Princess Victoria's official Governess in 1830 – a choice brought about by Sir John Conroy. (As Heiress Presumptive she had required a lady of rank as Governess; Lehzen being her Sub-Governess). The Northumberland family adopted Conroy's grandson to an extent beyond the call of mere friendship. The Duke of Northumberland was made the legal custodian of The Conroy Papers (although he never received them) and finally they were left all the royal mementoes accumulated by the Conroy family.[24]

It seems very probable the Northumberlands believed Lady Conroy's illegitimate descent through Charlotte Clarke to be true, although no further rumour of such an association now remains and it was never mentioned by Edward in his death-bed confessions.

In Elizabeth Fisher, then, Conroy had found a woman he considered to be related to at least one of the greatest families in the land. We do not know when he came to learn of his wife's supposed origins, but it is clear from Edward's memorandum that he believed them during his career with the Duchess of Kent and it is likely he was told of the suspicions many years before. Small wonder he became ambitious; small wonder he had, as Lord Melbourne had noted, 'a great deal of assumption'; small wonder too that he was over-familiar in his manners with his royal mistresses. (Perhaps he had hinted to Princess Sophia of the close association of his children to herself. She was after all scarcely in a position to disbelieve him.) Certainly, for the Conroy family, nothing less than a peerage would ever be good enough.

On 26th December 1808, in her family home at Stephen Street, Dublin, Elizabeth Fisher was married by Special Licence to John Conroy.[25]

They made a handsome pair – John Conroy was described as 'a very fine looking man'[26] and indeed his portraits, albeit of a later date, confirm this. He was six feet tall, with black hair and grey eyes, and even his enemies were to concede that he had a considerable presence and charm of manner. His young wife would have matched him well, being five feet ten inches in height with striking dark brown hair. She was amiable, kind and very musical and brought with her a large marriage settlement (Conroy did not) but, in the words of her grandson, her 'mental powers' were 'below average a perfect cipher'.[27] Even the Duchess of Kent was to describe her as never doing 'any harm to anyone only to herself as she was very indolent'.[28]

This indolence and lack of critical insight was disastrous for her family as well as for herself. She would follow her husband blindly, the passive and apparently innocent repository of his fantasies and ambitions. Had she been able to criticise and confront him more, much might have been salvaged, for he obviously had a true regard for her, as small snatches of verse and allusions in his letters bear out: 'My dearest Eliza!' he wrote, when they had been married for over ten years.

This little watch, when last in gay Paris
          for you I bought;
Which ever since I've kept to try to match
With gold seal – I ought *from thence* to
          have brought.

Alas! All my efforts have proved vain!
Pray therefore accept – in its present state,
First month eighteen hundred and nineteen
        the watch, the chain, and the
        key – for my sake.[29]

But in 1808 they were at the outset of their married life: six children would be born and Conroy would have achieved much in his army career before the arrival in England of the Duke and Duchess of Kent, and the birth of Princess Victoria at Kensington Palace, entirely altered the course of their happy life together.

3

'AN EXCELLENT PEN AND INK MAN'

By the time of Victoria's birth, Kensington Palace had become something of a shelter for redundant members of the Royal Family. The inhabitants consisted of the kindly Duke of Sussex, who with his chiming clocks and library of bibles lived in the cheerful south wing, whilst his sister Princess Sophia, with failing sight, sat alone at her spinning-wheel in the north wing and dreamt of the past. Silent, half-empty and disappointed, the Palace held little interest for the parading passersby – filled them even with dread, for the future seemed as equally bereft and uncertain.

Following the death in childbirth of Princess Charlotte in November 1817 the nation felt it had lost the one rejuvenating element in the Royal Family. The country was tired after its triumph at Waterloo in 1815; the war had sustained the farmers and fighting men but now the corn was not needed and the soldiers sent home; society was in the process of change from a rural-based economy to an industrial way of life, yet taxation was high, poverty extreme and general education almost nil. Against this discontent a great cry went up for a new order and a new world. The aristocracy took fright. They looked to the Royal Family and saw only the mad King George III and his degenerate sons standing between them and a revolution:

An old, mad, [wrote Shelley,]
   blind, despised, and dying king, –
Princes, the dregs of their dull race, who flow
Through public scorn, – mud from a muddy spring, –
Rulers who neither see, nor feel, nor know,
But leech-like to their fainting country cling,
Till they drop, blind in blood, without a blow.[1]

Despite this awful prospect the Tory Prime Minister, Lord Liverpool, still retained power, and the Duke of Wellington was to continue to exert a stabilising, balanced and unifying influence on the Government and nation. But they were essentially eighteenth-century figures; many of their contemporaries still living in the past – aristocrats who sat, as one young man complained, 'in their libraries and fancy things and men as they were twenty years ago'.[2]

Yet, with all, England possessed the greatest Empire in the world: her mines and mills of the Industrial Revolution produced an unequalled richness – and the great factory owners were themselves giving rise to a new class and a new type of Englishman who found neither a reflecting image in its present royalty, nor comfort from the thought of revolution. In them lay the country's hope.

Following Princess Charlotte's death the unmarried sons of George III embarked on a comical race to the altar. At least, so it appeared, but it is unfair to think so. It is clear from their letters that negotiations with various ladies had been long underway but only now had marriage become an imperative. Necessity to provide an heir served too to provoke the dislike and rivalry that lay between the brothers and from which only the married Dukes remained aloof.

The Prince Regent had his detested wife, Princess Caroline, and although charm and humour could still flow from him, he was petulant, ill and disappointed and glad to be out of the race. His brother Augustus, the forty-four-year-old Duke of Sussex, washed his hands of the business as well: he had two children by his first wife Lady Augusta Murray and later was comfortably married to a widow, Lady Cecilia Buggin. Both marriages were outside the provisions of the

Royal Marriage Act. The brothers the Duke of York and the Duke of Cumberland were legally married: the former was childless, but the Duke of Cumberland had only recently married in 1815 the widow of the Prince of Solms-Braunfels. They were an extraordinarily unattractive couple: he with a terrible scar on his face was destined to be the pantomime ogre of Queen Victoria's childhood, whilst the Princess – who had been formerly engaged to the Duke of Cambridge – broke his heart by unexpectedly marrying Solms-Braunfels instead. Queen Charlotte refused to meet her when subsequently she married the Duke of Cumberland. Cambridge showed resilience however, and only ten days after Charlotte's death asked Augusta, Princess of Hesse-Cassell, to marry him and was accepted. Likewise negotiations were soon underway for the sea-faring Duke of Clarence (then third in line to the throne) to bid farewell to Mrs Jordan his mistress of nearly twenty years, and his ten children – the notorious 'Bâtards' – and marry Adelaide, Princess of Saxe-Meiningen. This left the Duke of Kent to find himself a bride.

Edward, Duke of Kent, would not have cared to be described as 'mud from a muddy spring'. At fifty he took very good care of himself, rose at five with regimental discipline and dyed his balding hair and whiskers black. He had for twenty-seven years been living with his mistress Madame de St Laurent – she who had accompanied him to Canada in 1791 – but for some while he had evidently been restless to provide a legitimate heir. (He had had one child – not by his mistress – a fact which may have fuelled the Conroys' erroneous beliefs.) A gypsy had once told him the crown would come to him and his children: this prophecy inspired him now, and he reopened previous negotiations with the thirty-one-year-old Victoire, Princess of Leiningen, sister to Prince Leopold of Saxe-Coburg the husband of Princess Charlotte. (Madame de St Laurent fainted at the news he was likely to marry, which rumour she had the misfortune to learn from a newspaper.)

Victoire had been married formerly at seventeen years of age to the Prince of Leiningen who was twenty-three years her senior and by whom she had a son and daughter. He treated her more as a niece than a wife (his little 'goose' in fact), allowing her no say in the running of the household. On his death she was assisted in her Regency by an attractive young Equerry, Captain Schindler (who was to remain a beneficiary on her Coutts account), and who acquired considerable power within her small Court. Victoire never knew a loving relationship with a man of her own age and this made her exceptionally vulnerable to the influence of attractive young courtiers. Equally, she was used to others making decisions for her and – lacking in confidence and believing herself to be unintelligent – trusted their judgement; her whole outlook was totally straightforward and quite incapable of suspicion and malice.

There is an advantage in such unprejudiced natures; they will not assume unprincipled behaviour in others unless it is proved, and because they see only the good in people they tend to bring out their better qualities. However, such innocence cannot long survive in the real world.

In 1818 the Duke of Kent again asked Princess Victoire for her hand in marriage and this time was gladly accepted.

*

In 1818, on the Duke of Kent's marriage to the Princess of Leiningen, Captain John Conroy was made his personal Equerry. The appointment did not give him more than executive powers (although Edward Conroy described him as 'Chief Administrator' of the Duke's affairs), since General Wetherall remained Comptroller of the Duke's Household. The appointment however brought him within the sphere of the Royal Family and a potential intimacy was created that Conroy would have felt to be his family's natural inheritance.

Since his marriage in 1808 Conroy's career had been useful without being crowned by the achievement expected of an officer during the Napoleonic Wars. Indeed, it was with evident contempt that his fellow officers noted that he never volunteered for active service: 'In the war,' complained Sir George Couper to the Duchess many years later, 'whilst we all resigned our staff appointments at home and joined the army in Spain, Sir John preferred to retain his Staff situation and remain in Dublin.'[3]

Why was this? Captain Conroy was young and strong, an excellent horseman and fond of the outdoor life. Whilst it is possible that courage and a sense of adventure were lacking in his temperament, the more likely explanation lay in the curious circumstances of his marriage and family. Undoubtedly personal success in the army would have come more readily to him had he had experience in the field, and Conroy would have realised this; yet his natural ambition did not drive him to take the opportunity available. Later, the Duke of Wellington was to find this very lack of experience on active service an excuse for denying him promotion.[4] It would seem probable therefore that Conroy's ambitions were directed first and foremost towards his growing family whom he believed to be of royal descent. Left without a father – as were both he and his father before him – could they have achieved the way of life he felt their background demanded?

Nevertheless, Conroy had done well. He had been made Captain on the 13th March 1811, and two months later became Brigade Major to General Staff Engineers Department in Ireland.[5] The following year, however, General Fisher was transferred to England and, as his aide de camp, Conroy and his family joined him at Portsmouth. Later Conroy returned to Dublin Castle to wind up the General's affairs, which he did apparently to everyone's satisfaction dealing with the enormous sum of £300,000.[6]

However, the stay at Portsmouth was to last only two years, for on 10th October 1814 General Fisher died. For the first time Conroy – to whom his father-in-law had doubtless stood 'in loco parentis' – found himself alone.

'The papers will have informed you before you receive this, of the death of a brother of the Bishop, Gen. Fisher', wrote the Bishop of Salisbury's nephew to his great friend John Constable. 'I am down here with his family acting the part of Comforter where no comfort can be administered. Of all the scenes of distress I ever witnessed nothing has equalled what I have seen. His Son in law Capt. Conroy a fine manly soldier weeping like an infant. His only daughter I tore from the coffin as they were conveying the remains from the house. The widow is a little short of a state of distraction.'[7] The Bishop of Salisbury himself described his brother's death as 'a source of great affliction to the whole of his family. He was a very valuable member of Society, both in his public & private capacity.'[8]

Added to this untimely blow Conroy's own family circumstances had not been easy: of the six children left by his father only three survived – himself, his youngest brother Deane and his brother Llewellin, now an army officer in India. George, a Midshipman, had died at sea in 1805, and William and Laetitia both died young. Even his mother, Margeret – so romantically courted by his father – had been married since 1801 to John Waldron of Black Rock, Dublin. (Emma – her daughter of this marriage – was also married twice; secondly to Carden Terry, Conroy's land agent.[9]) In 1814 Conroy's own family consisted of Edward, born in 1809, Elizabeth Jane, born 1811, and Arthur born two years later.

Following General Fisher's death Conroy was removed from the Artillery Staff at Portsmouth and a flurry of recommendations blew about as he looked for a new job. A letter to General Douglas from Colonel Chapman, Secretary to Lord Mulgrave, apparently produced the desired result: 'My friend Captain Conroy', it read, 'is anxious to have your recommendation for one of the situations of Adjutant to the reformed Drivers Corps: you are aware, I believe, that Lord Mulgrave's determination that the Adjutants shall be selected from the Artillery. As I understand it, the intention is, to have one Adjutant at Woolwich, another in Ireland, and one in France.

'Either of these, would suit Captain Conroy. Woolwich is the first instance, and Ireland secondly, for he has a wife and family, and the Widow of my lamented friend General Fisher, to whom he affords an asylum . . .

'. . . Captain Conroy is the Person most likely to be *most useful to you at Headquarters* – for added to his qualification, he is an excellent Pen and Ink man, possessing great knowledge of horses and the care of them, great zeal and activity and a very early man in summer and winter – my opinion is, that I think him equal to almost any undertaking, where zeal, activity and talent are requisite.'[10]

In 1816 Conroy took up his command at Woolwich as Officer in Command and Charge of the Artillery Drivers (whose reorganisation he was to oversee) and moved his family to a new home in Shooters Hill. The move was an admirable one: Mrs Arbuthnot – the great friend of the Duke of Wellington – described riding to Woolwich and Shooters Hill at this time 'over a most beautiful country'. Conroy was now the father of four children (Stephen being born in 1815) and Shooters Hill was a delightful place to bring up a family.

It was whilst at Woolwich in fact that Conroy came into contact for the first time with the Duke of Wellington, then Major-General of the Ordnance, and their relationship did not bode well for the future. Wellington – whose detachment and sense of proportion were remarkable – clearly felt ambivalent towards Conroy. His Irishness and Ponsonby connection appealed to him (they actually looked a little alike) but this early encounter was to set him on his guard. Wellington and Conroy had what Edward Conroy was to describe as 'Military disagreements', and Conroy 'flung up his command at Woolwich in disgust'.[11] Following this fracas Wellington was to deftly fend off all future requests for advancement and rank for Conroy. In 1824, writing to William Knighton, Private Secretary to George IV, Conroy suggested that Wellington might not 'be sorry to have the means offered to him of allowing justice being done an old friend and officer, who he has materially injured'. Wellington's continued silence was, one suspects, very painful to him, for 'Military rank', he admitted, 'is very dear to me'.[12]

This unfortunate introduction to Woolwich seems to have had not the slightest effect on Conroy's admirers; once again he was job hunting, and once more the references bowled in: 'in every respect a treasure', saluted the Duke of Kent from Amorbach, 'as well as from experience and practice as from talent and a great habit of application'.[13]

Conroy's talent equally – perhaps one might even say ominously – enjoyed creating systems and reforms. Whilst at Woolwich he had drawn up a Reform of the Field Artillery which seems to have received polite enthusiasm and been quietly shelved: 'I have had the pleasure of receiving yours of the 14th together with *the Book* – the Plan therein proposed for the reform of the Field Artillery, is by much the best and *most feasible* I have yet seen . . .' wrote Colonel Maclean from Dublin, in July 1818,[14] and Colonel Jenkinson averred that he knew it 'from long and frequent conversations with the Duke of Wellington, to be that which His Grace has ever been most anxious to seeing carried into affect'.[15] Apparently His Grace had not been quite as anxious as Conroy would have liked.

Following the Duke of Kent's marriage (a ceremony in the Great Hall of Giants at Coburg had been followed by another double ceremony with the Duke and Duchess of Clarence at Kew) it was made clear to the Duke that he could not remain in England. He was hopelessly in debt – he continually complained, as did most of his brothers, that he had not been given sufficient money to maintain his princely station – and the acquisition of a wife with an expensive taste in hats had not helped matters. His rooms at Kensington Palace and his house at Ealing (an extraordinary place filled with artificial singing birds and waterfalls in cupboards) were shut up at the instigation of his financial committee and the pair returned to Amorbach. The Duchess was already pregnant, however, and the Duke wrote repeatedly to the Prince Regent desiring that his child should be born in England, claiming finally that Amorbach was unhealthy and too far from proper medical attention. On learning that the Duke's committee (formed by the Duke's creditors to manage his income) were willing to foot the bill the Prince Regent reluctantly agreed to the hair-raising proposal of driving the eight-months pregnant Duchess from Germany to Kensington. Captain Conroy was deputed, as the Duke's new Equerry, to organise the adventure.

Conroy had been known intimately to the Duke over

many years. As the son-in-law of his old friend and a Whig by tradition (the Duke himself was staunchly of the liberal persuasion) he was a man the Prince felt he could trust. However, it is unlikely that Conroy, at this stage of their association, was committed to his service. Until 1822, when he resigned on half-pay, he remained a full-time officer in the army and endeavoured to find preferment within it. Conroy later maintained that the Duke of York had offered him advancement which he had refused (but it was in fact Wellington who had rejected York's request on Conroy's behalf) and he further insisted that had he remained in the Artillery he 'should have risen to emolument and rank'; but one suspects that in fact his career was at a standstill and the Duke's offer was opportune.

The cavalcade which Conroy steered across Europe was described by one onlooker as 'unbelievably odd'. It consisted of a motley selection of carriages – some especially built for the Duchess's condition; carriages of maids and cooking equipment, a doctor, Madame Siebold the obstetrician, the Duchess's Lady-in-Waiting, Baroness Späth, and the cooks and footmen who brought up the rear. In a post-chaise (with her Governess) came the little Princess Feodora.

Travelling twenty-five miles a day, they made their slow way across Europe with 'the finest weather under Heaven and not an accident of any sort . . .' (The voyage was in fact of considerable dynastic importance: 'I should advise to say as often as possible that you are *born* in England,' wrote King Leopold of the Belgians to Victoria many years later, 'George the III *gloried* in this, and as *none* of your cousins are born in England it is your interest.')[16] The Duchess flourished on the journey and despite a rough crossing, was driven in a curricle by the Duke himself 'all the way', as Edward Conroy recounted, 'from Dover to Kensington Palace, & on the third day arrived at Captain Conroy's private residence on Shooter's Hill in Kent & remained there to rest'.[17]

Kensington meanwhile was in a flurry of expectation. Curtains were hung at the windows on the ground floor looking across to the Round Pond; furniture and a cradle were placed in the north-east bedroom; the clocks ticked and chimed with anticipation, and Princess Sophia could now look forward to a more interesting life than she had ever known before.

On a cold damp morning in the early hours of Monday 24th May 1819 the witnesses to the birth of Princess Victoria gathered in an adjoining room – the Duke of Wellington was there; the Archbishop of Canterbury, the Bishop of London, George Canning and the Duke of Sussex. Also present according to the Duchess, who described him to her daughter as being 'present at your birth'[18] (although not officially listed), was Captain John Conroy.

*

The Conroy family was now complete. On 12th August 1819, Conroy's second daughter (and sixth child) was born. She was named Marie Louise Victoire after the Duchess of Kent who became her Godmother. Little Arthur had died in 1817, aged only four years, but in this same year Henry George their youngest and most good-humoured son had been born, on 4th June.

It would be difficult to exaggerate the importance of the part the entire Conroy family was to play in the life of the Duchess of Kent. Arriving as she had in a country she scarcely knew, a by-no-means welcome member of the British Royal Family, she leaned thankfully on the un-doubted kindness of Mrs Conroy and the hard-working zeal of her husband. Mrs Conroy's recent confinement brought the two women closer together; the Duchess – despite being the mother of two grown children – found herself nervous and uncertain with Victoria and the seasoned advice of Elizabeth Conroy was a comfort. Doubtless they discussed 'maternal nutriment' – a favourite topic of the Duke of Kent. Discussed, that is, as well as they could, for the Duchess could speak no English at all and communicated in French . . . 'C'est bien conjoinment du fond du coeur, que nous rendons le tribut . . .' wrote the Duchess to Mrs Conroy in October 1819, 'à votre bon mari qui nous rendons le chaque jour à l'un et à l'autre, de nouvelles preuves de son zèle et de son attachement.'[19] Indeed one of Conroy's great achievements with the Duchess would be to turn her into an acceptable English woman: 'What pain did he not take with me to make me quite English', reminisced the Duchess to Jane Conroy twenty years later, 'he has *succeeded* and my *gratitude will never change*.'[20]

Such care and attention made a great impression on the Duchess at this time, for the bleak truth was that no other such help existed. The Prince Regent was not interested in the Duke of Kent nor in the child at Kensington: he was wrapped up in the affair of his hoped-for divorce from Princess Caroline, and besides, his brother Clarence was married and certain to have a family. Clarence himself did not care for his brother, and Cambridge and Cumberland were away in Germany intent on their own contribution to the succession. The Duke of York according to the Duchess was 'unkind'; whilst Prince Leopold, the Duchess's brother had shut himself up at Claremont grieving for Princess Charlotte. Many viewed the Duke and Duchess of Kent with derision and contempt and it was to ill-become those who, several years hence, were to complain that the Duchess kept her own company and council when they themselves had remained aloof at such a critical time of her life. The Conroy family were totally unsuitable for the Duchess and Princess Victoria (far more unsuitable indeed than anyone then could ever have guessed), but nevertheless it was they who were to create a home at Kensington and a family environment for Princess Victoria. That the Duchess remained loyal to their friendship was no more than natural gratitude. The foundation for tragedy had been laid in the summer of 1819. When, years later, others were to try to extricate her from her involvement it would already be far too late.

It was, however, to the Duke of Kent that the Duchess chiefly looked for support. Their marriage had been entirely successful and for all the enmities and difficulties the pair encountered they could look forward to many happy years together. The Duke had softened considerably with marriage, feeling his daughter's arrival compensation for the difficulties and set-backs of his life. The Duchess, for her part, relied on him entirely and, once again, had no responsibility at all for the organisation of the Household or the life at Kensington.

However, that Household was becoming increasingly difficult to run. The Duke was very seriously in debt – which fact he managed to keep from his wife whom he showered with gifts he couldn't afford. His only asset was Castle Hill which no one wanted to buy, and at last it was arranged with his 'Committee' that a tontine be set up and the property sold in shares. Meanwhile the Duke would have to remove himself from London and the expenses of Kensington. On the pretext of health and sea-bathing for the Duchess's rheumatism, it was decided to spend the winter at Sidmouth where the true reason for their evacuation need not be known. ('How he could think during such a dreadful cold season of leaving his comfortable apartments at Kensington is to me inconceivable,'[21] Cumberland was to write from Berlin.)

Tragically, the Kents could not have chosen a worse winter for their exodus to Devon. The season set in early and the household arrived at their rented cottage on Christmas Day in a snowstorm.

The severe weather continued and the Duke caught a cold which he neglected. Despite the freezing temperatures he insisted on going out with Conroy 'looking after the horses', returning home with wet feet and thoroughly chilled. The fever progressed and there followed a desperate two-week fight-for-life against the horrifying medical practices of the day. The Duke was bled incessantly until he wept at the torture and the Duchess kept vigil, horrified and helpless. Her brother Leopold and his Secretary Dr Stockmar were sent for and Stockmar (who had been present at the death of Princess Charlotte) pronounced the case hopeless. The Duke rallied somewhat to the voice of his old friend General Wetherall, and with difficulty signed his Will – a Will that was useless, he having nothing to leave – and the next day, 23rd January 1820, he died. The Duke of Cumberland echoed the feelings of the entire nation when he exclaimed: 'I can safely declare that I never was so struck in my life as with the late melancholy account of poor Edward's death . . . this event has made a deeper impression on my mind than anything I almost ever felt, for it was the last I should have looked forward to.'[22]

The immediate situation for the Duchess after the death of the Duke of Kent was terrible: she had quite literally nowhere to go, and only a plea from Princess Augusta to her brother the Regent enabled her sister-in-law to return to Kensington. Leopold, however, who had previously found the presence of Princess Victoria a painful reminder of Charlotte, behaved magnificently and gave his sister – who, as Edward Conroy was to describe it, 'had not a silver fork of her own'[23] – sufficient money to make the journey home. Captain Conroy, who but the day before had been the Duke's 'intelligent factotum', now found himself the servant of the wife and daughter, arranging the Duke's Lying-in-State and the melancholy journey of the Duchess and her family back to London.

Indeed, Conroy persistently maintained throughout the rest of his life and career that the Duke of Kent had on his death-bed entrusted the Duchess and Princess Victoria into his care. He set great store by this gesture and rested much of his future conduct upon it. Yet Queen Victoria, in the margin of a memorandum on Sir John's career in the Royal Archives,[24] wrote 'untrue' by this statement and Sir George Couper, Conroy's successor, denied his assertion as well.

Usually, Victoria's totally honest and somewhat unimaginative nature gives the biographer a reliable yardstick for the truth, but in later life she had difficulty in remaining stable on the subject of Conroy. Indeed, it is hard to understand how at eight months old Victoria could have known what took place at Sidmouth (and of course Sir George Couper was not even there). Fortunately, however, her mother the Duchess of Kent was an equally truthful and straightforward woman, and she is clear that Conroy had been well-spoken of by the Duke: 'I cannot more strongly express the opinion which The Duke of Kent entertained of your qualifications and character', she wrote to Conroy in 1839, 'than reminding you, that in His last moments, His Royal Highness counselled me, who was about to become his widow and who was the Mother of His Child, to avail myself of your assistance, and to be guided by your advice.' Her Private Secretary, she had told Victoria in 1837, should be *'tried* honor, ability, firmness and *free from party*: That person, (I must repeat it to you again) your Father on his death-bed, considered Sir John Conroy to be'.[25] Clearly at this stage in her life Victoria did not want to believe her mother – or even perhaps her father's dying words – but it is equally obvious that in Sidmouth in 1820 the Duke did so recommend Conroy to the Duchess of Kent as to make a considerable impression upon her.

As the forlorn party – Victoria and her mother, her half-sister Feodora, Baroness Späth and Feodora's Governess Fräulein Lehzen – returned to Kensington Palace, they had but three close protectors: Prince Leopold, Baron Stockmar and Captain John Conroy. For the next twenty years these three were to watch over the little family, but the greatest share of the work and responsibility would be placed with Captain Conroy – a man who came to rule over the Duchess of Kent with (as Prince Leopold would one day admit) 'a degree of power which in times of old one would have thought to proceed from witchcraft'.[26]

*

The Duchess of Kent was to be no match for the enormously complicated situation in which she found herself at Kensington. She was unhappy in England and longed to go home (despite Conroy's diligence with the English lessons) and only Leopold's reasoning and the promise of an annuity of £3,000 a year persuaded her to stay. King George III had died just one week after the Duke of Kent, and George IV (who was very ill with pleurisy) refused to keep the Duchess and her child, asserting that Leopold, with a £50,000 a year allowance from Parliament, could well afford to do so himself.

Nevertheless, it has to be said that Leopold in these early days did not give the Duchess and her daughter his fullest attention. In fact the Duchess found her brother irritating. Introspective and pompous, weighing up each problem slowly (George IV called him 'Monsieur Peu à Peu') the Duchess, who was instinctively optimistic, found him 'slow on the uptake' (he was much cleverer than she was) and despite providing financial assistance he made no effort to grasp the situation at Kensington and bring order out of chaos.

Inevitably, it was to be Captain Conroy who set about rescuing the Duchess's finances, 'doing all he can', she enthused, 'by dealing with my affairs . . . His energy and capability are wonderful.'

'I saw Mr le Blanc today the Solicitor named,' Conroy wrote to General Wetherall from Kensington Palace on the 3rd February 1820, 'and as conversation put him in possession of many particulars, until we meet I can do no more. We must act with great caution,' he warned, 'I see Lord Liverpool tomorrow to ascertain, if the Government will admit any part of the Duchess's claims – the Duchess is determined to give up everything necessary – the notoriety of which is abroad in the Royal Family – therefore Prince Leopold communicates it privately to the King.

'We can learn nothing of what is to be done for the Duchess – I fear little or nothing, but something for the Princess Victoria.' (It was in the event five years before the Princess was given a Parliamentary grant, and the Duchess only received her husband's former quarterly allowance for the first quarter of the year of his death, despite Lord Liverpool believing she had 'an equitable claim'.)[27] 'There is a report,' Conroy added confidingly, 'that the King is worse – when at Carlton House this morning He was decidedly better . . . We are all to appear in Court suits of mourning,'[28] he concluded cheerfully. It is clear he was enjoying his part in the drama exceedingly.

The King recovered from his illness; his father and brother were duly buried (with some difficulty – the Duke of Kent's body was so huge the coffin stuck in a doorway) and the Duchess at length dried her eyes and surrendered herself to the management of Conroy.

Over the next five years the Duchess's dependence upon her Equerry and his family increased daily. In April 1821, Conroy joined with General Wetherall and the Duchess on a bond of £12,000 to Coutts, providing £6,000 plus interest;[29] he was also said to have pledged part of his own possessions to pay the Duchess's debts (as the Duchess herself acknowledged)[30] and the following year the families combined for one of their many holidays together at Ramsgate. By 1825 it was becoming clear, following the death of the nine-months-old daughter of the Duke of Clarence in 1821, that Princess Victoria would most likely succeed to the throne. Indeed, in May 1825 it was proposed by Parliament that £6,000 be granted to the Duchess for the education and upkeep of her daughter. It was the first real public recognition she had received. This did not however deter Conroy from drafting a letter to Lord Grey for the Duchess complaining that £6,000 from the Government would not increase her income 'in real terms' by more than £3,000 a year, nor indeed pay her debts.[31] (The Duchess had asked Leopold to cease paying his allowance to her of £3,000 because Princess Victoria was now Heiress Presumptive.) In fact, Cumberland had received an identical sum to support his own 'angelic' child, which doubtless had annoyed Conroy and the Duchess immensely:

> I am a babe of Royalty, [heralded
> Winthrop Mackworth Praed],
> Queen CHARLOTTE was my grannam;
> And Parliament has voted me
> Six thousand pounds per annum.

Conroy's personal situation was also changing, for in 1825 his much-loved brother Llewellin died of cholera in India. As aide de camp to the Marquis of Hastings, the Governor-General, Llewellin had remained loyal to Hastings throughout his supposed support of corruption in the Palmer banking family, until the Governor's resignation over the issue in 1822. Llewellin himself must have been much embarrassed by this incident for in 1822 he had married Claudia Palmer, daughter of the Calcutta banker John Palmer, by whom he had two children, John and George. ('Very pretty little boys', as Victoria described them.)

Conroy had found himself therefore with many dependants: John, George and Llewellin's widow now joined with his mother-in-law and Deane under his immediate protection; he had too a wife and five children – including three boys at public school – with the eldest, Edward, soon to go to Oxford.

The Duchess did her best to find him more lucrative employment than the Audit Office, writing frequently and unsuccessfully to the Duke of Wellington: 'Myself and Victoria have been *faithfully* served, and we have had, not only a good servant, but an *honest* and *discreet* Councillor on matters, I must have been placed in a state of *great embarrassment* on [sic] if we had not had, such a person near us – as Sir John Conroy,' she wrote in 1828, presenting Conroy for the office of Surveyor General of the Ordnance. '– And when I recollect, that for nearly *nine* years this devotion has *daily* been the same (without my having had it, in my power to give him any salary) I *feel* what *we both owe*, – and that without *your aid*, we are powerless, to reward these services.'[32]

The underlinings were the Duchess's own, but the letter was drafted by Conroy. (He is betrayed by the illogical punctuation, an art he never mastered.) The Duchess, who of course knew nothing of his transactions with Princess Sophia, doubtless felt sincerely her indebtedness to him – whilst it is equally clear that Conroy had begun to trade on her own need: 'A real Mephisto', so Leopold claimed, 'who had artfully and at the same time for his own interest, absurdly, acted in many cases, and who knew how to act to impress a generous and affectionate mind, with the *immensity* of his *service* and *sacrifice*.'[33]

Conroy's immediate task in 1825 was to arrange for Princess Victoria's education. She needed tutors; a governess to replace Victoria's nurse Mrs Brock – in fact a complete rearrangement of the Duchess's Household was called for.

Prince Leopold, who should have taken charge of these affairs (if the Duchess had allowed it), was instead to fall in love with an actress, Karoline Bauer, a cousin of Dr Stockmar's, whom he installed in a house in Regent's Park. He was a tedious lover for he spent his time gazing at her – she looked like Princess Charlotte – whilst she read aloud improving books and he extracted the silver from military épaulettes to melt down and make into a soup tureen. This diverted him from the Duchess of Kent.

'I am anxious to convey to you', wrote Stockmar to Conroy in May 1825, 'and indeed before you had thought of the changes necessary in your establishment, the Prince's wish, that in doing so, you should calculate upon the continuation of the quarterly payment made by him till now.

'The Prince', he hastened to add, 'of course will speak to the Duchess himself, but he thinks no time should be lost to enable you to arrange for her *what you* judge needful under present circumstances.'[34]

Captain Conroy had very firm ideas as to what he judged needful. No one else, let it be remembered, yet gave much thought for Princess Victoria – but Conroy (whose masterplan for the Field Artillery may perhaps be seen as a trial run) now held in his hands the education of the future Queen of England. The first rumbles of the storm in the teacup were beginning, and the Duchess's Equerry – his wild fantasies stretching triumphantly before him – was to set about his task with a will.

4

THE KENSINGTON SYSTEM

'From 1825,' wrote Conroy to the Duchess, after the accession of Queen Victoria, 'Your Royal Highness conceived and acted on a System, that was to make the Princess "The Nation's Hope", "The People's Queen", – it would take volumes to narrate, your difficulties, – your anxiety, – your efforts to accomplish this mighty design.'[1]

In fact by 1825 Victoria was already emerging as 'The Nation's Hope', and Conroy's 'great operation' – an operation dubbed in almost military style the 'Kensington System' – was to be securely grafted on to a prevailing public attitude. Indeed, to whom else amongst the depressing array of decaying Princes could the country look to represent a brighter future? The uncertainty of the times had led both Whig and Tory to see in the person of Victoria an embodiment of their own political hopes and ideals – the Tory Lady Wharncliffe as confidently anticipating that the well-bred distinction of the Princess would 'save us from Democracy', as the Whig leader, Lord Durham, urged Conroy that the use of the word 'People' should be 'as familiar to Royalty, as that of King is to the People'.[2]

The Kensington System, indeed, was to be Whig operated and Whig advised. Conroy himself was a Whig by inheritance, and his middle name – Ponsonby – now attracted influence and lent distinction. Did not John Conry's portrait still hang in Bishopscourt, Roscommon? When the Duchess claimed that Conroy was 'without Party', she was suggesting his first allegiance was to the Crown. It did not imply (given the highly political atmosphere of the 1820s and 1830s) that such loyalty was non-political in character.

Again, it seems unlikely that Conroy and the Duchess alone 'conceived' the Kensington System. Conroy himself was surrounded by advisers – 'Counsellors' as they were called in the Kensington System – and it is certain his thinking was influenced and supported by their joint consultation. Indeed, whilst Conroy was anxious the Duchess should not become the 'tool' of either Prince Leopold or William IV, it is more than likely that he himself was used by such ambitious and clever men as the first Earl of Durham.

Conroy, like many people with organisational skills, had neither depth nor subtlety. He was tactless and insensitive in the handling of others, and he was not especially intelligent. He was naïve. These characteristics are worth bearing in mind when considering the Kensington System. Only a naïve man could have believed, as Conroy believed, that his family was of royal blood; naïve too was his outrage when the world finally turned against him. Conroy had persuaded himself of the rightness of his course, and that he alone should play a leading part within it. He took others at their face-value – having as Edward Conroy revealed, a 'confiding nature' – whilst his limited political sense could not grasp the consequences of the vast changes underway, nor how soon they would make obsolete his own ambitions.

The years 1820 to 1825 had been politically uneventful. Certainly they contained the failure of Queen Caroline's trial to dissolve her marriage with George IV – her subsequent death – and the suicide of Lord Castlereagh. But Lord Liverpool had conceded in part to pressure from the 'Canningite' reformers in a way that must have worried the old men 'in their libraries' but appeased the more liberal elements of the Tory party. On Lord Liverpool's death in 1827 Canning himself became Prime Minister, only to die suddenly the following August, 'killed', as Creevey lamented, 'by publick life'. Lord Goderich feebly headed a stop-gap

Government until Wellington, in 1828, formed a working administration with Palmerston and Peel. The Whigs had refused to serve under Wellington, and their agitation over the next few years for the reform of the Rotten Boroughs was to bring about one of the most far-reaching parliamentary upheavals the country had ever known. Conroy, according to the Duchess's son Charles, Prince of Leiningen, 'always considered the condition of England as eminently dangerous, and so described it . . .'[3] It was against this unstable background that the Kensington System was born.

Conroy had been some time 'behind the scenes of the great world', as he liked to express it, when the contacts he had made in the foremost of the Whig houses began to stand him in good stead. His newly-acquired wealth and supposed background (although nobody knew about either) had given him self-assurance. He could as easily talk with the aristocracy about the management of their mines and estates (Conroy had begun with zeal to improve the workings of his estate at Llanbrynmair) as he was happy arguing military tactics with army major-generals. He was tall and handsome and cut a considerable dash in society; and if society, in some puzzlement, considered him vulgar and absurd, he was clearly hard-working and loyal. Even 'in the interior' few doubts about his integrity had yet begun to stir.

Prince Leiningen, in an account given in 1840 to Prince Albert's librarian, Dr Praetorius, on 'the Policy followed at Kensington'[4] (which he himself supported), argued that 'virtually no-one' would have withheld approval of the Kensington System if it had been faithfully pursued. And indeed disapproval would have been difficult, for the Counsellors Conroy gathered about him were a powerful body of men.

The Chief Adviser to Kensington, Lord Dunfermline, had been a careful choice. As Judge Advocate-General of Scotland and a future Speaker of the House of Commons, he was acceptable to all Parties; and if he was somewhat anodyne in character, he was at least uncontroversial. A son of Sir Ralph Abercromby, Commander of Troop in Ireland (and doubtless an old colleague of General Fisher's), the diarist

Charles Greville declared him 'a dull grave man, sensible and hard-headed'. ('It was always a matter of astonishment to me', he added, 'that they make as much of him as they do.') Yet he was one of the few people who had any real influence over Conroy, and with a judge's detachment he saw all sides at Kensington.

The casting vote in the Kensington System however was to belong to the former doctor, Baron Stockmar. As he juggled the interests of his master, Prince Leopold, on the one hand with the Duchess and Victoria on the other, he was clearly not as detached as Dunfermline – who later came to believe that Leopold was 'intriguing'. Nevertheless, Stockmar remained on civil terms with Conroy – an achievement which, in the unfolding circumstances, was almost miraculous.

Men as diverse as Lord Dover, Lord Liverpool and Sir Richard Vivian all joined the Duchess's Kensington circle. Indeed, Lord Liverpool, brother of the former Prime Minister and the only Tory member of the Council, was – so Edward Conroy claimed – actually 'made by my father'. His daughter, Lady Catherine Jenkinson, became a Lady-in-Waiting to the Duchess and a favourite of Princess Victoria's. And it was old loyalties and family ties – a commonplace in the political world of the 1820s – that brought Lord Duncannon and Lord Durham about the person of Conroy. For they belonged to the Ponsonby connection.

Lord Durham – known to society as 'King Jog', since he 'jogged along' on £40,000 a year – was Conroy's greatest friend and confidant. They were not unalike (Melbourne noticed this), for both were hot-tempered, ambitious and with considerable *folie de grandeur*. Durham's ostentation (financed by the success of his Durham coalfields) ran to a yacht, a London mansion and footmen outriders to his carriage. He was publicly rude to his father-in-law, Lord Grey, who bore him patiently, and unpleasant to his servants who could not bear him at all. Yet his family adored him, and much of his excitable temperament could be explained by a nervous disturbance producing frequent migraine headaches and sickness. He had a brilliant mind severely impaired by ill-health over which Conroy showed unexpected sympathy – possibly because he himself could suffer similarly: 'I have been so poorly with my head', he once complained to Durham, 'I have not been able to go beyond the Palace.'[5]

Durham had worked all his life for the triumph of the Whig cause, and now, seeing in Princess Victoria how Sovereign and People might one day relate to each other, he engaged in a considerable correspondence with Conroy. It is likely indeed that his dream extended to being Victoria's future Prime Minister, in which case Conroy could have counted on an ally at the helm. Over one hundred of Conroy's letters to Durham survive in the Lambton Papers, whilst those remaining copies of Durham's to Conroy outline his political doctrine, and were meant as much for the Duchess's and Victoria's edification as for that of his friend. 'She was trained to have very liberal opinions', wrote Conroy of the Princess, 'without reference to party.'[6] And although Victoria claimed she did not like him, in fact her political education owed much to the influence of Lord Durham.

Durham's eldest daughter was to marry John George Ponsonby, the eldest son of Viscount Duncannon (4th Earl Bessborough) a descendant of John Conry's greatest friend. Lord Duncannon – Secretary of State in 1834 and Lord Privy Seal from 1835 to 1837 – although not a 'Counsellor', was the Crown of the Kensington System. 'I have no secrets from him', wrote Durham to Conroy, '& he knows my inmost thoughts'.[7] Duncannon was to be loyal to Conroy and his old Ponsonby associations, but it is clear he came eventually to have his reservations about this particular family connection.

Nevertheless, in his conception of the Kensington System, Conroy did not stand alone. He had the approval and consent of Prince Leopold and the advice of powerful and intelligent men. The System had been created, so Conroy rather vaguely recorded, 'to give the Princess Victoria an upbringing which would enable her in the future to be equal to her high position'; and indeed, some regulation of the Princess's life had been vital. Her education, which Conroy devised (he engaged all her tutors), though scarcely adequate accentuated her talents in languages, music and art; whilst she was brought into adult society – and later before the country – in a way that early accustomed her to public life.

But the real strength of her upbringing could scarcely have been foreseen; for it was to lie in Victoria's own endurance of the bitter conflict that was daily growing up around her within the confines of Kensington Palace.

*

The Duchess of Kent was an anxious and disappointed woman. As Victoria's hopes for the succession increased so the Duchess realised that, in the death of the Duke of Kent, a great opportunity had been snatched from her. 'I said that she had told me once', wrote Victoria, in her Journal, 'that if my Father had not died, *she* would be in *my place*; not certainly *quite* in *my place*', she added complacently, 'as Lord Melbourne and I observed.'[8] But Conroy's plans for a Regency must have looked to the Duchess as a natural compensation.

The Duchess's anxieties for Victoria were considerable. She feared her daughter would be taken from her and brought up in the English Court; she feared for the actual life of Victoria which rumour said was threatened; and more than all this she feared that her child through her extreme youth would be unable to control her great position. Such feelings were not unreasonable, but her natural concern as a mother was exaggerated by her situation. She herself admitted that she loved her child too much, and her consequent lack of detachment and faith in Victoria's own integrity led her to heed Conroy's advice unthinkingly.[9]

There may have been truth in the belief that the Royal Family wanted Victoria brought up in the English Court; certainly the Duke of Wellington thought so. The prospect appalled the Duchess for the Court was decadent and corrupt and the country did not wish to see any more such 'dregs of their dull race'. On the other hand, the Duchess's own family, the Coburgs, were not much more of an improvement. The Duke of Coburg (the Duchess's brother, and father of the future Prince Albert) was divorced from his wife who had eventually run away from him. Detachment from the Duchess's family would therefore be equally prudent. But it was the Duke of Cumberland – next in line to the throne after Victoria – who appeared the greatest threat. His horrifying facial disfigurement and reactionary views terrified everyone, and the Duchess was 'in a great fright' at the prospect of his influence.[10] Gossip had it that he was plotting to remove Victoria from her mother in order to poison her to death – having set about rumours that she was 'diseased in her feet' and would never grow up. Queen Victoria claimed that it was 'well-known' that Victoire Conroy was the source of these rumours, although since Victoire was three months younger than the Princess herself it is difficult to understand how anyone could have taken her seriously.

Nevertheless, the Conroy family undoubtedly came to believe these fantasies, whatever their origin – for Henry Conroy's wife set down the traditions as fact in an 1875 memorandum which the Queen herself annotated. ('For I am sure the *truth* must always prevail, if properly told,' Mrs Conroy wrote to her nephew.) But did Conroy himself believe them? Or were they, as Queen Victoria insisted, 'all Sir John's invention'?

The thread of melodrama was strong in the Conroy family and fed by the atmosphere of the time. (Indeed the Duke of Cumberland was nothing so much as the giant who ate 'boiled babbies' in Stanfield James's *The Sleeping Beauty*.) Edward Conroy's own memoranda of the period are couched in pure Covent Garden rhetoric – the characters at Kensington ranging from 'true', to 'a base fellow', 'a double-faced villain', and even 'a blackguard of the deepest die'. But the passion that invests the Conroy notes and letters does not have the feel of duplicity. The family were capable of believing legend and of defensive lying; yet the deliberate invention of intricate plots and sub-plots would have been beyond their capacity to sustain. Like most people, they believed what it suited them to believe and once entrenched they believed sincerely. Conroy did not live in an age that examined its motives or explored its inner psychology. According to a person's point of view, black was black or white was white. For Conroy, the Duke of Cumberland was very black indeed, and there is no reason to suppose he ever believed otherwise.

Indeed, it was for fear that the Duke of Cumberland would be made Regent on the death of the Duke of Clarence that Conroy consolidated a further aim of the Kensington System – 'to assure a pleasant and honourable future for the Duchess of Kent as well'. The Duke of Wellington had independently upheld the status of the Duchess – too much so for the pleasure of Victoria and Melbourne, who later complained that her idea of her high rank and position was 'a parcel of nonsense'.[11] Yet Mrs Arbuthnot, writing in May 1829, reported that 'the Duke is, I see, quite determined that the D. of Cumberland shall never be Regent, but that if the Duke of Clarence dies . . . the Dss of Kent shall be Regent'.[12] A Regency would be a vital means of control over Victoria not only of course for the Duchess and Conroy but for Parliament itself. It was clearly Wellington's opinion that the Duchess and Conroy were a far safer proposition for the nation than the hated Duke of Cumberland ('The Duke knows Conroy perfectly,' observed Lord Melbourne). And certainly the victor of Waterloo was confident he could deal with the Duchess's Secretary should ever the need arise.

Knowing himself to be so strongly supported, Conroy had already set about keeping Victoria away from her father's family. As early as 1827 he refused permission for the Princess to join a family party at 'the Cottage' in Windsor Great Park because the Duchess of Cumberland was there – thus setting in train the first of a long series of frustrating encounters that were to anger the Princess Victoria.

'Whenever it was necessary', Edward Conroy claimed, 'for the Duchess to refuse her child for any little act of folly or when anything occurred *in any way* that was displeasing to

the wilful child Sir J. was made to bear the advice . . .'
According to Edward the Princess 'learnt to associate any
unpleasant thing with his name & to his agency . . . The
Baroness [Lehzen]', so the Conroys believed, 'always in
secret repeating to the Princess that the acts of Her Mother
were recommended by Sir John'.[13]

According to the Duchess of Kent it was Sir John Conroy
himself who suggested Lehzen should become Victoria's
Governess – and she took up her duties on the 19th April
1824, when Victoria was almost five years old.[14]

Among The Conroy Papers, in a bold, youthful hand, are
a number of notes headed 'Mem for Memoirs', recording
Edward Conroy's own feelings and opinions on his father's
career at Kensington. To read them is to be struck by their
loyalty: 'My whole soul was for him', he wrote once of his
father – and by his awe and respect: 'I have seen Kings *quail*
under my father's glance and polished manner.' But most
insistent of all is the bitterness over false promises made and
the family's detestation of Baroness Lehzen. Even given
Edward's lack of judgement and insight, there is something
impressive in the sheer force of his scorn and hatred towards
this middle-aged German woman.

'Miss Letzen', as Edward called her, 'was placed by the
good Duchess about the person of the infant Princess
Victoria, as being rather of a superior class to the ordinary
description of maid-servant. – She filled the duties of this
early part of her career very well; & satisfactorily to the
Duchess – who protected her against all the observations
made against her by members of the family, who always
recommended a person of superior grade to be placed about
the person of the Princess.'[15]

Lehzen's inferiority however was to prove a source of
difficulty, if not of ridicule. Her eating habits were curious –
she once said 'she did not know the feeling to be hungry'
and all 'she fancied were potatoes'.[16] Carraway seeds, which
she carried in her pocket, aided her digestion. (The food at
Kensington was terrible.) Her table manners were uncertain,
her bonnets hideous – and the final challenge came when the

Queen of Württemberg (Victoria's aunt) announced she
would not 'sit down to table with a maid servant'.[17]

According to Conroy himself, 'the difficulty which arose
was, that her sister having been one of Queen Caroline's
Dressers, she [Lehzen] could not well sit at the Princess's
table'. Conroy consulted with Princess Sophia (doubtless a
sure source of Court etiquette) and she suggested a 'nominal
Rank' could be given to Lehzen 'to get over the difficulty' –
Conroy himself being knighted and given the Hanoverian
riband to create an excuse for Lehzen's elevation. Sophia
trotted off to George IV's mistress, Lady Conyngham, who
in turn delicately suggested to the King that since Victoria
was likely to ascend the throne it would be good for her 'to
make friends where she could hereafter benefit by their
interests for herself & children'. Within five days 'to the
astonishment of the World', Lehzen emerged as a Hanoverian Baroness and was appointed Sub-Governess to the
Princess Victoria.[18]

Jealousy abounded. 'Thus became the Bonne – a mighty
German Baroness . . .' roared Edward, adding, 'and the
writer, as a boy, was employed by his father to sketch her
"*coat of Arms*"!!!'[19]

Unfortunately, Baroness Lehzen rose to her full height, and
'a struggle to always be taken out with the Princess, and an
attempt to take precedence of *Earls* daughters' duly ensued.

'Sir John soon stopped all that' (wrote Edward).
'"Madam," I heard him once say to her, in his most
dignified tone, "You have no rank in England: besides if you
had, common courtesy would induce you to waive it in the
house of your mistress to her guests."

'She looked like a fiend, and that speech was bottled up in
her black heart,' (hearts were usually 'black' with Edward),
'from this time she . . . was in continual opposition to Sir
John.'[20]

Henry Conroy, Sir John's youngest son, insisted in later
life that Lehzen would 'have been dismissed by my father –
only she was kept, because she was useful with the young
Princess – she dreaded *the Bastards* coming in'.[21] In this she
was supported by the Duchess and, as Edward rather

curiously pointed out, supported 'by the *Mother* what could *he* [Conroy] do?'.[22]

Obviously, both Lehzen and Conroy despised each other's pretentiousness; both, too, were misfits whose status was artificial. (The last straw probably came when Lehzen attempted to take precedence over Lady Conroy.[23] Not only was the Knight of the Guelph offended, but so too was his wife's blue blood.) The Royal Family abounded in such a class of people (usually Private Secretaries) whose snobberies filled George IV with glee. Intimate with Kings, yet not of them, they eventually came to grief and were disposed of with a peerage. Conroy not unnaturally assumed such an accolade for himself (although he was not yet the Private Secretary of a Monarch).

It was an unwritten understanding of the Kensington System (one, indeed, among many) that Conroy would remain Private Secretary to the Duchess should she become Regent. In the event of Victoria's accession at eighteen, he would then transfer his allegiance to her. The nervous Duchess undoubtedly felt this to be the safest plan for her inexperienced young daughter 'at the *beginning*' of her reign – and indeed, a number of the Kensington Counsellors believed so too.

Clearly it was her innocent hope that all four would journey, as friends, along life's road together: 'Hand in hand on our way.'[24]

*

It was shortly after the installation of Lehzen as nursery Governess to Victoria, and at the outset of the Kensington System, that Conroy encountered the first serious challenge of his career. For the Duchess was experiencing considerable anxiety over her daughter Feodora.

Princess Feodora – the Duchess's eldest daughter, by her first husband the Prince of Leiningen – was, at eighteen years old, very pretty and charming and becoming increasingly difficult to control. She had already attracted the attention of such eligible suitors as the Duke of Nassau and the Prince of

Schönburg, and even the aged George IV had shown her a flicker of interest. (Although much, one suspects, in the manner of an aged dog saluting a puppy with a thump of its tail.) Neither Conroy nor the Duchess however were prepared for the affair of 'Stephen – a Madman'.

Robert Stephen, an Irishman and furrier by trade, had conceived a passion for Princess Feodora. On his own admission, in a petition he submitted to the House of Commons in 1826, 'about the month of April 1824' (the date Lehzen ceased control of Feodora):

I met in St James's Park the Princess Feodora, daughter to the Duchess of Kent, circumstances occurred there and elsewhere, which induced me to declare myself to her in the month of June following, and I had several interviews with Capt Conroy, Sectry to the Duchess which tended to confirm my opinion that I was not disregarded by the amiable Princess, accordingly I wrote to His Majesty and every Member of the Royal Family, and also to each of the Cabinet Ministers requesting them to be informed of the real sentiments of the Princess; and stating if *she* would negative the affair I would immediately desist; but I have never received an answer.[25]

It is scarcely surprising that Stephen had been universally ignored. In fact, for the past two years (one has to applaud his persistence) he had been repeatedly rounded-up by Robert Peel's Government-Agents and shipped back to Ireland.

'I found out *Stephen* this morning at an Inn in Aldermanbury,' announced Peel triumphantly in July 1825. 'He was brought before Sir R. Birnie very early in the morning, and he is at present in Tothillfields Prison.

'I hope the Duchess of Kent will not be annoyed by the extravagant acts of this man who must be crazy. He was in possession of only a few shillings & several epistles to the Minister & others, all of which are in my possession . . . Reasoning was of no avail with him. I propose therefore to try the effect of prison discipline for a day or two & then I hope he will be effectively undeceived . . .'[26]

'I have Her Royal Highness's orders', replied Conroy gravely, 'to express to you, Her warmest acknowledgements for the very prompt and decisive steps you have taken, to free Her, from an annoyance, that has given Her a good deal of concern.'[27]

Six months later Stephen surfaced again.

'Most Royal Duchess,' he saluted Feodora's mother, 'I think it my duty to inform you, that not having had any reply to the letters I wrote to you and other members of the Royal Family relative to my imprisonment, I have petitioned both Houses of Parliament for an inquiry; this step I have thought necessary in justice to my character.'[28]

This was nothing short of the truth. Conroy hastily sent Stephen's letter to Peel, who replied that he doubted the petition would be taken up – particularly if the Duchess and her family were mentioned.[29] However, he had reckoned without the Whig MP Henry Brougham, who could seize any handle to turn in favour of his party. A copy of the Petition headed 'Stephen to Hamilton. Petition to be put to the House by Brougham', might well indicate that Brougham had agreed to take the matter further on behalf of the under-dog; but, if this was the case, he was effectively silenced by Peel. Lord Archibald Hamilton, a Whig reformer (and friend of Brougham) to whom the petition was addressed, had certainly not been taken in: 'The writer is probably crazy,' he commented succinctly.[30]

'I will not say more on it', wrote Conroy to Peel with a characteristic turn of phrase, 'than to observe he appears to be not only a fool, but a *knave*.'

'I cannot tell you', he added, 'how very much hurt the Duchess of Kent is.'[31]

Peel sent a 'confidential officer' to Newry to remonstrate with the young man – and there the alarming affair of 'Stephen' appears to have ended.

Nevertheless, something had to be done about Feodora. The effect of so many epistles to the King, the Royal Family and the entire Cabinet scarcely served to inspire confidence in the Kensington System. Clearly Feodora must be married as soon as possible, before yet another young man fell in love with her in St James's Park.

This was just the sort of personal problem with which the Duchess might have turned to her brother, Prince Leopold; but instead, Conroy himself had been turning the matter over with some degree of urgency. On the 14th July 1826, he wrote to the Duchess from Leamington, rejecting the Duke of Nassau and the Prince of Schönburg in favour of a marriage with Prince Hohenlohe-Langenburg: '. . . in that marriage', he wrote, 'I think the Princess would find that character, that dignity of conduct which would tend to preserve her own happiness, and that if her life was unmarked by anything very splendid it would be free from the disquietudes that would attend either of the other two.'

Beyond giving independence, riches carried no real benefits he added 'and I must unequivocally state to you, that it is not only essential to the interest and happiness of the Pss Feodora, that she should marry *soon*,' (everyone had had enough of Stephen) 'but that it is as necessary for yours and Pss Victoria's interest, that it should take place – the influence you ought to have over her, will be endangered if she sees an elder sister not so alive to it – as she should be – and recollect,' he warned the Duchess, ominously, 'once your authority is lost over the Pss V you will never regain it . . . Her character – Her situation – the objects of others – will prevent it.'[32]

In February 1828 Princess Feodora was married to Prince Hohenlohe. The King, who was to have attended the celebrations, fell ill at the last moment – but Victoria, dressed in her best, handed round the 'favours' herself, from a straw basket. It was not a brilliant match (Edward Conroy described Hohenlohe's estates as 'two miles square') but the Prince had charm and intelligence and Feodora considered herself lucky to have found him, 'for I might have married I don't know whom merely to get away. There was that odious Prince Schönburg who wanted to marry me; if Mama had wished it I think I should have done it without liking him in the least . . .'[33]

Kensington could indeed be boring and uneventful, and later the theatre for tragic and terrible scenes; but it is difficult to conceive how an alternative way of life could have been created for Victoria. Indeed, her childhood was doomed. As a young girl she was bound to be the victim of whoever was in charge of her. It was healthier perhaps to have been the pawn of Conroy and her misguided but well-meaning mother – even, indeed of the triumphant Whigs – than of elderly Kings and Dukes, however indulgent, who belonged to a fading era. (In her own time, even Princess Charlotte had feared for too much influence 'by the Castle'.) For better for worse, the Kensington System had been established, and deep within, the battle for power over Victoria had begun.

❈

5

'IT WAS ONE FAMILY'

The Conroys lived near Church Street on Campden Hill, a
short distance from Kensington Palace. They had a paddock
with ponies ('Isabel' was a favourite); stables, grooms and a
succession of dogs that Victoria loved. Appleby, the butler –
a gentleman of heroic loyalty – headed a household of
considerable proportions.

The Conroy home had become a haven for the Duchess of
Kent from her earliest days in England. Here she found
companionship with Lady Conroy, in whose home 'it was
impossible', Frances Conroy remembered, 'to look around,
without seeing – among her books – ornaments & jewels –
some touching momento of the Duchess of Kent. Some
gracious generous gift.'¹ Here too the Duchess could indulge
her love of music – for all the Conroy women were musical.
Lady Conroy had a number of pieces dedicated to her by
the famous teacher Bochsa; whilst 'poor Jane' (who was
always ailing, and breakfasted in bed) published her own
composition 'A Souvenir of Tunbridge Wells', which appeared in the catalogue of Willis & Co. under the heading 'a
new and popular Quadrille'.

Until well into their twenties the Conroy children enjoyed
their life together at Kensington, and Victoria's *Journal*
relates many evenings spent in their company. Christmas
and birthdays were special celebrations and the cause of
generous present-giving – 'I had one table for myself', noted

Victoria, on Christmas Eve, 'and the Conroy family had the other together.'[2] On Edward's birthday in 1832, Victoria described how 'we played on the piano and I sung to Jane's harp. At about 9 Mons Bégrez, [the French opera singer] came and sung with Jane and sung himself with the guitar. Mamma and me sung and we all joined in a chorus.'[3] Celebrating Lady Conroy's birthday, Victoria recorded how 'after dinner Jane, Victoire, me and Edward danced a quadrille, and afterwards the whole party except Mama, who played for us, danced, Aunt Sophia also'.[4]

Harps and pianos, singing and dancing filled the Conroy home; a household that greatly appealed to the Duchess's provincial middle-class instincts. It should have appealed to Victoria as well. That she does not seem to have enjoyed whole-heartedly the youthful entertainment it offered – and in which she joined ecstatically when her German cousins stayed at Kensington – must be attributed to the influence of her Governess, Baroness Lehzen.

'The Conroy family', as Edward recorded, 'lived on no ordinary terms of intimacy with the Dchss and Pss – It was one family and the . . . Conroys never presumed or imposed on the exalted Persons with Whom they lived.'[5]

Lehzen, however, would not have agreed. Her own hatred of Sir John was now entrenched and she conveyed her prejudice to Victoria with whom, curiously, she shared similar Hanoverian characteristics. Prince Albert was to find the Governess 'astonishingly self-willed and obstinate'; yet the same tendencies in her pupil were to be transformed by Lehzen's upbringing into character-saving virtues.

The Baroness was narrow and uncomplicated in outlook; she disliked 'weakness' – despising this in the Duchess (she was to feel even Prince Leopold to be 'too weak and wavering'); Queen Elizabeth, be it remembered, was 'her ideal' of a Queen, and she educated 'by example'.

'I have to be sure not created, but nourished in the Princess', Lehzen told the Duchess, '*one* quality *which is* to test, consider and to stand firmly by that which the Princess finds right and good.'[6]

Not unnaturally, that which Victoria found right and

Princess Victoria with her mother the Duchess of Kent, holding a miniature of her father the Duke of Kent, who had died in 1820.

Princess Victoria

Baroness Lehzen

Queen Victoria

Lord Melbourne

Princess Victoria was aged thirteen at the time of her first tour in 1832. Her governess, Baroness Lehzen, defended her against the scheming Sir John Conroy – as later, when she was Queen, did her revered Prime Minister, Lord Melbourne.

Sir John Conroy

Lady Conroy

abeth
Jane

Edward

Victoire

ephen

Henry

Sir John and Lady Conroy and their five children at the time of the creation of the 'Kensington System'. The Duchess of Kent, Princess Victoria, and the Conroys were 'one family'.

Princess Sophia

William Rea

King Leopold of the Belgians

William IV

Princess Sophia supported Conroy's schemes to an extent probably only known to the Duchess's accountant William Rea. Sir John had powerful adversaries in King Leopold of the Belgians and William IV who, in spite of having a head 'like a pineapple', brought Victoria to the throne without a Regency.

Sir John Conroy in the unattached uniform of the Royal Artillery adorned
with his Portuguese medals. He wears the sword given by George III
to his son the Duke of Kent, and which passed to Sir John after the Duke's death.

Earl of Durham

Sir John Conroy, 1836

Baron Stockmar

Duke of Wellington

The Whig leader, the Earl of Durham, and his friend Sir John Conroy conspired to make the word 'people' as familiar to Princess Victoria as 'King' was to the people. Baron Stockmar and the Duke of Wellington acted as advisers and arbiters to the domestic conflict at Kensington.

John Conry   Sir John Conroy c. 1850

Sir John Conroy

John Conry, Sir John Conroy's grandfather, gained his job as Collector of Cork through telling stories to the Lord Lieutenant of Ireland. There is a likeness to the elderly Sir John, under whose farming jacket can be seen the 'white white waistcoat' remembered by his grandson. His marble bust provides neo-classical dignity.

Following his marriage to Queen Victoria in 1840 Prince Albert was responsible for dismissing Sir John's claims to a peerage as 'not to be treated with him'.

good would be influenced by Lehzen herself. It is possible
that without her Governess's iron prejudice, her encouragement of the Princess to tell people 'they were wrong and
setting them down'[7] (Victoria had disliked this, but was
urged to do so by Lehzen) – without, even, her disapproval
of novel-reading – Victoria might have grown up with a
more flexible view of human nature. The Conroys themselves
were convinced that Lehzen had formed a 'project which she
afterwards accomplished – the *severing* of the Mother's
influence over the child and her own assumption of
authority on the mind of the infant Princess'. Victoria, they
claimed, was 'taught to despise her mother and to nurse her
feelings *in silence*'.[8]

There is no doubt this was true; and in so far as Victoria
felt she had never lived 'as Mother and daughter should',
Lehzen was much to blame. The Baroness needed a focus for
her theories of strength and firmness, and she could scarcely
have found better material than Conroy and the Duchess of
Kent. Yet in time the polarisation between them and
Victoria became so complete that any friend or colleague of
either Conroy or the Duchess became instantly the object of
the Princess's suspicion and dislike: this prejudice was to
grow to lengths so dangerous and absurd that it jeopardised
the monarchy itself.

'You could have spared me much grief', the Duchess was
to tell Lehzen, 'had you attached yourself more to me, then
you would have understood me better.[9] Yet as long as the
Duchess remained loyal to Conroy the more remote Lehzen
was to become.

Indeed, the Duchess's championing of her Majordomo
was, by the end of the 1820s, becoming increasingly obvious.
The Duchess of Clarence (later Queen Adelaide and a
favourite aunt of Victoria's) became the first to voice her
anxieties. She was in fact in a strong position to do so, for
she had been one of the few members of the Royal Family to
comfort the Duchess after the death of the Duke of Kent.

'It is well-known', she warned her, 'who Sir J.C. is; he
cannot make himself higher or lower than he is, nor does he
need to, as a man of merit; only he must not be allowed to

forbid access to you to all but his family, who in any case are not of so high a rank that they *alone* should be the entourage and the companions of the future Queen of England.'[10]

Her hints undoubtedly found their target. Conroy, indeed, had puzzled Victoria herself by telling her 'his daughters were as high as me'.[11] Such inexplicable arrogance was to anger a child of the Princess's temperament, quite independently of Lehzen's dislike; ('there's no Irishmen don't say he isn't descended from those Milesian Kings', commented the unsuspecting Lord Melbourne). Yet Conroy's belief in his family's consanguinity to Victoria undoubtedly explains his familiarity towards her – a familiarity that, as 'a born Princess', she grew to resent deeply.

Although Lehzen was the greatest influence and source of affection in Victoria's life, it is clear that the Princess believed she made up her own mind on all important matters. If this was true it was Lehzen who gave her the support and self-confidence to do so; but it is equally obvious that until her marriage Victoria held no opinion that was not in agreement with either her Governess or Lord Melbourne. Hers was never an original mind, and she was to be always much influenced by others. The great advantage of Lehzen's upbringing was that it was straightforward and clear-sighted, and gave Victoria a single goal to follow. It was however, neither subtle nor tolerant and the constant wearing down of other people's characters before such a young child had its effect.

The Duchess was aware of this. She knew that Lehzen's quarrels with Conroy led Victoria to 'under-value' him (and Conroy said the same to Lord Liverpool). She tried to bring herself closer to Victoria by attending all her lessons (which did not endear her to anyone). For fear of Cumberland the Duchess had Victoria sleep in her room until her accession; and it is said she was never allowed to walk downstairs without someone holding her hand. But in every move her mother made Victoria saw the influence of Conroy; forbidding everything she wished to do; turning her mother – so she felt – into a tiresome woman who wasn't fond of her, teased her and was 'wishing to order me about, and always thinking of her rights as a Mother'.[12]

Such are the classic strains of a daughter's rebellion, and the waves in the giant teacup were growing higher. Quarrels at Kensington became almost incessant; yet the motives of the combatants were curiously complementary. The Duchess and Conroy were concerned almost entirely with politics; with the Regency – with the promotion of Victoria in the public mind as the hope of the Nation. They were also concerned with their 'reward'. Lehzen concentrated on Victoria's education and the building of her character. She devoted herself exclusively to the Princess with no recompense but a German Barony for which, in fairness, she had not asked. This was, for all her faults, the great difference between herself, Conroy and the Duchess – and Victoria was well aware of it.

*

On the 26th June 1830, George IV died. A charming, highly intelligent man, he had led a life of extraordinary difficulty. The Regent of a deranged father; the husband of an unbalanced wife; he had endured the loss of his only child and seen the offspring of his detested brother become the probable heir to the throne. Yet he remained childlike and amusing, and the Duke of Wellington smoothed down the worst of his excesses as the country headed towards Reform. For his part the King, a staunch Tory, became increasingly bewildered by events ('these are strange times', he wrote to his Private Secretary, William Knighton, 'and . . . we have very queer and odd people to deal with') and the King's death – painful and pitiful though it was – opened the way to a political revolution he would otherwise have successfully obstructed. The Duke of Clarence, however, ascended the throne with no greater expectations of competence: his informality in the streets was alarming, and his mental stability open to question. ('What can you expect', commented Greville gloomily, 'from a man with a head like a pineapple?') Yet he was totally unpretentious and fair-minded – and history was to prove him blessed with a remarkable instinct for constitutional survival.

The death of George IV was the moment for which the Duchess and Conroy had been waiting and their request for the Regency (on the day after the King's demise) held a bundle of fears and ambitions, which were by no means lost upon the Duke of Wellington.

It is tempting, when reading the Duchess's official documents, to hear in them the single voice of Conroy. Most of her letters are drafted in his own hand and expressed in his individual style. He corrected the Duchess's spelling mistakes (had he not made her 'quite English'?) and wrote her speeches; his tricks of phrase had become part of her own vocabulary. Yet the Duchess was never quite the puppet that Conroy would have liked. As she grew older she gained in authority and although she relied on Conroy for advice, she felt – as did Victoria – that her decisions were her own. Conroy maintained that it was 'particularly not easy to account for the D/S';[13] and in a note to Lord Durham in March 1832 we find her complaining: 'I have just read a letter Sir John Conroy has written to you by my desire. I am not satisfied with the way he has expressed my wishes. It is the only subject I have any intention of pressing on Lord Grey; and I place it in your hands, as one, I wish to give *all* my weight to.'[14]

'The weight of my Maternal Station' (probably quite considerable) was a favourite phrase of Conroy's that the Duchess had adopted; and the fact that the Duchess spoke with Conroy's voice but not always with his mind, is one of which the biographer must be aware. On the matter of the Regency it is safe to assume the Duchess spoke for herself.

The Duchess indeed was familiar with the idea of a Regency; for on the death of her husband she had become Regent to the little Province of Leiningen, where Schindler had been her adviser. Now she and Conroy had formed a similar partnership on the grand scale. Indeed, Sir John openly admitted that all his calculations for self-advancement depended upon a Regency, on the attainment of which the Duchess intended to make him a peer: '– to be a Peer of the United Kingdom was my ambition', he acknowledged, 'to find myself placed with other Men, who from Military, Naval, Diplomatic or Law Services, had been so raised, was a fair object to aspire to.'[15]

It was of course not only a daring aspiration for one of his background, but a colossal gamble; yet by now Conroy had convinced himself of the role he was commanding (as good as any his father played in Fishamble Street) and so with his 'great assumption' he was successfully persuading others.

The Duchess's long letter to the Duke of Wellington contained immense demands. Following her request for a Regency, and detailing her finances and her daughter's education, she went on to suggest she 'be considered and placed on the footing of a Princess Dowager of Wales, – and with that income, I would consider it for the Princess's interest, that there was no grant made specially to Her; as then, I would defray every charge for Her maintenance, education, etc, until She is Queen, or becomes of Age.'[16]

The Duke was alarmed. The entire contents of the letter were in defiance of William IV's likely intention of taking Victoria into his own care. (Melbourne later confirmed that the King was always wanting to take Victoria 'away'.) The Duchess's and Conroy's fears were real; and they hoped that by denying Victoria any independent financial control she would be kept reliant upon themselves. The Duke (who undoubtedly sided with the Duchess) nevertheless found her demands premature and urged that she should consider the letter 'as never having been written'. The Duchess tartly rejoined that 'if I am not to express my wishes and feelings, I dare say it will occur to your Grace that I am not likely to be asked for them'.[17]

The Duchess's and Conroy's position was, however, unassailable for no one wanted Cumberland as Regent. (Conroy had in fact feared that Leopold might be made Custos, but that apprehension finally dissolved when the Prince was offered the throne of Belgium – thus taking him still further away from the centre of affairs at Kensington.)

*

Intent on taking all opportunities that this great moment afforded, Sir John now commenced upon the first of his many tours of England with Victoria and her mother. Support for the Regency from the people was his intention; but the country knew nothing of the little girl at Kensington, whose dynastic importance had magnified so dramatically.

This initial tour was to centre around the Duchess's holiday at 'Hollymount' in Malvern during the summer of 1830; her approach – via Oxford and Stratford – being made through Birmingham where she was to introduce her daughter to the great manufacturers. Conroy claimed that the Duchess moved to Malvern out of 'delicacy of feeling'; there was however nothing delicate in Sir John's immediate introduction to Birmingham of the Heiress Presumptive. William IV, whilst not yet crowned, can scarcely have enjoyed their progress, despite Conroy insisting that the tour was for the Princess's instruction: 'grafting upon *Home* education . . . a more extended knowledge of the internal concerns of the country which she could not fail to imbibe from visiting the great seats of Manufacture and Commerce.'[18]

The Royal Party's welcome in Birmingham was tumultuous and 'the youthful Princess was regarded by all with the deepest feelings of interest'. Victoria and the Conroys were introduced to a rolling mill and a button factory; papier maché, nail and glass factories and to the Rollason and Sons glass and china rooms in Streethouse Lane. (The Duchess's birthday presents later that month consisted of a quantity of bottles from every member of her 'family' – Sir John gave one of gold, the provenance of which was unmistakable. She was fortunate perhaps to receive no buttons or papier mâché.)

The high-point of the tour however was Victoria's visit to the Boulton and Watts Manufactury of Soho and Soho Foundry, where the party were shown (by Joseph Watts's son) the smithery, boiler-making, casting of brass and iron, boring mills and turning and fitting departments; a catalogue of nineteenth-century achievement, all employed in the making of a steam-engine. The Duchess indeed was moved to express 'her feelings of respect for the memory of their author, the late Mr Watt' and she and her daughter were then introduced to 'the venerable Mr Murdock, himself the inventor of the gas-light'.[19]

More excitement lay in store at the foundry where Victoria assisted in the striking of her own commemorative gold medal with the inscription: 'Victoria, Magnae Spes Altera Britanniae Soho, 6 Aug. 1830'. The Duchess had a medal, too: 'Felix tu quoque Mater!'[20]

An even more attractive opportunity of sealing the Princess's presence upon the nation was furnished by the Duchess's birthday celebrations, which Victoria described in a letter to Feodora from Malvern on 28th August:

I had the permission to keep Victoire the whole day. At 12 o'clock we were to go up a certain walk, to open it and it was to be called Victoria's Drive. The whole Conroy family, as well as Dr Maton, walked through our grounds to it. There, at the foot of the hill, were Lord & Lady Beauchamp, and a great many other people. When we arrived at the top, we tasted the water of the well, and then went down. As we were going down they fired some cannons on the rock; and as we approached our grounds, it was so loud, that I shook a little.[21]

Victoria then hurried home to 'Hollymount', where she and Victoire gave their dolls a tea-party.

On their return home the party covered Bristol, Bath, Badminton, Gloucester and even Stonehenge. At Bristol, the Mayor, discouraged from presenting an Address, yet 'proceeded in state to Clifton to express their loyalty and devotion and met with a cordial reception'.

The tour had indeed been a quiet, almost surreptitious success and Sir John now confidently awaited a further excuse to exploit the Princess and her future position in greater style . . .

Even before Victoria's journey, the question of the Regency had been raised in the House of Commons; and the following October an Act was brought before Parliament declaring that 'Her Royal Highness Victoria Maria Louisa Duchess of Kent shall be the Guardian, and have the Care,

Tuition, and Education of the Person of Her said Royal Highness the Princess Alexandrina Victoria, until Her said Royal Highness the Princess Alexandrina Victoria shall attain the Age of Eighteen Years . . .'[22]

Sir John Conroy was now in a position of very considerable influence and power. Power however has its degrees; it can only be sustained by character and judgement, and is difficult to transfer or to let go. In the complex power-struggle to come at Kensington it is easy to see that Victoria held all the cards. She would one day be Queen; and this certainty gave her a strength unknown to Conroy. She knew that if she held out against his schemes she could defeat him; he had no such certainty over her. Yet in fact the very power invested in Sovereigns was in the process of change. Monarchies all over Europe feared for their existence; even William IV was to feel the Crown 'tottering' on his head. The post of Private Secretary to a Monarch (as Conroy hoped to become) would never again be as influential as formerly. Governments would be chary of allowing the appointment; and even as Victoria's half-brother Prince Leiningen urged the Princess in 1837 to guard her 'interest and prerogatives, vis à vis of your Ministers',[23] so the idea of a Government being locked in combat with the Crown was becoming out of date. In England the battle had been essentially fought by Parliament in 1832.

'Let me wish you *many*, *many* happy returns of the day', wrote the jubilant Duchess on Sir John's birthday as the Regency Bill became law, 'to yourself, to your amiable family and to myself for whom you have *done*, and still *do* so much. Never can Victoria and her poor mother, recompense *adequately*, all what you did for us.

'May you and your dear family, enjoy all the happiness this world can bestow, and may Providence assist me to contribute my little share to it . . .'[24]

*

Rumour and gossip were once more flourishing as to the nature of the Duchess's relationship with Sir John Conroy.

The Duke of Wellington when asked by Greville whether he thought they were lovers, replied 'he supposed so'. He also believed the hatred that the Princess showed towards Sir John was the result of her having seen familiarities between them. Rumour of a sexual relationship between such a working partnership as theirs was of course inevitable; yet (as has been discussed) a good deal of evidence points to the contrary. Speculation apart – and rumours still persist of adultery and even of an illegitimate child – it is worth emphasising that no documentary evidence has ever been found of such an affair between them.

As a figure of fun, however, Conroy was delighting his audience (except those who had the bother of him, to whom he remained singularly unamusing); '– a ridiculous fellow, a compound of "Great Hussy" and the Chamberlain of "The Princess of Navarre"', commented Greville, neatly encapsulating Conroy's Irish theatricality. Edward Hussey (an eighteenth-century Irish suitor of the Duchess of Manchester) had been thus immortalised in verse:

> Look down, St Patrick! with success
> Like Hussey's all the Irish bless
> May they all do as he does;
> And still preserve their breed the same
> Cast in his mould, made in his frame,
> To comfort English widows.[25]

The Duchess had clearly been comforted – if not quite to the extent indicated in the verse. So indeed had Princess Sophia, who was busy spying on conversations at Kensington and smuggling out reports to Sir John. ('What an amazing scape of a man he must have been,' exclaimed Melbourne in admiration, 'to have kept three ladies at once in good humour.')[26] What Lady Conroy made of it all history does not relate. One must assume that with her 'below average' intelligence, she simply dealt with life as it came – although her grandson thought she was 'spiteful', and feared 'she made mischief'.

Indeed, the Duchess was evidently sensitive to the difficult situation in which her relationship with Conroy placed his wife: in 1829 she had made Lady Conroy her Woman of the Bedchamber, thus giving her the right, the Duchess promised, 'to act in a situation, where you may be of use to me; But where your delicacy might have given you the feeling, that you were more a guest, than a member of my family.'[27]

Even before the success of the Regency Bill Conroy had been rearranging the Duchess's court to be consistent with her desire to be 'quite English'. Initially Sir John advised her to put an 'English Lady' about the Princess, but on the Duchess's defence of Lehzen he was obliged to change his mind. He later told Prince Leiningen that he thought it 'inconvenient' to place any English woman with Victoria, for if she were 'troublesome' she would be difficult to get rid of. He then proceeded to demonstrate the ease with which foreigners could be removed by dismissing Baroness Späth.

This caused a sensation at Kensington. Späth was the Duchess's faithful companion. She had been with her in her years at Leiningen and on the adventurous journey to Kensington. The Duke of Wellington suggested to Greville that Victoria had complained to Späth of the familiarities she had seen and that Späth had remonstrated with the Duchess. However it is more probable that Späth's age, nationality and critical tongue had finally told against her. Conroy rather unconvincingly explained that Späth was dismissed from 'motives of the kindest consideration'. She was sent away to live with Feodora in Germany, and in fact returned to visit the Duchess and Victoria in 1833 whilst they were holidaying on the Isle of Wight.[28]

Nevertheless the episode gave Princess Sophia plenty of opportunity for gossip and in a letter to Conroy in October 1829 she eagerly recounted a conversation she had had with the Duchess of Clarence (disguised as 'Mrs Aquatic') on the subject of the Duchess of Kent.

'It would make a noise S's going away', 'Mrs Aquatic' had told the Duchess – who had replied that 'she did not see it so, on the contrary that by degrees she felt she ought to get rid of foreigners about her'.

'Mrs Aquatic' feared Lehzen would go too; whereupon

Princess Sophia laughed merrily: 'Dear me. What can you mean? L & S are quite opposite in situations but so far I do think V. [the Duchess of Kent] is very right about replacing her people by nice English, for you yourself your Husband *above all*, which She must recollect, and all the family have never ceased asking – well how odd She has no English ladies . . .'

'She ought to have an E[nglish] lady to attend the child', commented 'Mrs Aquatic'.

'Then it is you who wants Lehzen to go so why do you fear it?' snapped Princess Sophia.

'*No I do not want her to go,*' insisted 'Mrs Aquatic', seriously alarmed, 'but still another she should have & I have thought of one – Lady Chichester do you not think she would do very well?'

'As what?', queried Princess Sophia suspiciously.

'Lady Attendant she is so good and would not meddle.'

'*Meddle*', replied Sophia triumphantly, '*no-one would dare to do.*'[29]

Conroy would have read this production with glee. Indeed, Princess Sophia, throughout the rest of her life, was careful to keep her *cher ami* informed of Palace affairs: 'Tell her', Conroy wrote to Edward in 1840, 'how well she writes and always to write with the *blackest* stuff.'[30]

Indeed, as Sir John was rising to the height of his fame and success, so Victoria's life became even more guarded, gossip-ridden and hedged with Palace intrigue. It was vital to Conroy's plans that the image of the Princess in the public mind remained pure, independent and firmly Whig in character. Certainly Kensington was nervous of the Fitzclarences – and so indeed was Baroness Lehzen (whose ally William IV became).[31] Victoria therefore was forbidden their company and the Duchess ostentatiously left the room should any of them appear. (William IV and Queen Adelaide were in fact genuinely fond of their niece and such priggishness became painfully irritating.) However, Conroy claimed it was on the Fitzclarences' account that the 'Duchess had been forced . . . to draw a narrower line [with the King] for that Her own wishes *really* prompts Her to.'[32] The King himself detested both the Duchess and Conroy. He particularly despised the Duchess's relatives – Prince Leopold's water-drinking irritated him profoundly – and clearly went out of his way to be as unpleasant as possible. Conroy claimed he was 'a marked man'; that the King 'persecuted' him and his family and that his name was struck out of Lord Grey's Coronation Honours List in which he had been given a Baronetcy (promised by Canning).[33] Lehzen however had been rather more devious. She had struck up a friendship with a 'Miss Wilson' (a Miss Martha Wilson was Lady of the Bedchamber to Queen Adelaide) through whom, so the Conroys claimed, she quietly intrigued with William IV.[34]

Leopold, as King of the newly-created Belgian state, was in a particularly delicate position. Belgium had recently defeated neighbouring Holland (whose Royal Family William IV supported) and Leopold desperately needed the alliance with the British throne. As Victoria grew older he took decisive steps to influence her character and political thinking; attempting through Baroness Lehzen, to keep his niece clear of Conroy's influence (one wonders how much he regretted Stockmar's encouragement of Conroy in 1825?) without actually alienating either him or the Duchess. In a conversation in 1831 Leopold asked Lord Grey to 'have his eye'[35] on Conroy – going so far, according to Sir John, to tell the Prime Minister he 'must be got rid of'. Conroy, in spite of spending the self-same evening with the Duchess and Leopold (who, he said, left him 'almost in tears'), was convinced that Leopold and Lehzen hated him 'one because he would not allow him to make a tool of his sister – and the other, as he kept her in her place'.[36]

In fact, Kensington's 'Chief Adviser', Lord Dunfermline, was, in his detached and amiable way, inclined to agree that the 'real merit of Conroy was his keeping the Duchess of Kent and the Queen quite clear of the King of the Belgians'.[37] This was certainly wishful-thinking, but the Kensington System and its advisers were closing ranks against any interference. The power-lines were clearly marked; the spy-network carefully co-ordinated. (Lehzen, according to Conroy, 'went to watch him, through the key-hole'.)[38] On New Year's Eve 1830, Sir John was to be found conscientiously researching a scholarly memorandum: 'Powers of the Sovereign over the care and education of the Children of the Royal Family.' His chief adversary from now on would be William IV and he and the Duchess needed to be sure of their ground.

If malice, intrigue and suspicion were having their effect on Victoria, the atmosphere at Kensington was no less un-healthy for the Conroy children. Indeed, their upbringing was to have a far more disastrous effect upon them than upon Victoria who at least was the natural heir to her situation. The Conroys however were living a life above their station – the victims of their father's fantasies – and were swiftly growing accustomed to a social life they themselves could never sustain. Their whole existence depended upon Sir John's success (and Princess Sophia's generosity) without which their world would have fallen apart.

At a time when Victoria was still a child, Conroy's sons were growing up and passing out of his control. Stephen and Henry were away at boarding-school: Henry at Eton, where he acquired a taste for the classics, and shared with his brother Edward a talent for verse in the style of Winthrop Mackworth Praed; Edward himself had attended Charter-house (where his great-uncle Dr Philip Fisher was Master) before entering Christ Church, Oxford. He attained a pass degree in 1830. One reason for this undistinguished career may lie in a bill for an Irish Dinner at The Star 'including Waiters, Music, damages £45.5.6'. With wine, the cost of the evening extended to £75.15.0. Edward's fellow under-graduates William Gladstone and Martin Tupper – the future author of *Proverbial Philosophy* – would not have approved.

Indeed, Conroy's eldest son (who was being groomed as the Heir Apparent) was something of a disappointment – a fact which Sir John, with a family pride he did not always extend to Victoria, succeeded in overlooking. 'He is clever and steady', he told Lord Durham, when Edward clearly was neither, and sent him off on a Grand Tour that cost him a fortune. Edward later came to have a rather more realistic view of his own capacities: 'I am a small person,' he admitted to his mother after his father's death, 'I was satisfied to think that I should always have a competency. My father always said I was his heir. he always spoke of me as his eldest son . . .'[39]

In 1830, however, Edward was still exceedingly pleased with himself. After a false start as a Lieutenant in the army, he was apprenticed as an unpaid attaché to Sir Robert Adair, the British Minister at Brussels. Like most of Edward's appointments, however, it did not last long and he was soon back on the social circuit, 'breaking hearts' and writing poetry for his sisters that has a poignant ring:

> Man's life in various passions spent,
> Changing with times – and ne'er content,
> Too oft forgets midst worldly strife,
> The love he felt in early life.[40]

Edward, alas, was not to live up to his promises of undying affection for his sisters, or indeed, for anyone else. In this saga of not always very likeable people his character is the least attractive. Deceitful and undisciplined, he was of all Conroy's children the most spoilt by his privileged upbringing; the most shaken by his father's defeat.

This was a pity; for Stephen and Henry both had charm (Stephen kept a diary containing pressed flowers and poetic references to the moon and new-mown hay) and Henry was renowned for his 'buoyant' spirit and irrepressible good humour.

As for the girls, the enforced playmates of Victoria, they were harmless, dull and ever-present – on holiday at Ramsgate or over Christmas at St Leonards; touring the great houses of England and playing duets at Kensington Palace – there they were . . . Willing to dress up as 'Turks' or 'Nuns', play cards or romp with the dogs. Victoria's only childhood friends.

It was hardly the Conroys' fault that Victoria hated their father nor indeed that their company came to displease her.

It is possible that the Princess would have been happier playing with 'the Bâtards' and living with the King at Windsor. But then, she might have despised them, too. (She certainly did not like her legitimate cousins, Cambridge and Cumberland.) The suspicion however that the Conroy family would have been much happier living at Shooters Hill, leading the middle-class life of their forebears, is inescapable. As it was, they were destined from Victoria's accession to be ignominiously 'banned' from the only world they knew by the friend they themselves grew up with.

Indeed, when many years later the Duchess of Kent saw at last the consequences of her former life with the Conroys at Kensington, she was filled with pity and remorse: 'How unfortunate for that family', she sadly admitted, 'that their Father ever came near the Royal Family . . . it is a *sore subject*.'[41]

6

'VICTORIA – PRIDE OF OUR LAND!'

Sir John Conroy, it can be fairly claimed, invented the
Royal Tour. Certainly George IV had visited Scotland and
Ireland, but never, perhaps since the progresses of Elizabeth
I, had England seen anything like such pageantry – let alone
publicity – as was to accompany Princess Victoria and her
mother on their tours of England and Wales.

'Victoria – Pride of our Land!' hailed a popular song
dedicated to Sir John Conroy – proving that in the public
mind, he and the Princess were indivisible.

Indeed, Conroy was described to Victoria (by her half-
brother Prince Leiningen) as 'the man who has worked hard
many a year to create this enormous popularity for you,'
and it was on her Royal Tours – which William IV so
detested – that Sir John's organisational skills were seen to
their greatest effect. He took enormous pride in their
execution '– not clouded by any one occurrence,' he rejoiced
triumphantly to Lord Durham, '– not one screw loose' – and
the pleasure they gave the public in seeing the 'Hope of the
Nation' was touching and genuine.

Others however felt the 'Journeys' to be manipulative and
disrespectful of the King. Melbourne told Lord Liverpool he
strongly disapproved of them (Conroy was furious) and
Victoria herself, especially as she grew older, dreaded the
travelling. She found it tedious and tiring – for she did not
seem to possess the pioneering spirit of her mother, who had

cheerfully crossed Europe when eight-months pregnant. 'I was very much tired, by the long journeys and the great crowds we had to encounter. We cannot travel like other people, quietly & pleasantly . . .'[2]

Politically the Tours were of supreme importance. 1832 saw the Reform Bill passed in Parliament and the Whigs, headed by Durham's father-in-law, Lord Grey, finally in power. The country had teetered on the edge of revolution: 'down with Kings, priests, and Lords . . .' cried the revolutionary press; 'Reform! Reform!' were the shouts in the crowd at William IV's Coronation. Perhaps the King remembered them when he agreed to create the Whig peers who enabled the Reform Bill to be passed in June 1832.

Little more than a month later on 31st July – this second Tour had been hurriedly arranged to take advantage of the public mood – Victoria and her mother, together with the Conroy family, set off from Kensington in a great cavalcade.

In theory Victoria was without Party; staying impartially at Whig and Tory country houses. But in fact the itinerary was arranged entirely by Conroy and his colleague Lord Durham, who took pains to outline for Sir John his political intentions: 'I wish to rally as large a portion of the British People, as is possible, consistently with sound policy, round the existing institutions of King, Lords & Commons', he maintained. 'I do not wish to make new institutions, but I wish to preserve & strengthen the old . . .'[3] Conroy himself made it clear that 'I have *always* given my support to the liberal party, as far as I could, consistently with the situation I held.'[4] Indeed, it is certain many people felt Conroy entertained political ambitions: an undated cutting from *The Times*, carefully preserved in The Conroy Papers, claimed that Sir John was 'as little likely to embark in any political plot as he is to write an epic poem'. This certainly was true, but in 1832 no man was without political bias, and Victoria's tours could well have been seen as Whig propaganda.

Curiously, Victoria's mother, according to Princess Lieven, had not been in favour of reform[5] – and indeed the Duchess admitted to Lehzen in 1837 that Victoria did not share her political outlook.[6] Conroy claimed the Duchess 'held a trust for all parties', and it is possible she maintained her Whig attachment in loyalty to the Duke of Kent rather than from natural inclination.

Nevertheless, Lord Durham had become, as Greville described him, her 'Magnus Apollo', and to him Conroy on 20th June 1832 outlined his hastily contrived plans: '– as her [the Duchess's] route would be, not far from Liverpool and Manchester – in Her way to Matlock; she is desirous to receive confidentially the expression of your opinion, whether it would be expedient or not, to shew the Princess those two great towns – and whether their shelter there could be looked to, as divested of all opportunity to shew political feeling – but rather, as was the case on a previous tour, to unite all parties, into giving them, a cordial reception'.[7]

This ambitious project did not materialise, and neither, the following year, did a long-held dream to take Victoria to Ireland 'via Plymouth to Cork – to visit Killarney – the capital – the Giant's Causeway in the north – after which, to cross to Liverpool . . .'[8] As late as 1836 Conroy had still been hopeful of success 'there being hardly a place untouched in this country . . . but unless Their Royal Highnesses could have gone, in the King's name, the Duchess decided not to go, and She might have as well asked for the consent of the sun and moon, such is the sad and fatal jealousy that prevails, and the King and His family, have lost a golden moment, to tie to a very interesting Heiress Presumptive, the feelings of the Irish Nation, for', he added prophetically, 'in coming times, it would have been well to have left no stone unturned to draw the countries closer together . . .'[9]

The 'fatal jealousy' of William IV towards the Duchess of Kent was the cause of increasing animosity between Windsor and Kensington. The Duchess, fuelled by fear of the King's intention to take Victoria from her, did everything to enhance her position and dominance over her daughter; the King, irritated beyond reason by Conroy's exploitation of the Princess, took every opportunity to object to the Duchess's plans and to find fault wherever he could.

The problem of 'the three rooms' on the upper storey at Kensington, which the Duchess had requested after the Regency, became a running saga. The Palace, for all its charm, was shabby and in need of repair and it is probable that the dark, east-facing rooms Victoria and her mother occupied on the ground floor were undermining the Princess's health. (Indeed the Duchess, according to Conroy, was 'anxious' to have Marlborough House – and had even used King Leopold's home at Claremont to get away from the Palace.) The Duchess was certainly not the first royal resident to complain of the damp from Kensington's underground streams, but nevertheless the King refused her request.

He even objected to the Princess's use of the name 'Victoria' ('My favourite and dear name', as she called it) and 'Charlotte' had been suggested instead. This was a further insult to the Duchess since the Princess had been given her second name in deference to her mother; (George IV, in an unseemly squabble over the font, named the hapless infant 'Alexandrina' after the Tsar). At first the Duchess yielded to this latest indignity, but a pencilled copy by Sir John of a letter to Lord Grey indicates that he and the Duchess had come to the historic decision that Victoria should indeed keep her name: 'I fear – ', declared the Duchess, 'that the people are very indifferent about the change of name – that they are accustomed to Victoria – and do not dislike it – it being a high sounding name.'[10] (Only now perhaps can we appreciate that, but for Conroy, we might be forever encumbered with the 'Charlotteian Age'.)

The King, infuriated by the Duchess's independent stand, was further irritated by her claiming Victoria be called 'Royal' Highness (the King had omitted the 'Royal' in a communication to Parliament) as conferred on her by the Regency Bill.

'I gave you my advice', provoked Conroy, 'to call her so in future – as conferred on her by Act of Parliament . . . although it seems – it was not intended to be done so – as it deprived the King of conferring it, if he was pleased to do so, as a favour, by letters Patent.'[11]

Favours to the Duchess however were very far from the King's mind. Indeed, at his Coronation the following month he achieved the ultimate snub, by forbidding Victoria, as Heiress Presumptive, from walking immediately behind him in the Coronation procession.

The sequel was dramatic. A bitter attack on the Duchess appeared in *The Times* on the 7th September 1831, stating that 'it is with deep regret that we learned that Her Royal Highness had refused to attend! and that Her absence on this occasion is in pursuance of a systematic opposition on the part of Her Royal Highness to all the wishes and all the feelings of the present King . . . We should be glad to know who are the advisers of this misguided lady?'

The horrified Conroy appealed to Durham: 'Her Royal Highness had no reason to expect this attack . . .' – he exclaimed, 'Her Royal Highness considered that the King and Her, *concurred* in thinking, the Princess should be relieved of the fatigue . . .'[12]

(As a matter of fact this was technically true; the King had written that 'he would not on any account, have the health of the Princess Victoria exposed to the slightest risk . . .')[13] Conroy's opinion was that the article came from someone 'not far from the Court' – he was right, Lord de Ros was the culprit[14] – who had 'seized this occasion to insult, and to raise a clamour against Her, on grounds to injure Her popularity'. The Duchess and King, he declared, were 'divested of positive disagreement' (the chief problem being her refusal to acknowledge the Bâtards) but that there were many people near him 'to rouse Him against the D. of Kent: therefore to *them* and to Lord Grey . . . He may have spoken differently – '[15]

This was a shrewd and probably accurate assessment of the situation at that time. The King was weak-minded (and well-meaning) and doubtless as influenced by such as his Secretary Sir Herbert Taylor ('Taylor was in fact King of England' declared Melbourne) as the Duchess was by Conroy.

Whatever the Duchess's intentions the incident proved something of a turning point in her relations with the King;

no 'general ground' was found; (indeed, it is hard to see how
it could have been); and Conroy, in his Royal Progresses (as
William IV sarcastically referred to them) continued to
supply the King with every excuse for provocation.

However irritated William IV may have been with Victoria's Royal Tours the public were entirely enthusiastic.
'Englishmen like to see the Royal Family coming frankly
among them, and receiving with kindness those marks of
attention the people love to pay,' commented one newspaper
– and the reception given Victoria and her mother must
have warmed Conroy's heart. The Princess's youth and
innocence was emphasised by her wearing white and being
accompanied by the young children of the towns through
which they passed. Her likeness to Princess Charlotte and
the 'illustreous Stock' of her father's family was frequently
noticed – and indeed at Chester the resemblance was
described as 'complete'.

That the Tour passed through North Wales via Conway,
not far from Sir John's own birthplace, cannot have been a
coincidence. Here the children strewed flowers before their
path and at the Menai Bridge a male voice choir sang 'God
Save the King'. Even Sir John's old nurse was brought out to
see him as the party drove by. At Lord Anglesey's home, Plas
Newydd, the travellers took a much-needed rest; (nobody
was well, and even 'Sir was very unwell & was unable to
come to dinner'). Here Victoria and Victoire could ride their
ponies (Isabel and Rosa had followed the cavalcade from
Kensington) and play with Lady Conroy's little dog Bijou –
setting him in the sea and watching him run about.

'Their Royal Highnesses are quite well,' wrote Conroy to
Durham from Plas Newydd, 'they have been absent from
town, eleven weeks, and have had a very agreeable sejour:
they have come in contact with all parties and classes, as
well as denominations: and from all they have met with the
most cordial reception.'[16]

In early November the party began its slow progress south
to Oxford, where Sir John – in one of the highest points of
his career – was escorted through the cheering crowds to

receive his Honorary Doctorate of Civil Law before the alumni of Oxford University.

Despite such accolades King Leopold (whilst exercising the greatest tact) was keeping a sharp eye on Conroy. Care was needed, for Lord Durham was in Brussels during 1832 as Leopold's adviser, and Baron Stockmar himself continued to receive trusting and gossipy letters from Sir John Conroy, who wrote as if no suspicions were entertained of him. Indeed Conroy often spoke of Stockmar's 'constant friend-ship for me'.

In fact, like an impossible child, Sir John had no conception that his behaviour was unacceptable. Warnings were of no avail and fell from him like leaves off a tree. ('He was incorrigible,' exclaimed Leopold.) Nevertheless, Conroy was soon to realise that Victoria was receiving advice from her uncle as to how best to withstand his coercion . . .

'It is very odd', wrote Leopold to Victoria, 'and proves that I foresaw what has happened that in 1832 I wrote to Conroy that I should look upon myself as bound *to protect you*, and that whenever I thought fit I should take my measures accordingly.'[7]

Such warnings however had not the slightest effect upon the behaviour of Oxford's Honorary DCL as he and his family once more prepared to celebrate Christmas at Kensington Palace.

'I must say', continued Leopold, 'that if we had not gradually these last years prepared ourselves for the struggle you would and could not have been equal to it . . .'

*

In 1834 the Duchess of Kent acquired a new Woman of the Bedchamber who henceforth assisted Lady Conroy and accompanied the family on their Royal Tours and every formal occasion. Her appointment spelt serious trouble for Victoria, and she was received with almost instinctive dislike and suspicion. Her name was Lady Flora Hastings.

Lady Flora, the eldest daughter of the Marquis of

Hastings was, at twenty-eight years of age, a gifted and attractive young woman. The possessor of dark smooth hair and large intelligent eyes, she had a considerable talent for literature and languages. Born before her time, she made a natural secretary – 'My table is like a Secretary of States' – translated from the Italian, and produced a stream of verse of varying quality. (Her serious poetry does not wear well but surprisingly her light verse, including 'Ashby de la Zouch' where she undertook to find numerous rhymes for 'Zouch', shows a sharp wit, which doubtless had its effect.)

Lady Flora became a close friend of the Conroy family with whom she stayed before going into waiting at the Palace. Flora 'fears she will hardly be able to reach Kensington on Saturday', wrote Lady Hastings, from Loudon Castle, 'but if not hopes to be with you & Lady Conroy, early on Sunday, so as to have the quiet of Sunday under your Hospitable & Friendly roof'.[8]

Yet this innocent, high-minded young woman had walked

Lady Flora Hastings by Princess Victoria.

into a hornet's nest. She was to be branded 'a Spie of J.C.'[19] by Victoria and when it became clear that her affection for her adopted family extended not only to Jane (who became her most intimate friend) but to Sir John himself, her doom was sealed.

Lady Flora's father, Lord Hastings, had died in 1826, his health broken by the burden of the Governor-Generalship of India and by his subsequent disgrace in the Calcutta banking scandal of 1822. Sir John's younger brother Llewellin had been his aide de camp and doubtless this connection had given Lady Flora an especial intimacy with the Conroy family. She had never recovered from the death of her father whom she resembled ('Oh thou to whom my thoughts unceasing tend', she wrote, 'My Father, my Instructor, and my Friend'). Indeed, the Duchess felt Lady Flora had been 'unhappy at home'. Undoubtedly she regarded Sir John as a paternal substitute, for 'In much you resemble my Father', she told him, '– in much also your fate bears some analogy to his'.[20]

Not only was Lady Flora too intellectual and pious for Victoria's taste, but she had the added misfortune in being selected as Victoria's chaperone by the Duchess instead of by the Princess herself. At fifteen years old Victoria felt she should choose her own ladies, but this freedom was firmly denied her.

A grander appointment by far had been the installation of the Duchess of Northumberland as Victoria's Head Governess. Whether this great lady had been acquired because of her possible kinship with Lady Conroy we cannot know; but if so, Sir John was to be disappointed in her loyalty. The new Governess sided with Lehzen, to the extent, even, of writing to Feodora in 1835 that the Baroness was being treated 'with contempt and incredible harshness'.

'Dear Duchess', replied the horrified Feodora (whose experience of Conroy went back to the days of the Stephen affair), 'we must do everything to preserve Baroness L. The King is the person to uphold her and say she *must* and *shall* remain . . . for what sort of person may be put near her, to further the plans of that man.'[21]

As a respite from the atmosphere at Kensington which everyone found depressing ('anything is better than K', exlaimed Conroy), the Duchess had taken to holidaying at Norris Castle on the Isle of Wight. (The Conroys stayed nearby at Osborne Cottage, later the site of Queen Victoria's own home.) At Norris, the Duchess received her numerous German relatives, and from here too, Conroy launched the notorious mother and daughter on a tour of the West Country.

For this assignment, the Duchess had her yacht the *Emerald* – a naval tender put at her disposal by the King. It was not as large as Lord Durham's ostentatious *Louisa*, which accompanied them, but Victoria was very fond of 'the *dear Emerald*'; and it was in this vessel that she was to have 'the narrowest escape possible'.

A courtesy Conroy insisted of the Royal Yacht was that she should be saluted. William IV was furious. The 'popping' would have to cease. 'Their R.H's went to Portsmouth on Friday last', wrote Conroy to Durham in October 1833 '– salutes were ordered ashore – counter-ordered – authorities disagreed – all referred to Ld Hill I hear! But', he continued cheerfully, 'the people came to the waters edge to cheer them – and having a Regt saluting them with a private Battery!'[22] – An order in council had already been made to forbid all 'popping' except for the King and Queen. But that had not deterred Conroy; indeed, Victoria later described the salutes as 'all Sir John's doing'.

It was on 2nd August, however, as the *Emerald* sailed into Plymouth Harbour, that the narrow escape occurred. The yacht 'fell foul of a hulk', breaking its mast which was in imminent danger of falling on to the Princess and her party. Saunders, the Captain, grabbed hold of Dashy, the Princess's little dog, 'but', wrote Victoria, 'I was *dreadfully* frightened for *Mamma* and for *all*'.

Lady Wharncliffe (who probably quoted from a news-paper) claimed that the Captain took the Princess 'up in his arms, & carried her off to the fore part of the vessel' – however, since he was already burdened with a dog, this seems unlikely. Indeed, Victoria made no mention in her

Journal of being rescued by anyone. Neither did Conroy. 'The accident was a ticklish concern', he reported to Durham, 'and really no one's fault – we had the Admiral on board: you will be charmed to hear of the *courage* shown by their R.H's and all our ladies.'[23]

The organisation of even the shortest tour demanded great attention to detail. The Duchess's Groom of the Chamber, Nathaniel Date, was quick to point out Sir John's and even Saunders's short-comings: there were no boats and carriages for the servants, he complained; no drink on board the *Emerald*, and they were given no butter or cheese. 'Sir John', he grumbled, 'treated me on many occasions most infamously. Mr Saunders abused the confidence HRH and Sir John placed in him and treated me with disrespect, as did also Sir John on many occasions, as there was those that he wished to shew favours to and at the same time to deprive me of due respect.' He signed himself ambiguously, 'N. Date'.[24]

Whatever the discomforts of the lower orders (and in general Conroy was popular with servants) the upper strata travelled in comparative ease. The Royal Party toured in an open carriage, Lehzen beside Victoria, 'and Sir John on the box'. For the first time the Princess visited Sidmouth 'where my poor Papa died', and from Dartmouth drove to Torquay where there was, exlaimed Conroy, 'the prettiest reception I ever saw – upwards of one hundred children in white to receive the P covered with flowers . . . all the gentry, & visitors passed thro' the D's room – all the doings of the town as the children was done, by the tradespeople – it had the effect I hear of bringing them together, these having been disjoined from politics!'[25]

From Torquay they drove to Swanage – a 'hard days work' – and the 'entry into Exeter was really most imposing every window full'.

'The Bishop', Conroy added, 'was sick.'

Flushed with success, the Duchess and her party settled again at Norris to enjoy the rest of the summer of 1833.

Whatever the trials of Victoria's early life they were not

without respite and the sparkling freshness of her descriptions of Norris – the sailing boats; the rides and drives; Lord Durham's fête; the joyous visits of her German cousins; even the celebration of Victoire's fourteenth birthday with a 'sillabub' under a tree in the garden – have a happy holiday air as yet untinged with bitterness. Osborne Cottage was filled with young people and their family pets, and even possessed a swing. It was not long before a swing was placed in front of Norris Castle.

Conroy enjoyed Norris exceedingly, for 'there is no life to recover one so good', he declared, 'as that idle sea life'. He excelled in outdoor pursuits, for he was not in any sense

Miss Victoire Conroy 'from nature' by Princess Victoria, December 1836, Claremont.

intellectual, despite being described as 'an excellent pen and ink man'. He would read history in relation to his work and is found reminding Durham 'to let me have the book I lent you' – but he admitted his notes were 'shabby' and Durham, though glad to see his handwriting, commented that 'there certainly was not much of it'.

'It is true', acknowledged Conroy, 'I am a sad correspondent.'

As to the deeper side of life, it is unlikely Conroy dwelt there long. He could be moved (as on the death of his father-in-law) but, too, he proved defiant in the face of disaster ('– not a bit unhappy or put down'). He held orthodox Church of England beliefs – he had married into a devout family – and would piously invoke 'the Will of a Higher Power', especially when it looked to be in his favour. That he found superficial comfort in religion is likely, but nevertheless in later life he was to show distressing evidence of possessing a troubled conscience.

Yet he could not live without a dream – indeed his gifts for organisation (as exemplified in his tours) were essentially creative, and one of the more remarkable aspects of his life would be that no sooner had one great hope been shattered than another was to be laboriously constructed in its place.

So enigmatic was Conroy's central personality that while, to such as the Duchess and Lady Flora, he appeared strong, paternal and trustworthy; yet this scaffolding was deceptive. Within, money, ambition and power were at the service of his fantasies, by which he was deceived. In turn, others were taken in by him. Yet it was his ability to dream that lent him charm and gave, for the susceptible, his dangerous attraction. Sir John in fact, was his own invention. An Irishman, indeed.

*

In September 1835, Victoria and her mother embarked upon the last – and most spectacular – of their eagerly-awaited tours. At the last moment however, the Princess felt very unwell and declined to travel. The years of incessant domestic strain, and the unhealthy situation of the rooms at Kensington, were undermining her health: she complained of headaches and sickness, of backache and sore throats. She felt permanently tired. Her mother, whose constitution was robust, and whose own youth had never been subjected to the strains Victoria experienced, was unsympathetic: '. . . Can you be dead to the calls your position demands? Impossible! Reflect – before it is too late . . . Turn your thoughts and views to your future station, its duties, and the claims that exist on you.'[26]

Conroy did not like Victoria's illnesses, for he was afraid of anything that would throw doubt on her ability to reign. He had already had one 'scene' with Lehzen the previous Christmas at St Leonard's, where Victoria was ill and nursed by the Baroness; now another storm, more serious and far-reaching in its effects, was gathering on the horizon.

Conroy indeed, in his presentation of Victoria, faced two directions at once: on the one hand he needed to show that she was too immature to rule without his and the Duchess's aid; ('Avoid in future to say much about your great *youth* and *inexperience*', warned Leopold. 'Who made the latter? Was it yourself? Or came it from your Mother?')[27] On the other hand, to assert that the Princess was in any way inadequate would have cast doubt on the success of the Kensington System. 'Our interior is as usual here', Conroy wrote to Durham, 'devoted to bringing up the Princess well – to make her fit for the critical times, in which she will live –'[28]

It was now openly understood that Conroy, on her accession, intended to be Victoria's Private Secretary; and it was his and the Duchess's plan that the Princess would agree to his instalment before she came of age. William IV was showing signs of failing health, while Victoria herself, at sixteen years old, was demonstrating a distinctly independent nature. Leopold upheld this inborn tendency by writing regularly to his niece on the dangers of hypocrisy, of the 'wolves in sheeps clothing' and of the importance of self-knowledge and discipline.

Eventually 'the terrible scenes in the house', as Victoria described them, had become so frequent that the distracted

Duchess called in Stockmar in the hope that he would bring harmony to her household. Nevertheless, her own dream of sailing serenely into the new reign with Conroy at the helm was still intact, and she had no intention of being shaken from it by Stockmar or anyone else.

The Baron's long and frank letter shows that he had judged the situation correctly. In one area alone did he falter: he had underestimated the influence of Lehzen. Indeed he dismissed it. The true ground he believed for the 'differences' could be found in 'the innate personality of the Princess, in the inner circumstances at Kensington, and in the behaviour of Sir John towards the Princess herself'. (Had he not told her his daughters 'were as high as me'?) He refuted the idea of Conroy becoming her Private Secretary. In fact, he doubted if the Princess had the power to nominate him; let alone whether Conroy had the self-control and modesty for such a position. Stockmar reminded the Duchess that from childhood Victoria must have known she was a Princess; and yet within the home she saw 'Sir John as the regulator of the whole machine' – these impressions, he pointed out, went deepest in childhood and had laid the foundation for her later dislike.

'And therein', he contended, 'lies the whole affair. With every day that she grew older the Princess naturally became more aware of her self, more conscious of her own strength, and hence became jealous of what she must have seen as an exercise of undue control over herself.'[29]

It is true that Victoria had always insisted the trouble was '*not* between Lehzen and J.C. but between him and *me*',[30] and it is very likely that Victoria did not appreciate the full extent of Lehzen's hatred for Sir John.

In 1838 the Duke of Sussex complained to Melbourne that Stockmar (who had evidently discovered more of Lehzen's relations with Conroy) should never have told the Duchess of Kent that Lehzen so hated Conroy that she would not rest until she had completely destroyed him. Victoria records that she 'started' when she heard this. Melbourne had asked the Duke: '"Are you sure he said so?"' And the Duke replied: '"The Duchess told me so."'[31]

It was however the combination of Lehzen's and Victoria's independent hatred that was to vanquish Conroy. He had, after all, the support of most of the 'Kensington System' in his bid to be Private Secretary: Lord Dunfermline (Speaker of the House); Prince Leiningen and Lord Durham – they all believed it vital that Victoria should have the guidance of Conroy on her accession. It was to prevent this appalling eventuality that King Leopold in 1835 resolved to save the situation (where Stockmar had failed). In October he and his young French wife, Queen Louise, sailed to Ramsgate to join the Duchess and her family on a late autumn holiday . . .

The Princess's final tour of the North Midlands and the east of England had been, as Sir John described it, 'a most splendid and satisfactory progress . . . all parties and all classes agreed to shew their good will and respect to their Royal Highnesses, on those points all were united'.[32] However Conroy's claim that 'the tour was not clouded by any one occurrence' was something of an exaggeration.

Victoria, who had at the last moment been persuaded to travel, was very unwell indeed. At York the Princess was so ill that Lehzen felt it 'a marvel she did not succomb there',[33] and at a great ball at Burghley House she retired to bed with a headache after the first dance (leaving her mother to cope with a pail of ice that had landed in her lap).

By the time King Leopold's party finally arrived at Ramsgate (eagerly watched from the Albion Hotel by Lady Flora and Lady Conroy), Victoria's illness had developed into what Conroy described as 'a slight cold', but which in fact was a severe sore throat.

Sir John, terrified of illness 'from a political point of view', endeavoured to hush the matter up and refused to allow Victoria's physician, Dr Clark, to examine her.

Leopold, however, deeply worried at the state in which he found his niece insisted Victoria should see Dr Clark and actually *'forced his* admission'.[34] ('Can greater folly be imagined!', he exclaimed).

Dr Clark found Victoria to be suffering from an 'ulcerated

sore throat', but did not consider the matter serious, and returned to town. Meanwhile, an angered Leopold had taken Conroy for a walk along the sands and confronted him with the truth of his position: '. . . if in consequence of your folly', he warned him, 'anything happens to the Princess there is of course an end of all your prospects, if the Princess lives and succeeds the King, she will abhor you. Though late in the day', he acceded, 'still things may be placed on a tolerable footing for you.'[35]

'Still he imagined', Leopold was to tell Victoria, 'he might get you into a sort of *captivity* which myself being near you, at your commands, was impossible, strange madness.'[36]

What was this madness? What had turned a loving husband and father – one who had 'wept like an infant' at his father-in-law's death – into an insensitive, hot-tempered, single-minded fanatic? The explanation must lie in his desire to elevate his family to the status he believed their origin deserved through his acquisition of a peerage. His only way to this obsessive goal was through Victoria, whose trust he had foolishly undermined.

Incensed by Leopold's conversation and seeing his long-awaited opportunity slipping away, Conroy resolved to confront the Princess with his plan. But he had reckoned without Leopold who, foreseeing Sir John's intentions, armed the Princess with 'very valuable and important advice'[37] which Lehzen would soon be able to report Victoria had followed, 'and has thereby thwarted the plans of the worst of all men'.

Victoria, herself, under great emotional strain, felt ill and alone and unsupported by anyone but Lehzen. Having seen her uncle set sail from Dover (which Conroy considered 'unnecessary') she collapsed, and Dr Clark was again sent for.

He however took the matter as lightly as before, and went away.

'Victoria's whims and your imagination', dismissed the Duchess to Lehzen.

Within a few days Victoria was so ill she was, in effect, fighting for her life and insisted herself that Dr Clark be sent for. 'How can you think I should do such a thing?' exclaimed the Duchess, 'What a noise that would make in town.'

Conroy still maintained that to call a local doctor would be politically dangerous, but Lehzen – speaking with him alone for the first time since their 'scene' at St Leonard's – replied she 'would not gamble with the life of the Princess for any political considerations. Even he', she commented, 'was visibly upset.'

A local physician, Dr Plenderleith, was eventually sent for and cared for the Princess until Dr Clark arrived and took charge of the case the next day.[38]

Many have speculated on the precise reason for Victoria's detestation of Conroy: Wellington and his contemporaries believed it to be her having seen familiarities between the Duchess and her Private Secretary – but this in itself could never have given rise to such passionate antipathy as the Princess exhibited towards Sir John. Those emotions could only have been born out of a painful personal experience. Victoria herself told Lord Melbourne that if 'people had seen what *I* had, they would not like him; that I believed him capable of every villainy'.[39] Lehzen, she maintained, had saved her from 'perdition and misery'. Even allowing for the melodramatic atmosphere of the day (and Victoria had seen *The Miller and His Men* twice in a fortnight in 1834) Victoria's language is passionate and uncompromising, and remained so for the rest of her life. The reason almost certainly lay in her confrontation with Sir John and her mother during her illness at Ramsgate.

'I gave my excellent friend [Melbourne] an account of my illness at Ramsgate;' she wrote in her Journal, 'all I underwent there; their (Ma's and JC) attempt (when I was still very ill) to make me promise *before* hand, which I resisted inspite of my illness, and their harshness, – my beloved Lehzen supporting me alone.'[40]

Nothing goes deeper in a person than insensitivity and cruelty during illness. Nothing is less easily forgiven. In serious illness perception is heightened and centred on the vital matter of existence; life itself. Indifference to this state betrays a selfishness the patient never forgets. Stockmar may have warned that such impressions go deepest in childhood, but he might – as a doctor – have added that in sickness they go deepest of all. It was in this attempt to take advantage of the Princess's weakness to gain their own ends – however sincerely with one half of their minds, they believed them for her good – that the Duchess and Conroy finally lost their grasp of Victoria. They had revealed a lack of proportion and understanding that the Princess instinctively knew to be wrong – Lehzen and Leopold had been 'true' in the vital sense that Conroy and her mother had not – and there was nothing more to be said.

Sir John himself was at pains to stifle rumours to the outside world of the Princess's serious illness. 'All the stories you will have read, of the Princess's illness were not true . . .' he wrote to Durham. 'She was never confined to Her bed, or to Her bedroom. She was never carried up or down stairs, or shaded with screens, never having had any beatings in her limbs . . .' Leopold, he added ruefully, was 'most kind and amiable . . . but with a great deal more decisiveness of character'.[41]

The local press who made a 'special inquiry' into the rumour that the Princess was dangerously ill were merely informed that one of the servants had been taken sick and that the Princess laboured under 'a slight cold'.

From henceforward Conroy, the Duchess and everyone to do with them were to be passionately distrusted and forsworn by Victoria. The successful tours, the years of hard work – the presents, the games with Jane and Victoire (who had suddenly become 'the 2 Miss Conroys'), all these were discredited and forgotten. As Leopold had predicted, Conroy was 'abhorred', and the Duchess despised. Lehzen henceforth was 'her Mother'.

And yet in the entanglement that lay behind this dreadful event, it can be seen that all parties were to blame. Had Lehzen attempted to maintain better relations with Conroy and the Duchess they might never have been driven to adopt their desperate measures; had Leopold and Stockmar themselves not encouraged Conroy in 1825 (or if the Duchess had taken a firmer grasp of that independent streak in her nature and forbidden Sir John so much freedom) nothing might have happened at all.

But then, as Melbourne characteristically expressed it: 'Oh if one thinks what *might* have been, no one can tell what might have happened . . .'

7

'A CROWD OF PRINCES'

In 1836 Sir John Conroy sat for his likeness to the artist Henry Pickersgill RA. The portrait depicted Sir John in uniform, carrying a plumed helmet under his right arm, his sword (a gift from George III to the Duke of Kent and given to Conroy at the Duke's death) slung from the waist, and across his chest a battery of ribbons and medals borne with evident pride. The picture was displayed at the Royal Academy in 1837 'where as a work of Art it was much approved of by the Public'.

Indeed, it was not difficult to be impressed by the Duchess's dashing Artilleryman who smiled so spendidly down on his audience. Sir John's medals blazed across the canvas with starry magnificence (their acquisition had involved him in a lengthy correspondence of piquant absurdity) and like the French Envoy to Pumpernickel in *Vanity Fair*, he was 'covered with ribbons like a prize cart-horse'.

Nevertheless Conroy's decorations had been won in sober diplomatic exercise and although it may be difficult to take seriously such ambassadorial triumphs, he was in fact to be a trusty go-between to more than one important royal marriage. For the Duchess of Kent, in the full bloom of her influence (and with some success), was intent upon assisting her Coburg relatives into the ruling Courts of Europe.

It was Conroy's fate to embark upon his diplomatic career

amongst some of the most accomplished, eloquent and colourful Statesmen of all time. Yet he did not flinch from taking the stage with the Foreign Secretary, Lord Palmerston, or the Prime Minister, Lord Melbourne – and these remarkable men were to find themselves in a courtly dance with Sir John that surprised them considerably.

Lord Melbourne had first become Whig Prime Minister in 1834. Distinguished, intelligent and shrewd, he was possessed of a fatal streak of indolence and indifference that lessened his political stature. Neither of the old order nor of the new, he was caught – like Conroy – in a period of social change without the ability to adjust to its consequences. Unlike Conroy, he had been unhappily married (to Caroline Ponsonby) whose instability and wild affairs he endured for twenty years. Few people were less likely to prove a friend to Sir John.

Melbourne would have been alarmed by his Ponsonby connection; he despised vulgar ambition, detesting Lord Durham and disliking Dunfermline because of this; whilst, as a former Chief Secretary in Ireland, his opinion of that nation was unenthusiastic: 'like all Irishmen, if you drop one single civil word in your communication with them', he commented with foresight, 'they immediately convert it into a promise and charge you with a breach of faith if they do not get what they have asked.'

The Duchess's first essay into the marriage market was to champion the cause of her nephew Prince Ferdinand of Saxe-Coburg to wed Queen Maria of Portugal. Ferdinand, son of her brother the Duke Ferdinand of Coburg, was not a promising candidate: at nineteen years old, he was tall and stooping with a high-pitched nasal voice. But the stout Maria, who since the age of seven had been threatened with the prospect of marrying her uncle, Don Miguel (and at sixteen had married Augustus of Leuchtenberg, who had promptly dropped dead), was scarcely in a position to object.

Ferdinand's chances were keenly watched from Kensington, as Conroy commenced a memorandum on the response of the British Government towards the Portuguese match.

Palmerston, however, did not take the matter as seriously as perhaps he should have done: '. . . if he [Ferdinand] is tall and stoops a little', he assured Baron Stockmar, 'it will be said he is only *condescending*, for the Portuguese are generally short, and he will be considered as studiously *inclined* to *give ear* to his subjects.'[2]

The Baron, busy appeasing Duke Ferdinand whose demands for his son's safety even extended to a guarantee for the marriage contract ('nothing ventured nothing have', commented Stockmar), was not so amused. England would not protect Ferdinand further than providing a friendly reception at Court and a man-of-war for the voyage to Portugal, and the Treaty of 1703 was said to provide adequate protection against a Government engaged in almost continuous Civil War. 'Is it', Palmerston queried 'for the honour of the young Prince, that He (or His House) should cast doubts on the stability of that throne He is about to share –.'[3]

The Duchess however reminded Lord Melbourne that negotiations began 'through me' and sought assurance of 'some measures . . . to support and protect my Nephew, in the no easy task, of maintaining Order and good Government in Portugal'.[4] None came.

Finally Conroy, in his four-page memorandum, pronounced that the marriage could be put off no longer. The Loulé party 'would have time to work out their plans' and the English Government, he suspected, were beginning to wonder whether Ferdinand was equal to the task: in short, he recommended, the Prince 'should repair, to Portugal, without a moment's delay'.[5]

Within weeks Ferdinand was married by Proxy to Queen Maria and journeyed to England the following March, 1836. Victoria, who had been watching the negotiations with considerable interest (she was not much older than Maria and they had been described as 'the two little Queens') resolved to see the best in Ferdinand. Yet even she had to admit that his 'slow funny way' of talking was against him (although 'it very soon wears off').

Resplendent in his Order of the Tower and Sword, the

Prince attended a Banquet at Windsor with the King. Conroy loyally described his protégé as 'a very fine young man – full of spirit and promise, the admirers of D. Miguel', he added, 'represented Him, as a crying boy, with his destiny thrust upon Him, by an ambitious family.'[6]

Princess Lieven however was more forthright: 'They say he is a worm, and that his falsetto voice is something incredible . . . How on earth will he be able to manage that enormous Queen?'[7]

In the event Ferdinand managed her surprisingly well. He and Maria were married in Lisbon in April 1836 and the next year, following the birth of their son, he was proclaimed King Consort, Fernando II of Portugal. It was hardly Conroy's fault that in September 1836 the City Garrisons mutinied, tumbling Portugal yet again into bloody Civil War.

Following Fernando's marriage to Queen Maria, honours for Sir John flowed in from Portugal. They did not please William IV (without whose permission no foreign orders could be accepted or worn) and Palmerston too was clearly embarrassed: 'if it is not necessary for you to be presented', he admitted to Conroy, on his receipt of the Military Order of D'Aviz, 'it would be rather more convenient to me, officially, that so public an announcement of your having received the Order should not be given.'[8]

Indeed, Conroy, according to the Portuguese Minister, was the only British subject to receive the Order of D'Aviz ('most gratifying to my feelings'), but that did not prevent Sir John from accumulating further foreign prizes. In fact the collection of German medals for his service to the Duchess of Kent was already substantial and the Commander of the First Class of the Saxon Ernestine House had been followed eventually by the Grand Cross, in 1838. These last orders caused some trouble, the Duke of Meiningen having stated that 'his family connection did not allow him to confer such a distinction to a person so hostile to the present english [sic] court, and especially to the Q[ueen] [Adelaide].'[9] According to Prince Leiningen (Conroy's chief ally and negotiator) the 'gentlemen of the Queen' had refused to wear their Grand Crosses if Sir John received the honour. 'This is so absurd!' exclaimed Leiningen. 'It made the D of K [Duchess of Kent] very angry and she wrote over to Meiningen that, to cut short all farther discussions, he made you not only his private chancellor, but gave you also the title of "excellency". Whenever you come to Germany this latter will be very agreeable to you, as it gives precedence imediately [*sic*] after princely persons – and is only given to Ministers and commanding generals. Trifling and funny as the thing is in itself, it gets important by circumstances.'[10]

Conroy did not find it at all trifling or funny. It was a distinct drawback that he could only be called 'excellency' and have precedence after princely persons in faraway Germany: even his knighthood was of the Guelphic Order. Indeed, it had to be admitted that his sole British honour was a promise of the 'Master Gunnership' in St James's Park;[11] and there is no record of Sir John ever having received that. It was very disappointing.

He had however received a Warrant from Queen Maria for the Tower and Sword – Portugal's highest honour – but here again fate intervened. The Revolution in Portugal made it impossible for the Queen to bestow orders even upon her fellow countrymen, 'in order', as Dietz the Governor of Prince Ferdinand explained, 'to give those mighty persons no occasion to clamourous lamentations'.[12]

(In fact a certain mystery hangs around the Tower and Sword, for although it is prominently in place in Conroy's Pickersgill portrait, and the Star and Collar still exist amongst his collection of medals, no record survives in the Portuguese National Archives of his ever having received the order. Nevertheless the Queen of Portugal's Warrant for the Tower and Sword appears in The Conroy Papers, as does Queen Victoria's permission for Conroy to wear it.)[13]

For the time being however Sir John had to he content with the Grand Cross of St Bento D'Aviz 'and that is not inferior to that of the Tower and Sword', reassured Dietz, 'which you wished before'. Indeed, this offered even more exciting prospects, for whole guards could turn out drumming a march when Sir John walked by. It must have been very frustrating for Conroy that Princess Victoria and the King of the Belgians did not seem to appreciate him at all. 'I told him at Claremont in 1836 that his conduct was madness and must end in his own ruin,' recollected Leopold, 'that though late, it was still time – but no, he continued in the same way as the events of 1837 did show.'[14]

It is tempting, but mistaken, to believe that Conroy's career was as unique as his character. In fact this is not entirely so: his own path had been curiously foreshadowed by that of a certain Sir Benjamin Bloomfield, one-time Private Secretary to George IV. His life indeed had set a precedent upon which Conroy had clearly pinned his hopes.

Sir Benjamin, an Irishman from Tipperary, had joined the Royal Horse Artillery at thirteen years of age and eventually rose to be Colonel Commandant.

Whilst stationed at Brighton his social talents and musical gifts (he played the cello very well) attracted the attention of the then Prince of Wales who made him his Gentleman-in-Waiting. He became in swift succession Clerk Marshal, Chief Equerry and finally Private Secretary. Nevertheless, on the King's accession he fell from grace, resigned and in 1825 (after less than ten years service) was transmogrified as Baron Bloomfield of Oakhampton and Redwood, Tipperary. An Irish peer.

Conroy himself claimed that in 1833 Lord Dover had been asked to look into 'certain arrangements' on his behalf and consequently was told that the red ribbon and an Irish peerage would be forthcoming. Feeling that he (or perhaps his son) was entitled to an English peerage Conroy had nevertheless declined the honour.

'Lord Bloomfield,' he argued, 'who was only a Servant and not an adviser:- He retired with an Irish Peerage – the red ribbon – an Embassy – and £10,000, a year – having also made near £150,000!'[15]

Clearly the amalgam of military polish and Irish charm had worked its spell as surely upon George IV as on his brother. There was however one aspect of Bloomfield's character that differed markedly from Sir John's. Following his death a book was published with the unexpected title: *A Coronet laid at Jesus' Feet in conversion of the late Lord Bloomfield.*

One thing is certain: had Sir John ever acquired a Coronet it would have remained firmly on his head.

*

In the year 1836 marriage of an even loftier order than Prince Ferdinand's was being discussed at Kensington. For Princess Victoria, as Conroy proudly admitted, had 'grown into a very charming young lady – taller – pretty figure and very dignified demeanour with it . . .'[16]

Indeed it was natural, Victoria being now seventeen years old, that plans for her future should have been forming in the mind of her family. The Princess herself, however, had no such designs; marriage to her was as yet only a distant necessity, not to be seriously thought of. Nevertheless the rival claims of her two principal suitors – Prince Alexander (son of the Prince of Orange and grandson of the King of the Netherlands) and Prince Albert of Saxe-Coburg-Gotha – were to collide with almost comic rivalry at the throne of William IV.

The Duchess of Kent herself had hoped that Victoria would marry her nephew Prince Ernest of Württemberg[17] (eldest son of her sister Antoinette) but any plans she may have had – and Ernest and his family had visited Norris in 1833 – were apparently overridden. It had been a growing wish of King Leopold's that Victoria should marry Prince Albert, and both he and Stockmar had long been grooming Victoria's cousin towards this end.

Prince Albert, the younger son of the Duke of Coburg (the eldest brother of both Leopold and the Duchess), had grown into a remarkably fine young man. Prince Leiningen described him to Conroy in 1835 as 'bodily and mentally one of the most distinquished young men I have ever seen!'[18] and Stockmar had felt that the time had come to introduce Albert to the English Court.

'Now is the right moment for the first appearance in

England,' he advised. 'If the first favourable impression is now made, the foundation stone is laid for the future edifice.'[19]

The foundation stone however was not to be laid without a challenge. King William had 'a violent passion' for the Oranges whom he had asked to England at the same time as the Duchess had invited the Duke of Coburg and his sons. King William not only disliked the Duchess but detested Leopold, who clearly desired that Albert should occupy the position he himself would once have filled. (Indeed Lord Melbourne felt the King only championed Prince Alexander in order to annoy Leopold 'for, that he had disliked the King of the Netherlands very much'.[20] In turn the Prince of Orange loathed Leopold who had captivated his intended wife, Princess Charlotte, and overthrown his country, 'Voila,' he would say, 'un homme qui a pris ma femme et mon royaume.'

The King was furious at the Duchess's invitation. He had not been informed of the Coburgs' visit (the Duchess had written to Queen Adelaide, which she evidently considered as good as announcing her guests to the King)[21] and ordered Palmerston to write to King Leopold forbidding the visit. Worst of all the Duchess was also ordered to turn her nephews back into Germany.

The idea of 'turning back' Prince Albert caused consternation at Kensington, and Conroy hurried down to interview Palmerston at St James's carrying a letter for the King.

The Duke of Saxe-Coburg was already on his way, the Duchess argued (in Conroy's hand), 'and may be at Rotterdam tomorrow'. How could the King of the Belgians stop them? The Duchess saw no difference between her brother bringing his sons to England and the Prince of Orange having brought his. Besides, she had no power to stop them, and 'felt assured, He [the King] would receive these members of my family, with the same civility, as he does other distinguished strangers, and Relations of Members of the Royal Family'.[22]

Palmerston endeavoured to smooth matters over with the King, explaining that the Coburgs were only staying a short time (Conroy even offered to shorten the visit further).[23] Evidently the King began to see the foolishness of his position, for he agreed that if the letter Palmerston had written to Leopold did not reach him in time he would receive the Duke 'with all the attentions due to His high station'.[24]

'I must do His Majesty the justice to say', wrote Palmerston to Sir John, 'that although he seemed vexed and annoyed that the discussion had arisen. His manner was quite free from anything like irritation or from any indication of unkindness.'[25]

Nevertheless Leopold was 'really *astonished* at the conduct of your old Uncle the King', (as he exclaimed to Victoria), '. . . Not later than yesterday [12th May] I got a half-official communication from England, insinuating that it would be *highly* desirable that the visit of *your* relatives *should not take place this year* – qu'en dites vous? The relations of the Queen and the King, therefore, to the God-knows-what degree, are to come in shoals and rule the land, when your relations are to be *forbidden* the country . . . Really and truly I never heard anything like it, and I hope it will a *little rouse your spirit*: now that slavery is even abolished in the British Colonies, I do not comprehend *why your lot alone should be to be kept, a white little slavey in England.*'[26]

The Oranges by this time however had already arrived and were being sumptuously entertained by the King and Queen with a ball at St James's Palace. But they were lumpish and boring and Victoria wasted no time upon them ('So much for the *Oranges* dear Uncle').[27]

The arrival of Prince Albert was by contrast a very special occasion. Stockmar had been anxious that neither he nor Victoria should know of 'the real intention of the visit' so that the pair might be 'perfectly at their ease with each other'. But in fact both young people seemed to have been well aware, as Albert expressed it, of the difficulties attending it.

Conroy's task in the organisation of the Coburgs' stay, and in the arranging of the almost incessant entertainment provided, was considerable. Even Lady Conroy, on this single occasion, was drawn in to supply additional musical diversion. Sir John indeed was particularly practised in the organisation of concerts. The Duchess had given two musical evenings at Kensington Palace the previous year – an 'Italian' concert and an 'English' concert – the latter involving Sir John not only in an extensive correspondence with Sir George Smart the conductor, but in all the suspense of non-arriving singers, overrunning concert times, programme omissions, and the hiring of Broadwood pianos.[28] Evidently both he and Lady Conroy now felt sufficiently experienced to undertake such an event in their own right.

On 8th June 1836 Lady Conroy opened her home to Victoria and Albert with a musical evening of the highest calibre. The greatest singers of their day were employed – Grisi, Rubini, Lablache and Tamburini – with Costa at the piano. Amongst the audience were the Duke of Coburg, Prince Albert and his brother Ernest, Prince Leiningen and the Duchess of Kent. This was just the sort of concert to please Victoria who nevertheless was not so impressed by her surroundings. The heat was considerable, she complained, and the room was 'small and low for music'.[29] Indeed, it may have been the last time she ever visited Sir John's house. For in the year prior to her accession, she told Melbourne, she had refused to go there any more. Nevertheless, the occasion was Lady Conroy's finest hour.

Prince Albert – who had already been to a 'pre-ball' supper at Lady Conroy's the week before – was exhausted. (One fears the heat of Sir John's home tried him extremely.) He had collapsed after Victoria's birthday ball with a bilious attack, had retired early from various formal dinners and was clearly at his best playing the piano and perusing autograph albums at Kensington Palace.

Yet despite their differences in temperament (Victoria revelled in 'dissipation') Victoria and Albert suited one another. They shared a love of music and art and the enjoyment of simple things. Victoria had not yet fallen in love with Albert, but already on 7th June – the day before Lady Conroy's concert – she was telling Uncle Leopold 'how delighted I am with him, and how much I like him in every way. He possesses every quality that could be desired to render me perfectly happy.'[30]

Three days later Albert had gone. The University of Bonn, philosophical study and careful grooming by Stockmar awaited him. It would be three years before Victoria saw him again.

'We have had a crowd of the Princes here', wrote Conroy to Durham wearily, 'and until that matter is settled, of course every season, will bring Them over – But, they all went away as they came, the Duchess will never take a step in such a matter, for *anyone*, or *anything*, but that may suit the happiness of the Princess and perfectly satisfy the Nation . . .'[31]

*

It was in the year 1836 that the Duchess's conflict with William IV finally came to a head. Conroy had pin-pointed the Duchess's failure to appear at the King's Coronation (an event which he claimed occurred '*against his* advice') as the commencement of these hostilities. He admitted her absence was 'a blunder' and as a result 'a serious intrigue was set on foot to discredit the Duchess of Kent in the eyes of the Nation'.[32]

Sir John himself claimed that his persistent support of the Duchess had made him and his family enemies of the King; this was certainly true, and the Duchess felt responsible for that. Indeed, the King on several occasions publicly removed Conroy from royal ceremonies and drawing-rooms. Victoria's Confirmation in 1835 (an event fraught with bitter dissension) had seen Conroy ordered out of the chapel by the King; in 1834 the King personally forbade Sir John to wear the 'attached' uniform of the Royal Artillery at a drawing-room ('I desire Sir, that you do not appear in that uniform again');[33] and in 1836 Conroy and all the Duchess's gentlemen (including Sir George Anson, General Hill, and Colonel Harcourt) were ejected from the Throne Room, on the excuse that only gentlemen of the King and Queen were entitled to attend. It was in the same year that Victoria's proposed visit to Ireland was abandoned 'to avoid, at the present moment, any battle . . .'[34] All in all relations with Windsor were in a ragged condition by the time the saga of the additional rooms at Kensington once more surfaced.

Following Victoria's severe illness at Ramsgate it had become imperative that the Princess be removed to a higher level in Kensington Palace. Seventeen rooms were applied for but refused by the King; the Duchess however ignored him, and the rooms were appropriated and refurbished. Indeed, as early as 1833 Sir John had complained that 'so far does the K carry all this stupid & foolish annoyance, that three rooms – that the D/S was to have had fourteen months ago on one frivolous excuse or another, he prevents their having – '.[35] Now, in August 1836, the King arrived in person at Kensington to discover the reinstatement of the rooms at the Palace. He was on his way to Windsor to celebrate his birthday (to which event the Duchess had already departed). The King arrived at the castle in a fury: '– he had just come from Kensington', he thundered, 'where he found apartments had been taken possession of not only without his consent, but contrary to his commands, and that he neither understood nor would endure conduct so disrespectful to him'.[36]

Clearly the health of Princess Victoria had meant nothing to the King; indeed one wonders if he ever stopped to think of the immediate repercussions on Victoria of his incessant attacks on the Duchess and Sir John.

But worse was to follow. At his birthday dinner next day he let down the full force of his anger upon the Duchess and her court: 'I trust in God', he bellowed, in front of one hundred guests, 'that my life may be spared for nine months longer, after which period, in the event of my death, no regency would take place. I should then have the satisfaction of leaving the royal authority to the personal exercise of that young lady . . . the heiress presumptive of the Crown, and not in the hands of a person near me, who is surrounded by evil advisers, and who is herself incompetent to act with propriety in the station in which she would be placed . . .'[37]

The Princess burst into tears. The Duchess ordered her

carriage and could scarcely be prevailed upon to stay overnight. Chastened and angered she and Conroy went to ground at Claremont where they remained for the rest of the year.

It was clear that the possibility of a Regency would soon be over. William IV, determined the Duchess should never gain power, had resolved to survive; and despite Conroy's bulletin, the previous February, that the King was 'furthermore bent and as deaf as a post',[38] he approached the year 1837 in a frail but stable condition.

Like the pieces on 'Alice's' chessboard the players at Kensington were assembling for the final confrontation. The Duchess, frightened for her daughter, sincerely believed Victoria could not survive without the advice of Conroy and herself; the Princess she feared (being too young for her situation) would fall prey to the will of politicians and the schemes of sycophantic courtiers. Still nurturing the idea of her little family gracing the throne in serene and cosy triumph, she joined with Conroy in a persistent and desperate attempt to have him designated Victoria's Private Secretary.

(It is worth noting that in fact Conroy was virtually the Princess's Private Secretary already; he dealt with Victoria's personal correspondence, and as late as 12th June 1837 Sir John was writing to the scientist Charles Babbage that 'Your high attainments render your attention particularly acceptable to the Princess, who has been trained to regard with the highest feelings of consideration all those, who so labour, for the benefit of the country.'[39]

In the spring of 1837 the Duchess sent for her son Prince Leiningen to give her support in the struggle ahead. Before his journey to England Leiningen consulted with Stockmar, who warned him not to regard 'treachery, lies and fraud as the weapons of success'. Prince Leiningen however had long been Conroy's friend; he had, according to Edward Conroy, 'received nothing but benefits from Sir John whom he *toadied* . . .' Sir John, he added, 'liked the Prince, who imposed on his confiding nature'. But he too had his personal ambitions to fulfil through Victoria (he was not greatly liked by Stockmar) and Edward speculated that he would 'have supported Sir J. if the doing so, had not militated against his own interests with the Queen'.[40] Certainly, until Victoria came to the throne he was Conroy's closest ally.

Leiningen was genuinely alarmed by the extent of the enmity he uncovered: 'I found the situation inside Kensington substantially deteriorated', he recalled, 'the Duchess of Kent complained with much bitterness about Baroness Lehzen – but Sir John Conroy expressed the most terrible hatred against her.'[41]

Conroy claimed that Princess Victoria's aversion to him was 'a childish whim nourished by Baroness Lehzen, who wanted to avenge herself on him'. He explained quite openly to Leiningen that 'all his calculations' depended on a Regency without which he would not get his 'just reward'. Indeed, it was around this time that Henry Conroy recalled entering his father's room and found him looking very grave: 'Ah! Henry,' he said, 'I have worked in vain – & my heart is sometimes very heavy – very sad.'[42]

Not only did Conroy expect a position at Court for himself but he also wished for a place for Victoire too.[43] It was well understood within the Conroy family that he blamed Lehzen for everything, and that he believed (correctly) that Leopold had been against him since Ramsgate.

However, Leiningen was also to discover the considerable support there was for Sir John: even Stockmar and Lord Liverpool pressed Victoria 'to take him into her favour'. Indeed, Lord Dunfermline actually suggested that she 'must be *coerced*'.[44]

Charles advised against such a desperate measure and instead urged a reconciliation between Conroy, Lehzen and Leopold. Even the Duchess, swallowing her pride, was to entreat Lehzen to unbend sufficiently so as to show a united front. Indeed, the great fear of everyone was that the Duchess would be separated from her daughter: Prince

Leiningen wrote to Leopold urging him to persuade Victoria to take on Conroy 'so that *her mother* might continue to be with her and help her'.[45] ('Be steady my good child', persisted Leopold, 'and *not* put out by *any thing*'[46].)

Even Sir John himself – sensing the hopelessness of his situation – 'had actually already composed a letter in which he justified himself and *begged* Princess Victoria for forbearance and forgiveness'.

But this he threw on the fire.[47]

As the Princess's eighteenth birthday grew nearer, the King at last began to fail. He had, however, one final move to play: a move that was to rouse Sir John and the Duchess to intense anger and frustration.

The King informed Victoria that it was his intention to apply to Parliament for £10,000 a year entirely of her own. She would appoint her own Privy Purse and indeed possess the power to form her own establishment. The Duchess was horrified. She saw all her influence slipping away. Had it been Lord Melbourne's Government, she demanded, that supported the King's proposal? To which Melbourne acceded 'that for that advice they are necessarily responsible'.

'I trust that representatives of it [the country] will refuse to vote money for such a purpose,' snapped the Duchess. 'Passed over, wounded on every occasion that circumstances will allow, I still know what is due to my station and to my maternal duties, supported by the tears of my child; who has of her own free will, told the King that she desires nothing but to be left as heretofore with Her Mother – '.[48]

Lord Melbourne at last began to understand that something very wrong was taking place at Kensington. ('God I don't like this man', he exclaimed of Conroy, 'there seems to me to be something very odd about him.')[49] The King 'kept hinting' to his Prime Minister about the problems at the Palace, but was too shy to discuss them. 'I said, it can't be so, Sir,' recollected Melbourne, 'but he knew better.'[50] Queen Adelaide and the Duchess of Northumberland (who eventually resigned) had told Lord Melbourne that Victoria was not of her mother's opinions, and eventually Melbourne

sent Lord Duncannon to Conroy to ascertain if Victoria
agreed with the Duchess: '– much more so', replied Conroy,
'and much more angry with the King even'.

'Now that was an intollerable [sic] falsehood', exclaimed
Melbourne, 'and I knew it wasn't so from others.'[51]

Conroy himself told the Duke of Wellington that the
Duchess did not accept the £10,000 from the King for
Victoria, because she knew it was done upon Lord Melbourne's and the King's responsibility alone and without the
concurrence of the whole Cabinet.

'Utterly false', dismissed Melbourne.[52]

A few weeks later, Victoria herself dictated a memorandum of the events to Lehzen. She had wished, she said, that
the Dean of Chester might be her Privy Purse (as advised by
Leopold). This the Duchess refused. She had then asked for
a private conversation with Melbourne which was again
forbidden. At length, recounted Victoria, 'as an *answer* must
be given', she wrote to the King a copy 'of a letter written
by my Mother'.[53]

But the King was not fooled. 'Victoria has not written
that letter', was all that he had to say.[54]

Completely obsessed with their goal, Sir John and the
Duchess had thrown away all discretion; they lied, they
ranted, they brow-beat and wrung their hands. Years of
dreams were fading, but Conroy could not let them go
without a struggle. The manner in which he acquired a
peerage – the ultimate decoration – for his supposedly regal
family, mattered little to him now beside its final attainment.

On Victoria's eighteenth birthday Prince Leiningen recalled: 'Sir John Conroy celebrated his greatest triumph.' If
so, it was to be short-lived. At the Princess's birthday ball
Sir John kept his eyes upon Baroness Lehzen the entire
evening; for she, like the banshee of old who howled on the
eve before Charles Conry's death, well knew that hers was to
be the final victory.

8

'BORN AND BRED A BRITON'

During the final weeks of the life of King William IV, whilst Conroy and Victoria battled for their future at Kensington, Sir John's son, Edward, had been working out a personal crisis of his own. And when, on the 29th May 1837, Conroy was informed that Edward had eloped to Gretna Green with Lady Alicia Parsons of Belgrave Square, the news could scarcely have lightened his burden.

There survives a vivid, if somewhat self-satisfied account of this event written by Edward himself.[1] (To read it brings a kind of recognition in reverse: that the worlds created by Thackeray or Jane Austen were, after all, but records of the literal truth.) For Lady Alicia, we find, was the youngest daughter of Sir Lawrence Parsons, Earl of Rosse – the same Sir Lawrence described by Wolfe Tone as one of the 'few honest men in the Irish House of Commons' – and in this union with a family so connected with their own liberal past the Conroy history now seemed destined to turn full circle.

On the discovery of Alicia's flight Lord Oxmantown (Alicia's brother) made haste to the Conroy home, and finding Sir John already at Kensington Palace confronted him there. He was received so 'coldly and proudly', however, that 'the fat Lord was awed'. (Lord Oxmantown was renowned for his rotundity.)

'He came to vituperate', declared Edward, 'he went away

reconciled'. (Sir John's ability to deal with abusive and difficult people was remarkable, and indeed was one of the qualities that made him so useful to his royal mistresses: Sir Charles Phipps maintained that his power over Princess Sophia was in consequence of his being able to get rid of 'the bullying importunities' of her profligate son, Captain Garth.)[2]

It seems Sir John triumphed over Lord Rosse as well, for soon after the Earl's meeting with Conroy Edward was kindly received at Belgrave Square where the old man exclaimed he was 'now too happy to have got you for a son-in-law – and I am most grateful and happy that all matters have turned out as they have done'. Writing from Keswick on the 8th June, Edward told his father '– no time in writing to say (but most inadequately) how very much obliged to you we are for *all* your kindness, and for the able manner in which you have conducted, and terminated for the present our affair – Alicia's only dread and sorrow is now removed, and she is very much obliged to you for so well bringing Lrd R. round . . .'[3]

Edward's inopportune flight and marriage however put matters in a new perspective for Sir John. His son may have told a surprised Lord Rosse that as for his blood 'it was better than his own', but for Conroy – at that very moment striving for a peerage – the sudden introduction of Lady Alicia into his household gave an added incentive to his entreaties.

In addition, Edward's marriage settlement proved a considerable strain on his resources. It had been a condition of the Rosse family that Sir John's Irish Estate (the freehold of which he had bought only the year before) was to be made over to Edward before he received Alicia's money: 'By the kind liberality of my Father', admitted Edward, 'I was enabled to make as good settlement on Alicia, in the event of my death, as my brother-in-law Knox, heir to £11,000 a year made upon Lady Jane his wife.' Nevertheless, it is likely this settlement weighed heavily upon Sir John during the final weeks of the reign of William IV.

'The King had been desperately ill,' recorded Greville on the 2nd June 1837, 'his pulse down at thirty; they think he will now get over it for this time. His recovery will not have been accelerated by the Duchess of Kent's answer to the City of London address.'[4]

But the King was not to survive. Throughout the hot summer weather, the news from Windsor steadily worsened and once again Kensington Palace became an object of curiosity to the passerby. Yet although the public well understood that 'Vic is a person with a will of her own', for the time being it had to be content with cheering the little person (too short to nod over the door of her carriage) as she drove in state down the Kensington Road.

The representatives of the City of London however were to enjoy a closer view. On the 30th May (the day of Edward's runaway marriage) two Addresses of Congratulation for the occasion of Victoria's birthday were brought to Kensington Palace and delivered to the Princess and her mother.[5]

'It is scarcely possible for us to appreciate the feelings of your Royal Highness upon this joyful event,' they enthused (with some truth), 'but we beg to express our unfeigned hope that you may long witness the fruits of your care and attention . . .'

The Duchess, aware that this was probably 'the last public act of my life', determined to take advantage of the moment. Indeed, the good City burghers were to find they had taken on rather more than they had expected: 'The Disposer of all human events', announced the Duchess (in Conroy's highest tones) 'has vouchsafed to allow me to be rewarded far beyond what I deserve, by witnessing at this epoch, so dear to my maternal feelings, such general expressions of loyalty to our King, hope and confidence in my Child, and approbation in the way I have brought her up.'

Reminding her respectful audience that 'at great personal risk' she had returned to England from Germany in order (in the words of George III) that Victoria be '"born and bred a Briton"', the Duchess recalled that 'In a few months afterwards, my infant and myself were awfully deprived of

Father and Husband; we stood alone, almost friendless and unknown in this country – I could not even speak the language of it.

'I did not hesitate how to act;' she declared, 'I gave up my home, my kindred, my duties', (though with what hesitation only Conroy knew), 'to devote myself to that duty which was to be the whole object of my future life.

'I was supported in the execution of my duty by the country; it placed its trust in me, and the Regency Bill gave me its last act of confidence.'

Victoria's own appreciation of her mother's lengthy harangue (it continued in this now familiar vein for some while longer) was somewhat more precise: 'I thank you for your kind Address', she acknowledged, 'I have nothing to add to what has been said by my Mother, and in which I entirely concur.'[6]

In fact, for all its self-satisfaction the Duchess's Address held more than a modicum of truth. Memory is short; and whilst the dying of an old man gave way to a new age, few allowed themselves to remember the journey that had brought Victoria to this great position. Nevertheless, it was true that the Duchess had taken risks for her daughter to be born in England; it was also true she had been friendless and alone: these were uncomfortable facts. Under Conroy's guidance, she had gained in confidence, acquired the Regency and brought her daughter before the public in an unprecedented fashion. Lord Melbourne might feel her pretentions a 'parcel of nonsense', but they were not to be so easily cast aside.

Prince Leiningen himself came to feel his mother had 'thrown away' a splendid position in supporting Sir John. But the Duchess was loyal and knew what she owed to Conroy. She could not turn against him, as did her son, when she found things other than she supposed. She had believed in him. The fact that she never ceased entirely to do so, even when much damning evidence was placed before her, is one of the more curious elements of this story.

Neither was the City's gesture without impact in the wider world. 'The City of London made a grand address', recollected Henry Conroy many years later. '. . . Think of that and then *the other* part'.[7]

It was '*the other* part', however, that now preoccupied Victoria's mother and Sir John. The Princess herself claimed she had '*first* spoken up against Conroy when the King was dying'[8] and that her 'decision upon Conroy' had come 'rather suddenly upon them'. It is likely this was true. Both the Duchess and Sir John had long since distanced themselves from reality, being fully persuaded that Victoria – helpless and immature – was incapable of surviving without them. Indeed, the Kensington System had formed its own plans for Victoria's accession and Lord Dunfermline even described them to a surprised Lord Melbourne whilst dining with the Duke of Sussex: he outlined 'all that should be done', chuckled Melbourne. 'The Queen will be married by next Easter, it will be a very good thing!'[9]

Nevertheless, Victoria's 'decision upon Conroy' had now been made perfectly clear. As soon as it was certain the King's end was near, a 'violent fight and struggle' took place at Kensington which may well have led directly to the calling-in of Lord Liverpool as final arbiter. Liverpool himself was of the Kensington System, but could claim to be a friend of both Victoria and the Duchess. Perhaps he would succeed where even Stockmar had failed?

It was an intensely hot afternoon when Lord Liverpool arrived at Kensington Palace on the 15th June, for what proved to be an extraordinary series of interviews.[10]

He was met by Conroy in the Great Apartment and led to Prince Leiningen's bedroom. In this unexpected setting Sir John reiterated the history of the Princess's aversion to him and of Lehzen's particular hatred. The Princess, he explained, had an 'insurmountable objection to his being appointed to the situation of secretary or private political adviser'. Yet, he claimed, 'it was impossible for the Princess to go on without such a person, that she was totally unfit by nature for the consideration of business, & was younger in intellect by some years than she was in age – that her tastes were light & frivolous & that she was easily caught by

fashion and appearances . . .' (Here he particularly impli-
cated the Duchess of Sutherland, who was destined to be
reprimanded by the young Queen for being late for dinner.)
Lord Liverpool, it was fervently hoped, would 'bring her to
reason if possible'.

Lord Liverpool was adamant: Conroy should take no
position about the Princess; he was highly unpopular, and
the country would not hear of it. The days of Knighton and
Bloomfield were over; politically such a post was unacceptable; a common 'scrivener' alone being needed for the
secretarial work of the Queen.

What then, should he himself do? asked Conroy; 'His own
disposition was to resign or retire; but that he had two
feelings very near his heart his attachment to the Duchess &
what he owed his family.'

Soothing him down with promises of a pension, Lord
Liverpool held out the prospect of the position of Privy Purse
– so long as he did not stray from his own Department, nor
interfere in politics. Liverpool must have been persuasive for,
after 'some reflection', Conroy agreed to these proposals and
asked if he would so recommend him to the Princess.

Baroness Lehzen and Victoria had prepared their response
to Lord Liverpool that same afternoon. Under her Governess's direction the Princess had written the topics for her
discussion on a single sheet of paper, and it was with a sense
of business far from the feeble character depicted by Conroy
that she instantly took command of the meeting.

Lord Liverpool must be aware, she protested, 'of many
slights & incivilities Sir John had been guilty of towards her,
but that besides this she knew things of him which rendered
it totally impossible for her to place him in any confidential
situation near her, that she could not therefore think of his
being Privy Purse'.

As Lord Liverpool gently pressed her on this point she
grew more urgent: 'She knew things of Sir John', she insisted
desperately, 'which entirely took away her confidence in
him, & that she knew this of herself without any other
person informing her.'

This final decision Lord Liverpool broke to the Duchess

who was waiting for him alone in her room. 'Le Roi George in petticoats' had given her verdict and, declared her mother bitterly, 'it was all the doing of Baroness Lehzen'.

As for Sir John's response to Victoria's ultimatum, 'I will not', Lord Liverpool commented delicately, 'describe the feelings of exasperation which this seemed to produce in him . . .'

Even before Lord Liverpool's involvement the Duchess had made one last attempt to bring Lehzen into the fold. However, her muddled and emotional letter to the Baroness became as much a defence of Conroy, revealing too her own fear that should another take his place she and Sir John's successor would appear divided in their political outlook. (Clearly it had not occurred to her that few people would ever again be anxious for her opinion on politics or anything else.) Indeed she even believed that Victoria would be severely criticised for rejecting Sir John's appointment as Private Secretary.

'In this important, difficult moment', maintained the Duchess, with that combination of vacuous emotion and pathetic silliness which could make her so difficult to deal with, 'only love, trust, and unity, should surround the Princess. Thousands of dangers and intrigues await the dear young future sovereign. Ach, she has much, much to learn', she cried, 'she is also under the crazy illusion that she is prepared, and young and inexperienced as she is she believes herself mature enough to undertake the heavy duties.'[11]

But it was too late. Lehzen's final comment was brief: 'In all other qualities I am far beneath the Princess', she assured the Duchess, 'hence must my views also be subordinate to hers . . .'[12]

At half past five o'clock on the fine summer morning of the 20th June, the Duchess of Kent's maid came to acquaint her mistress that Sir John Conroy wished to speak to her.

The Archbishop of Canterbury and Lord Conyngham, Sir John told the Duchess, had arrived at Kensington Palace to announce the death of William IV.

'I awoke the dear child with a kiss!', recollected the Duchess, 'I do not say more about this great event: days of *care* and *anxiety* & all *kinds* of *distress* have followed *this day*.'[3]

*

The years had in no way diminished the sense of drama possessed by the leading characters at Kensington. No man wickeder than Conroy walked the earth; no woman fouler in her black arts than Lehzen ever breathed; no more scheming, foolish mother ever ill-treated her daughter more. Victoria however (like the young heroines she applauded so enthusiastically from her box at Drury Lane) rose shining and innocent to greet the golden morning of her reign to the admiration of her entire Privy Council.

The truth however was very far from the fantasy each had woven for themselves and one other: indeed, it was only the exaggeration of their circumstances that had allowed the actions of such ordinary people as surrounded Victoria to grow to such immense proportions. The storm in the giant teacup had broken and overflowed, but like most tragedy, perhaps, its beginnings lay in the simple misunderstandings, prejudices and irresponsibilities of everyday life. It may be perverse to begin a reign as remarkable as Victoria's with undertones of disaster; but they are here. In fact it would be strange were it otherwise. The Princess's entire childhood had been spent as the object of expectation and speculation in those surrounding her: their jealousies and rivalries did not evaporate as she ascended the throne; indeed, they deepened and hardened into a fossilised attitude from which no one could break free.

The long road from 1819 had, for the Duchess, been spent with Conroy. Only she knew what she owed him in emotional support. As she perceived it, he had given her power and independence; between them they had brought the Princess to the accession in a blaze of glory that should, by right, have been theirs to savour. The Duchess's dependence however had been founded on fear: fear for the future, of the Royal Family, but chiefly for Victoria herself – whom, like most mothers of young daughters, she saw as a helpless child soon to flounder under the influence of evil advisers. (The fact that Victoria was well-practised in their avoidance naturally passed her by. Conroy's own ambitions we have rehearsed; nevertheless, one aspect of his character is perhaps worth reiterating.

Sir John had little or no understanding of how others viewed him. Somewhere in the depths of himself – and despite being surrounded by his 'enemies' – he believed the world thought well of him. Lack of self-doubt was both his strength and weakness. He believed he was himself a great man; that Wellington's pat on the back was sincere; that Prince Albert was 'kindly about me'. If he boasted of his estates, his wealth, his background, he lacked the self-awareness to realise that others would not believe him. Indeed, the very idea that to anyone else his arrival as a peer in Parliament 'would furnish *O'Connel* with a better argument, than he has hitherto supplied himself with, for the *necessity* of a Reform in the House of Lords',[14] would have utterly astonished him.

Within days – perhaps hours – of Victoria's accession, the Duchess and Conroy began to realise 'that their influence upon the Queen *will be very little*, or *nothing* . . .'[15] The Queen declared at once that she would not alter her mother's rank, whilst the posts of Secretary or even Privy Purse, which Conroy had so violently desired, were finally closed to him.

Indeed, the whole question of Sir John and his 'rewards' were to occupy a considerable part of Victoria's first days as Queen. From Edward's memoranda it is clear that the Conroy family believed Lehzen played a more influential part in Victoria's decision over Sir John than was probably the case. 'Baroness Lehzen', Edward declared, 'altho in the Duchess of Kent's service – took the management and direction of all into her own hands superseding the man, who for 20 years had devoted time and heart to the service of the Queen.'[16] In fact, another had now entered Victoria's life who was to override even Lehzen in her youthful affections. Her Prime Minister, Viscount Melbourne.

It was to Melbourne, that Conroy addressed his claims on

the morning of the 20th June 1837. During the first sitting of the Council at Kensington Palace (where Victoria by her youth and composure was to make such a strong and favourable impression) Sir John walked in the Palace garden with Stockmar. Both men were anxious that what was to be done should be done with speed; and as soon as Lord Melbourne came out of the Council Chamber Stockmar pressed a paper containing Conroy's demands into his hand.

It was Baron Stockmar's hope that if Sir John's claims were granted at once he would then leave the employment of the Duchess of Kent and so bring peace between mother and daughter. Indeed, Conroy himself gave it to be his intention to retire if his wishes were fulfilled; and it is highly probable he would have departed graciously, had not a considerable snag arisen in the negotiations.

As it was, Melbourne considered Conroy's demands exorbitant: 'My reward for the *Past*, I conceive should be', he had written, 'a peerage – the red ribbon – and a pension from the Privy Purse of £3,000 a year.'[7]

'Have you ever heard claims, stated with greater audacity?' gasped Melbourne, his hand shaking so, he dropped the paper.[8] (Spring Rice – the Chancellor of the Exchequer – vowed that such demands '*took his breath away*'.) Again, the precedent of Lord Bloomfield was duly held up before Lord Melbourne, who only commented that if Bloomfield had behaved thus, 'he ought to have been hung for it'.[9]

Reluctantly, the Prime Minister agreed to advise the Queen to grant the Pension and a Baronetcy instead of a peerage, 'which as likewise the Bath', warned Stockmar, 'were out of the question'. The Baron described this conversation to both the Queen and the Duchess 'the very same hour', and Victoria herself, in a memorandum dated 20th June recorded: 'I have given Baron Stockmar the permission to speak to Lord Melbourne on the subject of Sir John Conroy. I have received a paper from Baron Stockmar containing the claims of Sir J. Conroy, which paper I shall take the earliest opportunity of putting into the hands of Ld Melbourne, & shall consult with his Lordship upon it & decide upon it as soon as possible.'[20]

(There is in fact some doubt as to how soon Melbourne was consulted, for although Stockmar claims negotiations were reopened on 22nd June, Conroy wrote in the margin of a copy of a letter from the Baron[21] recounting the incident that 'It all happened on the 20th'.)

Whichever the day (and the 22nd seems the most probable) Stockmar had previously consulted with Lord Palmerston, who deemed the necessity of getting rid of Sir John so great that he advised the promise of an Irish peerage, the Baronetcy being retained as 'a preparatory step' (or 'sop' as Edward saw it) to Conroy's elevation.

On the evening therefore of the 22nd June both Stockmar and Melbourne arrived at Kensington Palace to discuss the problem of Conroy. Lord Melbourne advised the Queen strongly against giving Sir John either a peerage or the Order of the Bath. 'It was only then, and not before,' maintained Stockmar, 'that I pressed the subject again very much . . . that the promise of an Irish Peerage might be given.'

'Very well,' the Queen had agreed, 'speak then again to Lord Melbourne about it, either tonight or tomorrow morning.'

Stockmar immediately visited Conroy who was in his office 'fully dressed, ready to kiss hands'.

'If it is an object with you, to set in the House, you may do it as an Irish Peer as well as an English,' he observed to Sir John.

'*No*,' exclaimed Conroy emphatically, 'for who would elect me?' adding tentatively: 'Are there any vacancies?'

'I have heard there is one or two,' replied Stockmar casually, 'but I am not sure.'

'A third may not occur for a long time yet,' observed Conroy. 'I will never attain of it, and I insist upon the English.'

Although his instincts were correct, Conroy does not appear to have insisted very hard. In fact he himself claimed that Stockmar proposed the Irish peerage to him 'by the Queen's Orders, and on my accepting, I was conducted to the Queen's presence, and I had the honor to kiss Her

Majesty's hand thereon'.[22] (Prince Albert considered this assertion an 'effrontery'.)

'I see I must submit!' he had written to Stockmar the following day. 'I therefore accept the Baronetcy and the promise of the first Irish peerage. Pray let the first be done speedily, and let me have the second in writing, in such a manner, that it must be done, who is in, or out, so as to put it *beyond doubt.*'[23]

Lord Melbourne was not to be duped. His promise was carefully worded to be binding upon himself alone. Victoria's promise, however, was to prove a very different matter indeed.

It was in the proposal of an Irish peerage that Stockmar, Melbourne and the Queen had made their great mistake. It was a decision taken under duress to rid themselves of Sir John, but they were to regret it deeply.

The special constitution of Ireland since the Act of Union admitted only one hundred peers – other than those entitled to an hereditary seat in the House of Lords. Of those one hundred, only twenty-eight could be elected to the upper house. Three extinctions had to be established before a new peer could be created and it was the absence of these extinctions that brought doubt and uncertainty to what should have been a quick solution to the problem of Conroy.[24] Melbourne indeed does not seem to have realised that at the time he advised the Queen to bestow the Irish peerage, the Crown was unable to fulfill its promise.[25] It was this hiatus between the promise and its achievement that not only induced Sir John to further acts of mania, but provoked Victoria into behaviour that seriously jeopardised the early part of her reign.

By mid-July it was clear to Conroy the peerage was not to be forthcoming. 'By some mistake,' he wrote despairingly, 'it appears, that there is not one extinction – that the honor thought so near, is but a Shadow!'[26]

It was discovered that far from awaiting the death of Lord St Helens (then eighty-four years old) two further extinctions needed to occur, thus making Conroy's claim 'a distant hope'. As he pointed out, enjoying the result of three extinctions 'would be very presumptious, at my time of life'.[27]

The possibility was discussed of exhuming a peerage that had become extinct before the Act of Union, but it was Melbourne's argument that this would have extended the construction of the Act.[28] The Duchess meanwhile, pursued by Conroy, continued to press her daughter for the English peerage. 'I seek it, to be bestowed now', demanded Sir John, like a spoilt child, 'as marking my services, and throwing a Halo over, the private life of a man, who has passed much of it, in a public duty.'[29]

Stockmar, however, lifted a warning finger: 'the assertion of a Competency of Wealth for the Station', he told the Duchess, 'is not very consistent for a demand for an immense Pension *and must not be taken* on the *Ipse dixit* of any man.'[30]

Conroy was undecided whether to leave the Duchess's Household. Ideas and possibilities drifted in and out of his mind. Lord Durham had returned from Russia where he had been serving as the British Ambassador in St Petersburg, and his investiture as Knight of the Bath was Victoria's first ceremonial act ('I knighted him with the Sword of State', she recorded, 'which is so enormously heavy that Lord Melbourne was obliged to hold it for me.')[31] This was undoubtedly a cut above Conroy's achievement, and after a joint consultation Durham endeavoured to obtain an English peerage for his old friend and collaborator: '– really & truly, I am too happy to be out of it all', Conroy told Durham wearily, 'and if this is done – I have nothing to care for.'[32]

By October 1837, however, he had already given up hope and, having decided against going abroad, seems to have settled on retiring to Llanbrynmair. ('I like your country plan,' soothed Lady Flora Hastings. 'You will be happier in the country than anywhere I am sure.')[33] However, in August, sentimental thoughts of Ireland and even of following in his grandfather's political footsteps had evidently assailed him: 'After an absence of a quarter of a century', he announced to Melbourne, 'I visit my native country –

Ireland; – it has occurred to me, that as I am to be raised to the Peerage of that Kingdom, that your Lordship would not be indisposed to recommend, that I should be made Privy Councillor there.'[34]

Melbourne's reaction is not recorded. Neither, however, is Sir John's visit to Ireland. In any case by the autumn of 1837 he had decided to remain with the Duchess, and his family was busy putting up a gallant front against the disaster that had befallen them: 'The young Conroys are going about everywhere even in the pastry cook's shops', chuckled Lord Liverpool, 'saying that Sir John is enchanted with the Queen that he is every day on business at Buckingham Palace!!!'[35]

Victoria, however, had banned the Conroys from her Court; neither did she soften in her attitude towards them until after the death of their father. Nevertheless, there was one intriguing addition to Sir John's family for whom she had made a notable exception: 'At 3', she wrote in her Journal on the 8th July 1837, 'came Lady and the Misses Conroy, and Lady Alicia Conroy. Lady Alicia (who is a very pretty young person) is the daughter of the Earl of Rosse and married Mr Conroy about a month or 3 weeks ago.'[36]

She was never to see her childhood companions again.

*

The young Victoria had surprised and delighted her Privy Council with her dignity and grace. If the Councillors were apprehensive as to what to expect from a girl of eighteen, the relief at finding such a self-contained, businesslike young woman was immense.

Yet it was Sir John himself who unwittingly had supplied Victoria with the armoury needed to attain a throne at eighteen. The years of strain, subterfuge and suppression – disastrous for an ordinary child – had, as Leopold pointed out, given her habits of '*discretion* and *prudence*'; whilst the very necessity to survive, and to maintain a clear-sighted view within such a tangle of conflicting passions, had given this self-willed young woman a strength of character it is unlikely the Court of William IV could ever have supplied: 'I am very young', she admitted to her Journal, 'and perhaps in many, though not in all things, inexperienced . . .'

Youth, however, was Victoria's greatest strength (a strength she was to need, for the battle with Conroy was very far from over). Indeed, as Queen the first skirmish with her mother arose over whether Sir John should be allowed to attend Victoria's proclamation at St James's Palace. ('Everybody knew Sir John was out of favour; his enemies would increase,' cried the Duchess desperately.)[37] It was the only struggle her mother was destined to win.

In the royal carriage Victoria, looking 'remarkably well' and in 'high spirits' under her black chip bonnet, sat in her mother's usual seat before the Duchess and Lady Conroy.[38]

Behind, following a detachment of the Royal Horse Guards, came a further carriage containing Sir John Conroy, together with the young woman who had already followed the little family through so much anxious tribulation to this triumphant day – the witty, pious and sadly ill-fated Lady Flora Hastings.

As they journeyed to St James's the thoughts and emotions experienced by Conroy would have been considerable. The conflict between his own thwarted ambition and the genuine belief in the nobility and importance of his and the Duchess's task had reached a painful climax. Only two months before he had compiled a long account of the Duchess of Kent's career, detailing her years of effort, the support by Parliament for her work and demonstrating the happy outcome of her toil.[39] This carefully written product (which eventually found its way on to the desk of Lord John Russell) was a defence of the Duchess's now disastrous financial situation and an appeal to British patriotism (as had been the Duchess's Address to the City of London). Nevertheless, there is revealed in the conclusion of Sir John's report a romantic, even – one may venture – a perceptive imagination that had sought outlet in a daring adventure: '. . . when the great Governor of all things shall appoint the time', he declared grandly, 'there is a cheering prospect that the Duchess will reap the sweet reward of Her Maternal counsels and example – and to use the words of Shakespeare in a more prophetic Spirit than that in which he penned them – to feel that

> The Royal Child, though young yet promises
> Upon the Land a thousand thousand blessings
> Which time shall bring to ripeness.[40]

9

'MONSTER AND DEMON INCARNATE'

'A worse school for a young girl', admitted Queen Victoria, 'or one more detrimental to all natural feelings and affections cannot well be imagined than the position of a Queen at eighteen, without experience and without a husband to guide and support her.'

Prince Albert himself observed that while he believed the Queen's character to be fundamentally good, he felt it to be flawed by wrong upbringing. Never more than in the first years of her reign was this handicap more detrimental. The lack of a father led her to romanticise paternal attachments (Melbourne she believed to be 'so like an *own* father, to me, poor *orphan* child'); the absence of proper relations with her mother forced her to lay that mantle inappropriately upon her 'Guardian Angel' Lehzen (even Melbourne admitted the Baroness had undertaken 'a great responsibility in standing between mother and daughter, however much circumstances may have justified her'); whilst the lack of normal relationships with children of her own age, and the constant awareness of her own position, detached her from exercising her naturally warm sympathies. It was a strong, eager but emotionally scarred young woman who came at last under the tutelage of Lord Melbourne.

Melbourne's position was difficult and without precedent. Victoria had no Private Secretary or adviser; she headed a Whig government with a small majority, herself being anti-

Tory (her mother begging her to be above Party and to beware that Lord Melbourne was not 'King'). Yet she had a strong sense of Sovereignty – which she separated from herself as a person – and of what she believed to be her prerogative. Melbourne, who could not afford to anger her, humoured all her whims and passions and felt his way in a relationship with the Queen that soon plunged a good deal deeper than was suitable between Sovereign and minister.

Many people criticised Melbourne's 'careless way of doing things', and indeed doing nothing was his first line of defence. It was easier and safer, he believed, to wait and see. As to the situation he discovered at Kensington, he took entirely Victoria's part, upholding her attitudes and behaviour against the Duchess and her entourage. This line of conduct was soon to have very serious repercussions.

Indeed, Lord Melbourne himself was peculiarly susceptible to the admiration of a young girl who was his to educate and form. Only the previous year he had lost his only son at the age of twenty-nine; his eccentric wife Caroline was dead and his consequent cynicism was to subtly underpin Victoria's own prematurely negative experiences. (When the Queen observed that there were not many very good preachers, Melbourne rejoined: '"But there are not *many very good anything*" which is *very true*,' Victoria agreed sagely.)[1]

Melbourne had worldly wit and charm and 'stores' of knowledge (qualities in short supply at Kensington) and in his presence the Queen's natural intelligence aired itself for the first time. He was, in short, a revelation. But his influence, much as she came to love him, was not wholly for the best.

The Duchess was jealous of Melbourne; it upset her to see Victoria's 'pretty young face' next to his – 'he looks old', she lamented, 'very old.'[2] She longed to be in the centre of affairs (in spite of evenings spent playing whist with the Duke of Wellington). Instead she was further cut off from Victoria and thrown upon Conroy's advice. In fact her worst fears for her daughter were proving all too accurate. The Queen had surrounded herself with Whig ladies (against

Stockmar's advice), and whilst the Duchess had hoped that she herself would be ensconced with the Queen's ministers – as in the schoolroom of old – it was Melbourne who sat alone with Victoria. Nor was it Conroy who held the strings of the Privy Purse, but Sir Henry Wheatley who found he could not pay any bills without their first being signed by Baroness Lehzen.

For the Conroys had been right when Edward suggested the Baroness had taken over Conroy's affairs: 'Overtures were made to all the old servants of the Duchess', he asserted, 'to forsake her service and to enter the Queen's in order to draw all nails from Sir John's boat.'[3] By all but a few this offer was refused.

As for the Queen's affairs they were in 'temporary confusion' without Sir John to act as Secretary – 'now all this would not be', protested the Duchess, 'if you were to employ Conroy'. People persisted in asking Sir John's advice, but 'naturally he must send everybody away'.[4] Baroness Lehzen was not a suitable Head of Household; she lacked authority and charm, her judgement was biased (Stockmar found her 'extraordinarily suspicious') and her own want of direction over Victoria's ladies was a strong element in the disaster to come.

Against this background of constitutional and domestic uncertainty Conroy and the Duchess were defiant. It was rumoured that many of Melbourne's own Cabinet were in sympathy with Sir John, who encouraged their support by giving grand dinners to which '*as many Members of Parliament as he can scrape acquaintance with*' were invited. However Lord Liverpool asserted that 'public indignation is gradually closing round him & will infallibly overtake him'.[5]

In fact, even now Sir John's background was being quietly investigated by the gentlemen of the Press, and he was about to pay for his secret financial dealings with Princess Sophia in a most unhappy manner. As early as 21st November 1837 Conroy was rumoured to have bought an estate in Ireland with the Duchess's money.[6] Whilst it is improbable the Duchess's funds were used for this purpose – there is indeed no evidence that Sir John ever used her money for any project of his own – Sir John had purchased the family estate in Ireland for £900 in about 1836 (the same estate which became Edward's on his marriage to Lady Alicia Parsons). It is possible however that this estate was paid for by the temporary sale of the lease of his Welsh mine;[7] for although the sum of £896.17.5 was paid to Sir John on 21st July 1835[8] on Princess Sophia's Drummond's account, Sir John's grandson never listed 'Bettyfield' as being amongst Princess Sophia's benefactions.

Sir John and the Duchess continued to maintain a united front. In July 1837 Victoria was removed to Buckingham Palace 'to be out of their fangs'; the Duchess, installed in rooms far away from Victoria, continuing to exert pressure in support of Conroy. 'The incivility and unkindness is done to me,' she wailed. 'You hurt me *deeply*. What has Lady Conroy and her daughters done, to be so marked?'[9]

King Leopold advised that it had now become 'necessary to adopt some system regarding Sir John which may induce him to thank his stars to get out of it';[10] the tactics selected being those of constant pressure upon the Duchess by Lord Melbourne (through Lord Duncannon and Lord Dunfermline) to persuade Sir John to leave the country. These two gentlemen played a remarkably adroit diplomatic role in the affair, each retaining Sir John's confidence and respect despite communicating with perfect candour to both Melbourne and the Duchess.

Lord Duncannon was seriously alarmed at the deteriorating relations between Victoria and her mother: the subject was 'the great topic of conversation all over London, and among all classes,' he warned; to 'embitter' the Queen's reign that had begun so auspiciously would, he believed, be a severe blow to the Crown.[11] The Duchess herself – miserable and upset – seemed at last prepared to entertain the idea of Conroy's departure, but only with 'honour'. Indeed, her 'eternal plans' for finding employment for Sir John included his being sent to Canada as Lord Durham's Lieutenant-General (Conroy and Durham had conspired over this); and even to Sir John being made Governor of the

Ionian Islands ('that would suit me', agreed Conroy perkily). Duncannon however felt it unlikely he would be given work whilst still in the Duchess's Household (the Duchess shrewdly guessing he would not be employed outside it either).

Nevertheless, the Duchess was wavering. Although Conroy's hold on her was still great, King Leopold had, in March 1838, half-succeeded in bringing his sister to heel, 'but that *diabolical* man has got a power which I do not comprehend'. Lord Melbourne interpreted Sir John's influence as one of constant intimidation: '– "that's the way both men and women generally keep their power"', he explained to Victoria, '"they keep up a continual interest;" she thinks every morning what he will say to her; he says to her "I'll go away and leave you, if you don't take my advice", and I dare say is very savage with her.'[12] ('In all that has been going on and is doing for and around the D/S,' Conroy instructed Edward in 1840, 'believe me, every turn *tell* her, the loss of me.')[13] That the mainspring of Sir John's influence however lay in the Duchess's earliest years in England, was never appreciated by Melbourne: significantly the Duchess advised him to consult Lord Dunfermline on the question of Victoria for 'he *knows* a *great deal* of the past'.[14] Sir John nevertheless had other ideas as to who had the greatest influence over the Duchess of Kent, for he himself was firmly convinced that his position had been undermined by none other than the Duchess's financial clerk, William Rea.

At this sensitive moment, when revelations over Conroy's association with Princess Sophia were on the edge of exposure, Rea had begun to sow seeds of doubt about Sir John in the Duchess's mind: '– the D/S lent herself to the trick (of that great trickster) Rea to get rid of me', alleged Conroy, 'since 1837 she was then different – '.[15] The Duchess herself had admitted to being frightened of Rea – he was 'rough' and had given himself 'airs' since declining to enter the Queen's service at her accession.[16] Added to which William Rea may well have had more than a financial hold over Conroy.

It was in fact believed by Rea's family that he himself was the illegitimate son of George IV:[17] whether or not this was true, such a belief would have set him well above Conroy in the fictional family tree. Even Lady Conroy (who was ignorant of her supposed parentage) had described him as 'a good master to begin with'.

'Rea's language all changed about me', admitted Sir John, 'shows Charles up, he hurried on – the greater villain of the two'.[18] Certainly, Prince Leiningen's betrayal (for so it must have seemed) in the spring of 1838 would undoubtedly have swayed the Duchess's allegiance – despite Leiningen admitting that nothing he or Princess Feodora could do or say, had any influence over her.

Indeed, the Duchess endeavoured to reassure the doubting Sir John that she hoped in time he would come to see 'I never *ceased* to be your most *sincere* and *true* friend'.[19]

*

The Times newspaper of the nineteenth century had as great a reputation for the exposure of scandal and corruption as *Private Eye* came to possess in the twentieth. The *Thunderer* too had a similar propensity for plunging its owner – John Joseph Lawson – and its editor – Thomas Barnes – into constant hot water with the law.

On 9th March 1838 Lord Melbourne, in his daily audience with the Queen, directed her attention to an article on Sir John Conroy in that day's *Times* which provoked certain disagreeable suspicions:

The British public, we believe [Victoria read], was aware of the demands of a certain newly-created Baronet attached to the household of the Duchess of Kent when her Royal Highness's daughter ascended the throne of these realms 'a red riband' [the Order of the Bath] (to be sure one little thought how that decoration would be afterwards bestowed) [to Lord Durham] 'a peerage! a pension!'. We wish he had had the red riband promised him: it would have been as much honoured by his wearing it as by its present possessor.

We believe the chief merits of the person who made these

demands were his respectful conduct to the estimable monarch then just defunct, and the happy state in which the pecuniary concerns of the illustrious lady whom he served were found under his management. The amount of the latter obligation of the nation to him, it is perhaps hardly possible to compute: it may be thought to be in hard cash somewhere about £80,000; and the large annuity of £30,000 was granted with an understanding that a gradual liquidation of the £80,000 would silently take place. Happy be the end of the affair! we say; but a matter which has come to our knowledge may throw some doubt on its success. We learn that the Baronet of whom we are speaking, having been so happy in conciliating the respect of the late King of England, is desirous of exercising the same amiable and modest qualities towards the King of Sweden, and to be sent to that Court in the character of ambassador! And we have been told that the Premier was disposed to acquiesce, for the purpose of getting rid of him; but the highest personage did not approve of such a representation of the Crown of England.

Should he quit his present position, we ask where are talents to be found capable of applying a due portion of the £30,000 to the liquidation of the £80,000, and who can so well understand wiping off as he who has chalked on?

There is another matter also worth notice. There is a certain estate in Wales, purchased and paid for not long ago . . . If any public inquiry should take place whence the money for the payment came, who so competent to answer the question as the Baronet?[20]

No sooner had Conroy read the offending article than he sought an interview with the well-known advocate Sir William Follet. Sir John instructed him to prosecute the editor of *The Times* – saying the ministers were in his favour – and indeed was 'determined to carry things with a high hand'.[21]

'I asked Lord Melbourne who was the editor of *The Times*,' noted Victoria in her diary.

'– a Mr Barnes;' replied Melbourne, 'but that a Mr Stirling was the person who wrote all the articles about Sir John C'.[22]

Edward Conroy had described Stirling as a 'low writer' who, he alleged, was paid by the Court to attack his father.[23] Indeed Conroy himself believed this, even claiming the article to have been written with Queen Victoria's knowledge.[24]

This was of course untrue; but the eventual discovery of Sir John's Welsh Estate had been certain: indeed the greatest flaw in his grand design had been the curiosity that would be aroused as to the origin of his immense wealth. Inevitably, the finger pointed to the Duchess of Kent: by a miracle, it never occurred to anyone to hint at Princess Sophia.

Queen Victoria, however, clearly had suspicions which she did not fully disclose even to her diary: 'Lord Melbourne then told me he had seen Mr Stephenson who spoke of him about S.J.C. and how S.J.C. said he had got a certain estate; spoke of S.J.C. and Princess Sophia with Lord Melbourne for some time, and *how* it happened that Princess Sophia was quite in the power and *à la merci* of Sir J.C. at which Lord Melbourne was quite horrified.'[25]

The evidence in fact points to both Queen Victoria and King Leopold having some knowledge as to the extent of Sophia's contribution to Llanbrynmair. Indeed, neither she nor any other member of her family ever accused Conroy of using the Duchess of Kent's money for the purpose of buying an estate – although, as will be seen, Victoria held Sir John responsible for her mother's debts (which she had undertaken to pay). As for the Duchess, she gave no indication that she knew anything about Sir John's background at all.

The Times trials were to excite enormous public interest and employed the services of the foremost lawyers of the day. Although Sir William Follet finally acted for neither party (being retained by *The Times* to keep out of the fray), the *Thunderer* eventually fielded Sir John Campbell (Attorney-General since 1834) and Conroy secured Frederick Thessiger, who himself was destined to become Attorney-General and Lord Chancellor of England.

Sir John, in an affidavit, denied all charges laid against

him; swearing that the money for his mines and estate were his own 'and that he never did directly or indirectly appropriate any part of Her Royal Highness's Income or Pecuniary means to his own use'. Furthermore, he assured the Court, 'he is possessed of an Estate in Wales, the largest part of which was agreed to be purchased by him in 1826.'[26]

Insisting on Lawson's behalf that a denial was insufficient, the Attorney-General provoked a rebuke from Lord Denham who pronounced that 'all that the rules of the court required was a full denial of the slander and everything that implied dishonourable conduct to the party'.

The Rule was made absolute, and Mr Lawson was removed to the Queen's Bench Prison to which indeed he was no stranger. It is comforting to learn that he had there 'a very commodious suite of apartments . . . He lives in good style and has a foot boy to attend him'.

So thrilled was Sir John by this outcome that he told Lord Durham, he was 'inclined to let them off' – and so some of his more prudent friends advised him. Nevertheless by 11th June 1838 Conroy had filed 'Criminal Information' against *The Times* and battle truly commenced.

The Times, desperate to prove they could make a good case against Sir John if allowed, summoned (without success) Lehzen, Stockmar and even Lord Conyngham to appear on their behalf. Finally Lord Melbourne himself was subpoenaed as 'being cognisant of J.C's disrespect for K[ing] W[illiam] IV'.

'You know you can't examine me,' exclaimed Melbourne angrily, 'my oath as a Privy Councillor prevents my telling anything; it's a disgrace to your profession.'[27]

Courage to persist with his fight arose chiefly from pique and anger engendered by Queen Victoria's Coronation in June 1838, from which Conroy had been conspicuously absent. 'When I glanced my eye yesterday from mother to daughter', wrote Sir John's friend the explorer Basil Hall, '& then to the bearer of the Sword of State – & then ran it along the line, in the rear, & missed *you* – my resolute, constitutional, clear minded & good hearted friend – I sighed very deeply to think of the wanton waste of opportunities which nature had provided for on this very trying occasion.'[28]

Strength too came from the support of such friends and relations as the Common Sergeant John Mirehouse – husband of a cousin of Lady Conroy's – who appears to have acted as a legal adviser to Conroy.

Mirehouse had long been known to the Conroy family since his marriage to Bishop Fisher's daughter Elizabeth, in 1823. In 1826 he acted as party to the release of the fifth part of three parcels of land incorporating the Llanbrynmair Estate.[29] Indeed, since his brother, the Reverend Thomas Mirehouse, was at one time Chaplain to Princess Sophia, it is possible that John Mirehouse was acting on the Princess's behalf over this transaction. In fact, by September 1837 Mirehouse had become trustee of the marriage settlements of both Sir John and Edward Conroy and an intimate family friend.

(Mirehouse's advisory role in the Conroy trial seems to have been known to Melbourne, who described the Common Sergeant as 'a good man' – a verdict not shared by John Constable who when faced with painting his portrait could only exclaim: 'Angels, & ministers of grace defend me.')

Mirehouse evidently had an ear to Sir John's Counsel, for prior to the trial in December Edward Conroy wrote to him begging that he make certain suggestions to Mr Thessiger:

[Sir John's] affidavit [Edward pointed out] did him an immensity of good, by setting forth the truth, of which no one had any conception . . . I am unable of course to point out what Mr Thessiger *should* say:– But when showing up the malevolence of the libel published in *The Times*, could he not touch upon the unworthy treatment that has been the reward of a man to whom the Duke of K. on his death bed confided his wife & child . . . Reflecting the Trial itself – I hear with regret that the Attorney General has the right to speak last – that is after our Council has done. – Now I know the effect the '*last say*' has upon weak minds – I therefore hope Mr Thessiger . . . will take the bull by the horns and cut up the Attorney General's arguments even before he utters them. – The latter will say, that had Sir John Conroy adopted another course of proceeding *The Times* would have been able to have produced Witnesses to prove their allegations.

This is all vapour – Bosh – I know on that Lawyer's part but may not his artful words have weight with the ignorant of the law . . .

In short my dear Mirehouse you see my object – it is to arm the old Governor's cause at all points – and if you shall see any point in my observations that is likely to strengthen our case, I am sure you will give Mr Thessiger a hint.[30]

Mr Thessiger, who has been described as having 'a fine presence and handsome features, a beautiful voice . . . and a gift of natural eloquence', scarcely needed Edward's advice in pleading Sir John's case, and true to a future Lord Chancellor, Conroy's Counsel prevailed.

Gloom descended over Buckingham Palace. Victoria, Sir John alleged, 'came to dinner with red eyes',[31] despite Melbourne asserting philosophically that Sir John's success 'was to be expected'.[32] The old *Thunderer* had picked up a misleading scent and the trail was false. The old Governor had got clean away.

*

Sir John Conroy attributed the events that now unfolded as being the direct result of *The Times*' failure to prove their case against him. Indeed for Baroness Lehzen it is not unlikely that all the old jealousies and hatreds of the past surfaced again, and it would have taken little to incite the Governess to revengeful feelings in the totally hostile climate that now prevailed at Buckingham Palace.

In fact the Baroness and Lord Melbourne were about to behave with considerable irresponsibility. Life had ingrained in both a cynicism that made unprejudiced judgement difficult; whilst Victoria herself, young and inexperienced, would unthinkingly attack anybody who allied themselves with her mother and Conroy. In her violent dislike no steadying hand or warning voice (such as Melbourne himself should have provided) was to prevent her gleeful suspicions from running riot.

In the spring of 1838, Lady Flora Hastings (the unwanted presence of Victoria's girlhood) had returned to Buckingham Palace as the Duchess's Lady-in-Waiting. The Queen had warned Lord Melbourne that Flora was 'an amazing *Spy*, who would repeat everything she heard, and that he had better take care of what he said before her'.[33]

'I'll take care,' agreed Lord Melbourne in cheerful collusion. He quite unreasonably pronounced Lady Flora plain, of a bad character (like the father she had so much adored) and more disagreeable than Lady Mary Stopford. Nor indeed had Lady Flora's affection for Sir John gone unremarked by the gossiping Court.

Following Conroy's downfall in 1837 the entire Hastings family had proved staunch defenders of Sir John. Quite apart from their own association with Llewellin Conroy, they likened Sir John's situation to that of the former Marquis of Hastings who himself had been dismissed as Governor General of India by George IV. In October 1837 Lady Flora replied to a letter from Sir John in tones which betrayed an undoubted attachment: '– how kind in you thus to allow me to enter into your feelings,' she wrote, 'to think me worthy of sharing them to tell me I can be a comfort to you! & I can say so little of what I feel but you know me; you know my heart is not ungrateful.'[34]

Perhaps Sir John had been indiscreet. It was rumoured that he had travelled from Scotland in a post-chaise alone with Lady Flora some time before she returned to the Duchess at Buckingham Palace in January 1839. (Conroy actually seems to have claimed they were in a steam-boat. Among the answers to a lost questionnaire in the Hanmer Papers he replied: 'Yes – between London and Edinburgh, but as Conroy himself was in a steamer, with Lady Flora, that failed, but they came at court to develop this calumny. . .')[35] Lady Flora had felt exceedingly unwell over Christmas and her mother was very worried about her. On 2nd January 1839 the Marchioness wrote to Sir John from Loudoun Castle informing him that Flora had 'just left us' – evidently alone. 'I think however', she continued, 'the change of air & exercise will be very good for her, & the change of scene in the exertion of her Duties of her place which is very dear to her . . . I am really glad of an excuse', she added, 'to write to you My Dear Sir John to thank you & Lady Conroy, for all your kindness to My Dear Child & to say how I have felt all your attention . . .'[36]

Arriving at Buckingham Palace on 10th January Lady Flora immediately consulted Sir James Clark who examined her over her dress and prescribed rhubarb and camphor. She was however much troubled by an unexplained swelling in her abdomen.

'Lady Flora had not been above 2 days in the house', recorded an excited Victoria on 2nd February, 'when Lehzen and I discovered how exceedingly suspicious her figure looked, – more have since observed this, and we have no doubt that she is to use the plain words – *with child*! Clark cannot deny the suspicion; the horrid cause of all this is the Monster and demon Incarnate, whose name I forbear to mention . . .'[37]

Melbourne undoubtedly shared Victoria's and Lehzen's belief. As early as 18th January he had asserted to the Queen that the Duchess was jealous of Lady Flora, 'looking sharply, as if he *knew more* than he liked to *say*; (which God knows! *I do* about *Flo* and which others will know too by and by)'.[38]

By 2nd February therefore Lehzen, Victoria and Melbourne all believed Lady Flora to be 'with child' by Conroy. Since Victoria had said that 'more have since observed this' it is possible, given Sir John's observations of 'calumny', that the ladies-in-waiting (Lady Portman and Lady Tavistock) may also have shared this view.

It was later publicly averred that Lady Flora found it 'remarkable' that from the second day [after Lady Flora's arrival from Scotland] the 11th January, to the 23rd February, 'the idea, however or by whomsoever suggested . . . was so strong in the Queen's mind, that she never opened her lips to me!'[39] Conroy himself was certain the origin of the rumour lay with Baroness Lehzen who, he claimed, wanted to 'destroy him' through Lady Tavistock.[40] Nevertheless Victoria in her diary said specifically that '*I* had observed it',[41] and Lady Portman admitted she talked often with the Queen on the subject 'especially when she found it was Her Majesty's own idea'.[42] Later Lady Portman denied Lehzen gave her the information.

It was well known however that Lehzen colluded with Victoria in mutual suspicion. Even Stockmar, in another context, complained that Lehzen 'instead of calmly examining the matter is more violent than the Queen, says she is right . . . sees more ghosts than the Queen herself . . . The elements we are dealing with', he had conceded gloomily, 'are as inadequate as they could be, and we must take them and treat them for what they are.'[43]

The ghosts haunting Buckingham Palace were menacing indeed. Lady Tavistock had already spoken to Lord Melbourne of her suspicions regarding Lady Flora when (about 1st February) the Prime Minister sent for Dr Clark. This extraordinary doctor – whose competence following the Ramsgate affair must have been doubtful – despite finding 'little derangement of health' in Lady Flora, and believing that 'suspicions ought not to be readily listened to', evidently suspected pregnancy.[44]

Nevertheless, Melbourne – true to his nickname 'Pococurante' – advised the ladies of the court to be quiet; and even Lehzen had considered waiting a further month.

At this stage, as the Home Secretary Lord John Russell was to observe, it would have been better if Clark had voiced his fears to Lady Flora's mistress. 'But', objected Victoria, '. . . he did not speak to me . . . and that we, not being on good terms with the Duchess, couldn't have done so, to which Lord M. assented.'[45]

Non-communication between the opposing factions was the chief cause of the unfolding tragedy. Conroy was to point out that had the Duke of Wellington been Prime Minister the disaster would not have taken place; this was almost certainly true. Wellington, as Melbourne himself admitted, 'always heard both sides'. Lord Melbourne, for both constitutional and personal reasons, sided with the Queen.

Indeed, far from insisting that his advice was obeyed,

Lord Melbourne drafted a statement which Lady Portman considered her 'duty' to communicate to the Duchess of Kent suggesting that 'if the suspicion is unfounded it should be removed as speedily as possible'. Later Lady Portman pleaded that her only motive was to clear up the suspicions cast on Lady Flora.

The Duchess, certain of her Lady-in-Waiting's virtue, was appalled; but Lady Flora pronounced herself 'strong in innocence' and her courage 'equal to any endurance'. She needed her courage. Clark was insensitive and over-excited. Urging her to confess her guilt 'as the only thing to save me', he stated (averred Lady Flora), that 'his own conviction agreed with that of the ladies'; that it occurred to him from the first; that no-one could look at me and doubt it'.

When the unfortunate woman protested that her waistline was reduced he replied: 'Well, I don't think so: I think you grow larger and larger every day; and so the ladies think.'[46]

Clark's irresponsibility was soon to be exposed. The women's specialist Sir Charles Clarke was in the Palace. With Lady Portman, Sir James and her tearful maid in attendance, Lady Flora submitted to Sir Charles's examination. He pronounced her a virgin. Indeed, she was even given a signed certificate to prove it.

'Clarke [*sic*] pushed the ensuing beyond all calumny', declared Sir John '– and Lady Portman looked on without any feeling – '.[47]

This revelation – if such it was – produced even more hideous complications within the Court. The Duchess, having dismissed Sir James Clark from her service, retreated still further from Victoria and refused to come to dinner. The outraged Lord Hastings, very ill with influenza, stormed down from Scotland proclaiming his intention 'to find out the originator of the slander and bring him or her to punishment'.[48] This was certainly a terrible possibility and the young Queen reacted with angry bravado.

Indeed Victoria's defiance was maintained by the lingering conviction that Sir John and Lady Flora were still the guilty parties. Both doctors, despite their public verdict, had

privately voiced their prevailing uncertainty over Lady
Flora's condition, and Victoria in a confused note insisted:
'Sir C. Clarke had said that tho she was a virgin still that it
might be possible . . . that there was an enlargement in the
womb like a child.'[49] The tacit opinion of both the Queen
and Melbourne remained one of underlying belief in Sir
John's and Lady Flora's culpability.

The Duke of Wellington, fearing for the Crown, now
urged that mother and daughter be reconciled (flattering the
Duchess 'as the Highest in Rank and Dignity of Her
Majesty's subjects' which Victoria grumbled 'put foolish
pretensions in her head'). To a 'grateful' Lady Flora
however the Queen made a gesture of reconciliation which
her natural good-heartedness rendered partially sincere: 'I
sh'd like to see Lady Flora in my *own* room *now*', she
demanded of her mother imperiously, 'if she does not wish to
come later but I think the sooner I see her, the better.'[50]

Lady Flora, temporarily overawed by the situation,
humbly acquiesced to Victoria's plea that 'all shld be
forgotten, & that for Mama's sake she shld suppress every
wounded feeling'.[51]

Victoria later reported to Lady Portman that she had seen
Lady Flora who had been exceedingly agitated and nervous
but had expressed 'what I think is real and sincere gratitude
at my kindness'.[51] Content she had exercised her duty
Victoria hurried happily off to the theatre.

Lord Melbourne, however, was concerned that Conroy
still wanted to bring the affair to 'a quarrell'. Sir John was
well aware of the suspicions cast upon him and he still
believed Lehzen was their sole perpetrator. It is certain that
he made known his beliefs to the Hastings family, and
indeed Lady Flora's sister-in-law stated '*positively Lehzen
instigated the whole*'.[52] (This Lord Melbourne thought very
wrong.)

Lady Tavistock (like Lady Portman) nevertheless denied
Lehzen's influence; indeed Lord Hastings (perhaps tipped-off
by Conroy) asked of her husband the crucial question: 'was
NOT Baroness Lehzen the first person who originated this
foul slander, and mentioned it to Lady Tavistock; and if she

be not the individual, who was?' The question remained unanswered.[53]

Nevertheless Lady Flora herself was convinced that Lehzen was the culprit. In a letter to her uncle Hamilton Fitzgerald, graphically detailing her recent experiences, she stated the hatred of a 'certain foreign lady was no secret'. This letter the hot-tempered Fitzgerald circulated privately and later published in *The Times*; while on 24th March he published a letter of his own in the *Examiner* (dated 21st March) which was widely syndicated, summarising the events of the past weeks. Finally in mid-April, Lady Loudon (Flora's mother) published her own bitter correspondence with Lord Melbourne.

Victoria and Lord Melbourne were shocked. 'I said I was quite furious', wrote Victoria, 'and that it was too bad to have to endure this for such *a nasty woman*, as I said, and shall and will say, Lady Flora is.'[54]

The story was public at last, and the facts of Lady Flora's ordeal, and the question of her accuser's true identity had become the chief subject of debate in every London coffee-house. 'Never we believe', exclaimed the *Church of England Gazette*, 'since the days of the royal profligate, Charles the Second, has the Court of England been in such a state as at the present moment . . .'

Writing eight years later Stockmar (who was not even in the country at the time) reserved some of his strongest words for the part Sir John had played in the drama:

It was particularly in that most unfortunate case of Lady Flora Hastings [he declared] that the entire genius of his unprincipled and malignant nature broke forth. All the advice he gave to the Duchess of Kent and to the Hastings family was conceived and given in the most venomous spirit of personal revenge on Baroness Lehzen, whom Conroy believed to be the only and real author of that mournful event.

If this advice had had its intended and full effect, its consequences must have been much more ample, more dire in their nature, and they must have entailed on a greater number of persons a still greater proportion of mental agony and distress than actually lighted on a smaller circle from this unhappy affair.

For these last assertions we certainly have no legal proofs, but we have evidence of such convincing clearness and moral truth that in order to transmute the moral evidence we have into lawful testimony nothing would be requisite but the practibility of sifting the part Conroy had taken in this affair in a court of law.[55]

Time spreads its cloak of judgement over all parties, and indeed the intimate revelations of diaries and letters have long since rendered Stockmar's muddled and ill-thought-out statement inappropriate. Sir John himself had been successful once in a court of law; it is not improbable that at some ideal judgement seat, such as Stockmar evidently envisaged, with access to every hidden instrument of proof, he could well have triumphed again. To be believed an adulterer (and an adulterer who begets children) is no small accusation even in modern times: to be thus maligned (albeit privately) by a Prime Minister and a Queen is accusation on the grand scale. It was certainly Sir John's own behaviour that had prompted their suspicions; but trial by reputation is clearly unsatisfactory. Besides, if Baroness Lehzen was not 'the only and real author' of the Flora Hastings Affair, then history still waits to know who its true originator was.

Nevertheless by the spring of 1839 it had become all too obvious that Conroy was not only preventing a reconciliation between the Duchess and her headstrong daughter, but that his presence was a positive liability to the Crown in the eyes of the nation: a liability which the Duchess, bowing to the advice of Dunfermline and Duncannon, reluctantly perceived she would be rather better without.

The Queen and her mother were not however to be so easily rid of Sir John. Within the Conroy family's volume of cuttings from the *Morning Post* on the Flora Hastings Affair there may be found written on the inside cover in Edward Conroy's hand, these warning lines:

. . . and if we do but watch the hour
There never yet was human power
That can resist – if unforgiven –
The patient search and vigil long
Of him who treasures up a wrong.[56]

10

'A PONT D'OR'

The Duke of Wellington – whose service to his royal clients had been much that of a distinguished family solicitor – was now obliged to turn his professional attention to the deplorable subject of Conroy. Perhaps, it had been suggested, Wellington could bring the Duchess's Secretary to reason?

Despite the fracas at Woolwich more than twenty years before, the Duke was one of the few men Conroy respected. Wellington himself had studiously avoided him – the occasional note conveying money he owed the Duchess at whist (or, on one occasion, thanking her for eau-de-Cologne for a sprained thumb) being the full extent of his communications: 'I take Sir John to be too insignificant a person to be able to hurt the Queen of England', he assured the Duke of Coburg, 'the greater indifference he is treated with the better –.'[1]

Conroy himself however was open to suggestion. Indeed, he had already seen the writing on the wall. It had after all been an exhausting year. Two legal actions, culminating in the Flora Hastings Affair, had worn him out: 'don't you think it would be best for me to get at once whatever I can?' he confided to Prince Leiningen. 'I see what I shall nòt get today, I shall never get. I'll set at work at once.'[2]

Quite what Sir John had hoped to achieve other than his proposed peerage, is uncertain. A Baronetcy and a pension

were his already. Nevertheless Wellington seized the initia-
tive and invited Sir John to a ball at Apsley House. Queen
Victoria was 'schocked'. Wellington however had his motives
and was applying 'plenty of butter' – thus smoothing the
way for Lord Dunfermline who launched the offensive with
a carefully-worded letter.

The Speaker had long maintained the role of the fair-
minded overseer of the Duchess's Household: pronounced a
bore by Charles Greville he was yet 'sensible and hard-
headed', and the shrewdness of Dunfermline, and the tact
and flattery of Wellington, were to prove a formidable
combination. Conroy admired them both. Melbourne even
went so far as to say that Dunfermline, because of his
friendship with Conroy, was Victoria's 'worst enemy': had he
known of the judge's letter to Sir John of 25th May 1839, he
would have thought otherwise.

In fact, Conroy had already asked for the Speaker's advice
on his proposed retirement and had agreed to abide by his
decision. 'My business', acknowledged Dunfermline, 'is main-
ly to consider how the change, which you contemplate will
affect yourself, the Duchess of Kent, and as far as it is
permitted to me to do so, to look at the public interest of
Her Majesty and the Monarchy.'

Sir John's retirement, the Speaker decided, would not be
'fairly construed'; neither, he predicted gloomily, would it be
likely to alter relations between Victoria and her mother –
despite it being asserted that Conroy was the supposed
reason for their conflict: Victoria herself had said Sir John's
departure would make no difference as she could not abide
her mother in any case.

'– I do advise you to say', proceeded Dunfermline, 'that
you will no longer continue liable to the charge that is made
of being an obstacle to that, which is so much desired by the
Public. As your withdrawal leads to cordial union between
Her Majesty and her Mother; you will I am sure rejoice in
the happy result. If it fails to produce that effect, you will
have the satisfaction of proving that what has been so
generally asserted is untrue, and you will also have the
consciousness of having taken that course which all reason-

able men must approve . . . I have looked at the whole case, as one of the greatest public importance, and as involving the security of the Throne.'³

Sir John's course was set. 'The sentiments expressed in his Lordship's letter, confirms the views I had taken', he submitted finally and irrevocably to the Duchess on 1st June 1839; 'but, as I had great diffidence in my judgement, as it was naturally much weakened by my feelings, I felt, I could not resort to a more competent authority, – from his Lordship's intimate knowledge of all that has passed . . . I close my service, as I would my life, with my solemn assurance to Your Royal Highness, that I had never any other object, than the Queen's and your Royal Highness's honor and interest: and I shall carry into the retired situation I am now about to enter, every respectful and sincere feeling for Her Majesty's and Your Royal Highness's welfare.'⁴

It was a devastating shock. Much as the Duchess had come to realise that Conroy's leave-taking was inevitable, his letter of resignation horrified her. For over a week she was unable to accept the truth and searched wildly for an excuse to delay his departure. Her loss was indeed appalling. Not only had she apparently been deprived of the love of her daughter, but she now faced the removal of Sir John himself, who had been the most important man to have entered her life. For twenty years he and his family made up the common round of her everyday existence. Neither one of her husbands had been associated with her for so long nor had made such a mark on her experience. She knew Conroy had faults but she accepted them. In short, she loved him. Sir John did not love her – his own family held first place in his affections – but in so far as he secretly believed Victoria to be his wife's sister, he felt a degree of closeness and affection for the Duchess that the more detached official would never have assumed. This attachment was emotional and familial for both of them and was never to be broken for the rest of their lives.

Excitement and relief at the news of Sir John's impending departure spread swiftly about the Court. Yet the Duchess still could not bring herself to reply to his letter. ('What a great event', exclaimed the Duchess of Gloucester to Melbourne. The Prime Minister was puzzled: 'this resignation', explained the Duchess. 'Very good thing,' agreed Melbourne solemnly.)[5] It was not until the 3rd June that the Duchess of Kent at last sent for Wellington who, being shown Lord Dunfermline's letter, spoke to her 'pretty roundly'.

'I won't hear of any reasons', he warned the Duchess, brushing aside her excuses for retaining Sir John, 'it's quite enough if the Queen disapproves of it.'[6]

'You are a very fair and just man, and I will do what you say,' she acknowledged humbly, nevertheless begging the Duke should write to Conroy to say that he 'approved his conduct'. (Since, however, Wellington had already been softening Sir John's path, it is likely this was not entirely the Duchess's own idea.)

'I cannot but think that you are quite right in the course which you have taken,' ran the Duke's grave letter to Conroy a couple of days later, 'and considering the sacrifices which you make; and that it is liable to misrepresentation, it is an honorable and a manly course.'[7]

Thrilled by such an accolade, Sir John hurried round to Apsley House. Wellington however was 'busily engaged'. Scurrying home again Conroy wrote excitedly 'to convey my acknowledgements in this manner – for I consider a favourable opinion of your Grace's the most distinguished and valuable a man can receive'.[8]

'My object in writing it', confided Wellington to Lord Liverpool, 'was as far as I could to insure his going away by giving him a *pont d'or* to retire over'.[9] In fact Conroy had already 'set to work at once' to arrange his honourable departure. Only three days before on 2nd June he had secured a curious interview with Lord Melbourne: 'He had nothing to say', Melbourne reported to Victoria, 'he came in, was very civil; I saw he wished to shake hands; I only bowed at first, but then I saw he wished it, so I shook hands with him.'

Conroy had sat down and the two men contemplated one another awkwardly. Sir John then suggested that there must have been some mistake, as he had understood from Lord Duncannon that Melbourne wished to see him.

'No', replied the Prime Minister, who knew from Lord Duncannon that the reverse was actually the case.

'So I entered into nothing', sighed Melbourne, who suspected Conroy had only come to establish the appearance of friendship between them.[10] (Or even perhaps a symbolic transfer of the Bardic 'white wand'?)

In truth, Conroy was swiftly adjusting to his fate and showing those first signs of an ability to turn disaster into triumph that was such a startling and remarkable aspect of his character. Far from languishing in ignominious ruin, delightful possibilities now spread themselves before him: fresh vistas lay open to be explored; a new life, far from the cares of the Court, beckoned enticingly.

'I have taken a step', he declared firmly, 'by which I'll abide, and I have character to do so. I trust by degrees to bring my mind to know all that by account, with a better feeling altho' that feeling will ever be the same, as to my opinion of the conduct displayed to me. Nothing can alter my attachment to the D/S [the Duchess] my anxiety by her – but I hope I may be allowed to conduct my life in more tranquil scenes . . .'[11]

Sir John, it was currently rumoured, had dismissed his servants and was going abroad, first to Ems in Germany and then to Italy. In fact the Household in Kensington flourished, with Edward and Alicia presiding over Vicarage Gate (doubtless to Edward's relief, for he had lived long enough in his father's shadow). Appleby remained in charge of domestic affairs, whilst Conroy, and his wife and daughters, prepared for what they hoped and expected to be a leisurely journey across Europe.

Nor was Sir John's leave-taking quite so unheralded as supposed. It was a fact that the Duchess of Kent's tradesmen were on good terms with Sir John and his family (who possessed 'the common touch'): indeed Edward's runaway marriage had been financed by the shopkeepers of Kensington whom William Rea, on Edward's behalf, had cajoled into raising £300 on a single Sunday afternoon. These selfsame gentlemen had presented Sir John with an engraved candelabrum (worth 400 guineas) which they had conveyed by a special deputation, representing ninety tradesmen, to Kensington Palace.

'It is presented to you – Sir – ' they explained, 'not more as a token of our personal esteem & respect than as a testimony of the Ability, Urbanity, Kindness and Integrity with which you have so long directed the Household, and performed the Arduous duties of the several situations you held under Her Royal Highness's orders, during the Minority of our Beloved & most gracious Queen Victoria.'[12]

Conroy glowed. 'I shall always look at this Memorial of your feelings towards me with pride & pleasure', he had acknowledged benevolently, 'it is the record of an intercourse of twenty years, during which long period, I had but one object the honor & interest of my Royal Mistress & Her illustreous Daughter.'[13]

At last the Duchess braced herself to accept Sir John's resignation. Without him, and his wife and family, the life she had made for herself twenty years before was over. The dreams they had shared had been shattered by her daughter's will. Lady Flora lay dying and the young Queen – obstinate and selfish – seemed heading for disaster. The immediate future was indeed fearful and had to be faced alone. Whatever doubts about Sir John William Rea may once have placed in the Duchess's mind, they deserted her now: 'For twenty years', she wrote to Conroy with deepest feeling, 'I have availed myself of your assistance, to the fullest extent, and have profited from your ability, exertion and zeal. You have possessed my *entire* confidence, – I gave it to you *freely*, – because I knew that it was reposed in one, who would not abuse it. I shall *always feel*, *how much* I *owe* to your *friendship*, and shall *ever retain* the most unshaken esteem for your character.

'The future welfare of yourself and of your family will

always be *anxiously desired* by me, – and it is with *the utmost pain* that I consent to be *deprived* of the continuance of your services.'[14]

'– most touching', [15] conceded Sir John graciously – adding the Duchess's letter to the burgeoning catalogue of praise he believed his sacrifice had earned him.

*

Sir John was not the only figure who, in the public mind, cast a shadow over Victoria's early years as Queen. Indeed Lord Melbourne and Lehzen vied with one another, among the pages of the pamphlets and broadsheets, as the two principal villains of the Flora Hastings Affair. In a 'Warning Letter to the Baroness Lehzen' it was Lehzen herself who – variously described as 'a rouged old woman' and a 'Palace Washerwoman' – was blamed for the deteriorating relationship between the Duchess and her daughter; whilst 'The Palace Martyr! a Satire' deplored that 'a vain old dandy's "glozing" prate should sway the interests of a freeborn state!' The coffee-houses seethed with gossip and condemnation from which sinister letters, penned in haste, found their way to the Palace: 'Dr James Clark' (breathed one such missive from Burton coffee-house, Cheapside) 'he had better be sent away, else he will to a moral certainty be *taken away*. Ladies P– LT– are degraded to all eternity . . .'[16]

Certainly Ladies P and LT were having a difficult time. The Hastings family continued to demand moral vengeance – Lady Hastings publishing the 'Horrid Details' in April, and the doomed Lady Flora refusing to make peace with Lady Tavistock. In May, this 'wild wilderness of women' was to find itself in the centre of an even greater furore.

The Duchess of Kent, Conroy – and even Baron Stockmar – had long urged Victoria to political impartiality in the choice of her ladies-in-waiting; Victoria – to whom all Tories were villains – had taken no notice and surrounded herself with Whigs. On 7th May the sugar planters of Jamaica, in refusing the measures for the abolition of slavery, brought down the Whig government and Lord Melbourne was forced to resign.

'*All all* my happiness gone!' wailed the Queen, 'That happy peaceful life destroyed . . .'[17] That Victoria's life had been anything but happy and peaceful was something she would shortly come to realise; it had been however an immeasurable improvement on the past, and without Melbourne as a stabilising influence all her old insecurity now returned.

Sir Robert Peel – whose smile had been described as like a silver plate on a coffin – was civilly received by the Queen, but his departure reduced her to fresh misery and with an underlying resolve to stand firm.

Even before her daughter's accession the Duchess of Kent, in an anguished letter to Lehzen, had foreseen just such a danger as Victoria now faced: she had however attempted to protect her daughter by relying on the hope of Conroy becoming the Queen's Private Secretary[18]; a hope that was defeated by Victoria herself. However, the Queen's strength of will contained its share of obstinacy and defiance; ultimately, an embattled position was not one Victoria could sustain without those two-edged characteristics turning against her. Self-destruction was, and always would be, very close to the surface of the Queen's complex nature.

Sir Robert Peel now objected to Victoria's Whig ladies and asked for some changes. To Victoria 'some' was as good as all. Archaic as the matter of the Bedchamber Plot may now seem, the immense influence of the aristocracy in a still limited franchise was supreme. If Victoria could not change certain Ladies, Peel would be unable to form a Government. Victoria not only hated the Tories, she feared them. It was they, she believed, who maintained the attacks on herself, Melbourne and Lehzen over the Flora Hastings Affair (although Conroy, who was also a Whig, remained unscathed). More Tories meant more misery. ('Monsters!' she cried, on a question of Prince Albert's precedence, 'You Tories shall be punished. Revenge! Revenge!')[19] Revenge was hers now: she refused to change her Ladies and Peel retired, defeated.

The Bedchamber Plot further reduced Victoria's sinking popularity. Greville concluded shrewdly that the Queen's feelings for Melbourne 'which are sexual though she does not know it, and are probably not very well defined to herself, are of a strength sufficient to bear down all prudential considerations . . .' Melbourne, it must be said, took advantage of Victoria's emotions; he encouraged her to stand firm over Peel and certainly did not argue with the outcome of her defiance. (That, at least, was the Tories' reading of the 'Plot'.) Indeed, whatever else the Bedchamber crisis proved, it demonstrated that Victoria's iron will, so fostered by her beloved Lehzen ('I could pardon wickedness in a Queen but not weakness'), was – in a nation tentatively feeling its way to full democracy – a potentially dangerous commodity.

*

Underlying the tragi-comedy of the Bedchamber Plot, Lady Flora's life (like the slow beat of a muffled drum) was drawing to its close. As the Conroys gathered their belongings to leave the country, the unhappy victim, fully aware of her fate and almost too weak to hold a pen, had written a 'Swan Song' to her sorrowing friends and relatives:

> Grieve not that I die young. – Is it not well
> To pass away ere life hath lost its brightness?
> Bind me no longer, sisters, with the spell
> Of love and your kind words. List ye to me:
> Here I am bless'd – but I would be *more free*;
> I would go forth in all my Spirit's lightness –
> Let me depart![20]

She was, Flora told them, 'quite happy': she was prepared for her end, and 'had forgiven all those, who had offended them'.

Queen Victoria and Lord Melbourne, once more united, were not happy at all. Still clinging to the conviction of Flora's culpability Melbourne found it 'odd' when the young woman's abdominal swelling returned: it was inconvenient and demanded a post-mortem should she die. Indeed, when such an operation was performed, it disclosed liver disease of long standing. The liver so enlarged as to produce the effect of pregnancy.

By 22nd June the Duchess, who had nursed Flora devotedly, had written to Lady Loudoun in Scotland enclosing a letter from Dr Chambers urging that Flora's family be informed of the graveness of her condition. Flora's sister Sophia immediately left for London – first travelling by steamer to Liverpool and thence by 'rail road'. Lady Loudoun, however, was quite unable to grasp the reality of the situation: 'I cannot think Flora has any chronic complaint', she told the Duchess pathetically, 'this is the first serious illness she ever had in her life & other circumstances induce me to think that Dr Chambers would think so too, if he knew more of her.'[21]

Lady Flora, unable to eat and drifting in and out of a laudanum-induced sleep, cast a grim spell over the Palace. Forced to cancel several balls and dinners Victoria was nevertheless more irritated than moved; her dislikes were profound, and she remained obdurate in the face of an experience that Lady Flora's mother would feel 'must prove to H.M. in her youth & High Station a striking instance of the mutability of this world'.[22]

Nevertheless the Queen did gather together the courage to visit the patient whom she found 'as thin as anyone could be who was still alive'. Upon Victoria expressing the wish to see Flora again when she was better, the dying woman grasped her hand 'as if to say I shall not see you again'.[23]

On the 5th July Lady Flora died 'without a struggle and only just raised her hands and gave one gasp'.

It was the Queen's opinion, with which Melbourne concurred, that Sir John's departure had hastened Flora's death 'as she felt he deserted her'.[24] Victoria's remark gives further proof that she and Melbourne still persisted in their belief in Sir John's and Lady Flora's liaison; in fact the Conroys would hardly have wished to invite further suspicions of Sir John's involvement by delaying their journey any longer despite coming away, as Conroy expressed it, 'at such 6's and 7's'. Besides which, Flora was well aware of their departure, and her last days were filled with the happy remembrance of former times.

To her great friend Elizabeth Jane Conroy she left her yellow shawl, her 'Flora' seal, a smelling bottle and a mother of pearl fan 'they gave me'; 'these little things', she felt, 'will remind them more of me than most things'.[25]

Indeed, it was to Jane Conroy that she wrote her last known letter; (undated, it must have been written before the 16th June – being the approximate date of Sir John's departure for Germany). Carefully inscribed in pencil, it marked the end, not only of a life, but of a friendship and of an era:

My dearest Jane, [it read] I did not think when we parted that we shd meet no more but I desire earnestly to wish you my love & Blessing – God be with you dear Jane & strengthen & support you & preserve you thro' all the trials of this life & lead you to that whch is to come. Give my love to yr mother & Victoria & all yr family.

> Always yr affec friend
> Flora Elizabeth Hastings[26]

*

And did Sir John's departure bring an improvement in relations between Victoria and her mother? The short answer has to be 'no'. Lord Dunfermline had been right in his suspicion that life at Buckingham Palace would continue much the same as before. Nor did the Duchess's friendship with the Conroys cease. On the contrary, she remained in constant touch with Edward while Sir John was abroad – and, through Elizabeth Jane, persisted in keeping up her connection with the entire Conroy family for many years to come. Every nugget of news was savoured; little presents exchanged; surreptitious meetings hopefully projected. Edward Conroy, in fact, received a generous allowance from the Duchess – from which even her god-daughter, Victoire, claimed a share.

As for Sir John – his spell was not to be so easily cast off. As late as April 1841, the Duchess was still pleading his cause: Conroy she protested, was 'pining to death for want of occupation'. But the Duchess was sternly told that she must look on the difficulties of finding employment for Sir John as 'insuperable'.[27]

Princess Feodora, however, believed she detected in the Duchess a change for the better. In June 1841 she found her mother 'quite her own self again . . . it was so melancholy before', she confided to Victoria, 'the dreadful influence he had over her and all her feelings . . .'[28] But even as Feodora wrote, the Duchess was watching anxiously for news of Stephen Conroy who had found refuge with her brother-in-law in Vienna.

Victoria herself scarcely believed Conroy had really gone for good. 'Mischievous pains', Dunfermline warned, were keeping alive suspicions in the Queen's mind that her mother was still under his influence.

Indeed, in a less tangible way, the Conroys still exercised a subtle power over the Duchess – for they had belonged to her inner life; when Sir John left the country she became totally alone. His children had been as her own children – they had been 'one family'. It would be many years before the Duchess learned to live without their support and friendship.

One person however was about to change the life of Victoria and her mother for ever. Conroy, Lehzen, Lord Melbourne – all were at last to be superseded.

Indeed, Lord Melbourne himself had judged the newcomer to be 'a very agreeable young man, he is certainly a very good looking one, and as to character, that we must always take our chance of . . .'[29]

11

AN EXPENSIVE WHISTLE

Sir John left behind him accusations that were not so easily swept away. *The Times* trial may have found Conroy innocent, but in the minds of a puzzled and curious public, serious doubts had been raised. Among his own colleagues too, rumours of embezzlement from the Duchess were rife. Here indeed remained the great imponderable of Sir John's career; one that was to pursue him across a century or more and turn a man pronounced by Wellington as so 'insignificant' into the Duchess's notorious 'evil genius'.

From the beginning of his royal service there had been an ambiguity in Sir John that laid him open to suspicion. He was secretive of his origins and from where he had obtained his wealth; he was arrogant, presumptuous and openly ambitious. Upon his shoulders he now carried the burden and penalty of his strange hallucination. He bowed out of public life not with the glory he had dreamt, but with the reputation of an adulterer, a thief and a fraud.

Naturally, he himself did not perceive his career of service and sacrifice in this light; and the letters Sir John was to write home to Edward from Italy – during perhaps his greatest trial of all – gave no indication whatever of resisting any specific allegations. In time, proofs of his gallant spirit were to be defensively underlined in note books, and in the inevitable memoranda; but now only an aggrieved, yet optimistic defiance dominated his mood.

If Sir John himself had any long-term plans for his future, however, they were as yet vague: a gentle sojourn in Europe would rest the family's nerves; a couple of German spas could be visited for Lady Conroy's neuralgias . . . winter beside the Mediterranean Sea – possibly a cruise on one of the new steamers that plied the coast – and then home to a country house and the care of his Welsh Estates.

There was too the promised Irish peerage – work in the House of Lords – a dynasty for his regal offspring to be firmly established. On the whole the future appeared to hold more for Sir John and his family than might at first have seemed possible.

In fact the Conroys were about to embark upon one of the greatest tragedies of their family life. An ordeal that would place the events of the last few years into sharp perspective. Indeed, Sir John was to say of this time that 'As nothing occurs in life, however distressing, that does not carry its good with it, so my long detention abroad, the rambling life I have led, and being forced to occupy myself with new pursuits, has succeeded, in breaking up habits, I could not otherwise have succeeded in changing.'[1]

Conroy's second son, Stephen (a captain in the Coldstream Guards), had for some years been showing signs of having inherited the Fisher family's tubercular taint. He had lived in a 'fast set' in London and Dublin, and as early as 1836 it was rumoured that 'his voice had become very hollow – a bad sign . . . he may thank himself for his early ill health', his Aunt Mary Harley chided, 'drinking and tearing about . . .'[2]

By the time of Conroy's exile abroad, life had clearly caught up with Stephen. The Conroy family, on the move across the Continent, journeyed first to Ems and then to Baden Baden (where Sir John, to her great delight, met Princess Lieven: '– he blames Leopold *for everything* absolutely', she reported to Lady Cowper. 'He says that from the year '35 onwards he [Leopold] had plotted with the governess to deprive the mother of all influence over her daughter, in order that his influence alone should prevail').[3]

Whether Stephen accompanied the party from London or joined them later in Italy, he is discovered in September 1839 on the brink of death from tuberculosis in a hotel in Pisa. His illness was to be described in a series of distressing letters from Sir John to his son at Kensington.

The Italian summer had gradually descended into autumn: fires in the grate kept the patient warm but already the Simplon Pass was closed, leaving no way over the Alps for the travellers to return. Besides, Stephen was too ill to be moved: only an endless vigil by the Conroy family – 'every minutes change' being watched – and the devotion of a Scottish doctor, who had been persuaded by Sir John's entreaties to remain with Stephen, kept him alive. 'I do what I can, and he needs me, more than anyone else', Conroy wrote to Edward, 'you can happen, how we are cut down – and almost everything against us, but only hope in God'.[4]

Pisa was noisy and the air was bad; gradually the family fell ill with renewed strain and fatigue, and the trials of the past year seemed almost impossible to bear: 'I cannot even grasp it', admitted Conroy, 'and if I was not more than ever disposed to bow to all misfortune, with a good feeling, I really should hardly know where to turn, or what to do.'[5]

The Duchess, keeping in regular touch with the Conroys, was horrified by this unexpected turn of events: 'God be praised he is out of danger', she wrote to Elizabeth Jane. 'The difficulty will be to have patience not to move him too soon! I heard with the *greatest dismay* from Edward that your dear Father had also been unwell! And what must your dear Mother have suffered! And you all!!!'[6]

By the end of October Stephen, having rallied, suffered a relapse: 'I do not despair', confided Conroy to his son, 'but I am very uneasy – internally, I am the only one, of the family who knows the real state of things – and 57 days of care and sorrow, it is today to us all . . . It is a sad scene – years of hopes are going . . .'[7]

The decision having been made to travel to Rome, Conroy – who always found solace in organisation –

occupied himself with the complicated paraphernalia of moving the sick man: 'At ½ p. 12 S is to be carried down stairs in a chair to the Boat and laid on a sopha in it, rolled up in blankets, it will be a good half-hour's journey to the vessel, then he will be carried up the side – and put into the bed carriage on the Deck . . . It has been a feverish and protracted matter and but for the feeling of exacting a great duty, even I, though as strong in mind, have been at times, nearly worn out.'[8]

The journey proved dull with 'see nothing' places on the boat but Stephen, though no more than 'a bag of bones', seemed to respond to the change of environment (101 steps up from the street in the Hotel Europa) and by mid-December Conroy could write that his son was out of danger: 'Explain all this', he urged Edward, 'with every feeling that is affectionate and grateful to the Pss S [Sophia] . . . Apprise her, that I feel *her* steady and understanding feeling for me, and that I am most grateful. I have many worries from England. I have been placed in a position to feel, I could not return to the Dchs it would compromise her interest – so I have completed *my sacrifice* – my place is ere this filled up. The Dchs has been very kind, I feel deeply for Her you and P/s S. I'll tell you all, it is too long to write. I have had enough to break me down, *in my way* . . . But I always come to the surface, perhaps my heart could be broke, but not my nerve.'[9]

His son's illness, as he had recognised, proved a turning point in Conroy's life. It also brought out the best in his character. His devotion to his family and friends was undoubtedly the finest thread in his personality; and those who experienced the small and incessant kindnesses that he rendered – the helping of colleagues into new employment;[10] the giving of presents ('dabs' as he called them) and the fulfilment of the most menial and unpleasant tasks of family life – found, not surprisingly, these generous acts hard to reconcile with the demonic image projected by the Royal Family.

It was his ambition for his family that had been his undoing – but his own family were remarkably true and forgiving. His desire for a peaceful life for them was as genuine as had been his dreams of turning Victoria into the 'people's Queen'. Alas, as with all his fantasies, self-importance, restless energy and an over-reaching imagination rose up and took control. There was after all the granting of Victoria's promise to be considered and prepared for; a suitable 'seat' still to be found as the backdrop for the family's future aristocratic career.

From the depths of despair in a Roman winter Conroy's chirpiness remarkably reasserted itself – 'the climate is just the thing for you', he told Edward, 'it is *healing* as well as mild. No snow, no frost, oranges out of doors!' – and Sir John began to renegotiate his future.

Edward had been given *carte blanche* ('do not fear responsibility') to find Sir John a country house. With the aid of Princess Sophia he had discovered Hurst House in Berkshire (evidently through the Princess's son Captain Garth, whose uncle, Thomas Colleton Garth owned neighbouring Haines Hill House).[11] Hurst House was a sixteenth-century manor of ample proportions whose lease was conveniently vacant.

'I leave *you* to *decide* about the House at Hurst for *me*, as *you* may consider *best*,' Conroy assured Edward. '. . . It is of great moment to me, to have a place *all ready*. You and I do not disagree at all on our country ideas. I see no reason why we should not take the residence of the lease.'[12]

Sir John's anxiety over Stephen thus temporarily eased, he could once again find comfort in the indulgence of his fantasies. A tour of the Mediterranean by paquet boat, culminating in a month's stay at Lisbon occupied his thoughts for some time. Lisbon in particular awoke cheering emotions; Portugal, he felt, certainly owed him something: even now, Sir John perceived, whole guards might turn out to drum a march as he took his early morning stroll, the sun glinting on his plumes and sword and medals.

'Will you make Appleby pack my uniform;' he wrote excitedly to Edward, 'boots, cocked hat – and sword carefully in their tin boxes – as well as *all my orders* – of *every sort* –

ribbons – so that, I have all that sort of thing – even to ribbons in *pieces* to use if I think fit . . . I would rather not be called on to *appear* at Lisbon', he added modestly, 'but it would not be proper, after the favours I have received, not to be *ready* to show.'[13]

There is no record that this delightful prospect materialised. Two days later on the 13th January 1840 the family are found setting off on an overland journey ('All my sadlery – four carriages – the little post-chaise is coming . . .') and Lisbon appeared to be the destination ('a little Portuguse acid, would be better than Prussic, my dear Ned'); however by 21st February the party had settled in Nice and were anxious for home: 'I shall try and make our long journey as easy as I can – to my Pilgrims they are dead sick of the Continent'.

The Conroys returned to a different world. In their absence Queen Victoria's marriage to Prince Albert had taken place, and the momentous changes that great event induced were underway.

'– I only arrive', commented Sir John, 'to find, all the actors in present scenes, in the new places, they will occupy from the marriage. It will carry with it something advantageous', he recognised, 'that I have not mixed or meddled in anything . . . I hope', he added piously, and in fact not without some justification, 'my new situation will allow me to be of more use and comfort to others.'[14]

The rural peace the Conroys found at Hurst House was to bring its own healing. The village life, untouched since the eighteenth century – the rhythm of the agricultural year; the quiet beauty of their surroundings – gave a refuge much to be desired after the events of the past months.

'I am "growing" to like the old house *here* with its many imperfections . . .' admitted Stephen in May 1840, as he slowly grew stronger – enjoying the moonlit country drives and gardens thick with the scent of roses and new-mown hay.'[15]

Conroy himself had taken up country pursuits with vigour: 'Papa commenced his fishing today at Sandford

Mill', reported Stephen, 'he caught one of his old friends "a Pike".'

The Duchess roared with affectionate laughter. 'The description you give me of your dear father's fishing talent amused me very much', she chuckled to Jane, 'does he wear a gentlemanly costume when he indulges in that amusement?'[16]

Fishing, however, was by no means the only gentlemanly pursuit in which Sir John had plans to indulge. Indeed, there was forming in his mind a grand scheme that would consume his energies for the remainder of his life. The past was never to be forgiven (indeed, 'the patient search and vigil long' for his just reward would become an increasing obsession) but the outward scaffolding of Conroy's life was to acquire a more robust and purposeful expression than it had ever known before.

All that was required to bring his new schemes to fruition would be the ever-indulgent aid (and apparently bottomless purse) of the faithful Princess Sophia.

*

Arborfield Hall stood at the end of a long drive surrounded by rich parkland. Replete with limes and firs and meadows – threaded by the River Lodden that flowed under the terrace walk beyond the Hall rose-garden – the park held the Old Church of Arborfield (with its ancient yews) and a large farm.

The Hall itself had lately been rebuilt in the Elizabethan style when Sir John Conroy and his family came there to live from neighbouring Hurst in 1842. Edward Conroy maintained he had brought his father to Arborfield; having found this, the family seat – and having persuaded Princess Sophia to buy it – for the sum of £20,000.[17]

It was no ignominious retreat. Pleasure grounds and walks encircled the mansion; fountains could be induced to play in the River Lodden; there was fishing (Sir John's new-found sport) and punting from the ivy-clad boat house – and tucked away behind a grove of trees, the buildings of the home farm. Conroy hastened to impose his initials upon the farm yard wall: 'J.C. 1843'.

Following his elevation to the Baronetcy, Sir John had had no intention of letting fall the standards to which years of royal living had accustomed him: the large and elegant reception rooms at Arborfield were furnished with 'costly Marble Chimneys' and 'rich Gold Paper and mouldings': a stained-glass window lit the broad oak staircase that swept to the light and airy bedrooms with their large bay windows. There was even central heating. The house, the prospectus was anxious to inform its new owner, was 'particularly cheerful'.[18] Cheerfulness was needed. The previous autumn Stephen had given up his struggle for life – ending his days in Vienna at the home of the Duchess's brother-in-law, Count Mensdorff; ('How frightened I was at his appearance!' wrote Mensdorff to the Duchess, 'he is really very ill, a dreadful cough and considers himself as lost.')[19] The Conroy family hastened once more across Europe to be at Stephen's bedside. He died on 9th September 1841.[20]

'Give my kindest remembrance to your excellent father', wrote the Duchess just before Stephen's death, while staying with Feodora in Germany, 'and tell him that if he does although not write to me, my thoughts are not less occupied

Arborfield Hall c. 1842.

with him tell him, how it distresses me, that I cannot *comfort* and that I cannot be of any use to him.'[21]

In 1842, Sir John's youngest daughter, Victoire, was married to Edward Hanmer, 'a whole-hog-going' friend of Edward Conroy's. Hanmer had assisted in the daring abduction of Lady Alicia from Belgrave Square in the fateful year of 1837. Victoire herself was more conventionally married in a veil of Brussels lace given to her by the Queen of the Belgians (presumably in happier days); while Sir John escorted down the aisle her mother-in-law (who had recently been widowed) for all the world, Charlotte Hanmer exclaimed, like his grandfather, 'rollicking Johnny Conroy'.

The Conroy family filled the cheerful rooms at Arborfield Hall; Victoire, Edward, and their baby son, lived with Sir John for twelve years; while his elderly mother died at Arborfield in 1845 (she being the first Conroy to be buried in Arborfield Old Church); Edward Conroy and Alicia settled at Arborfield Grange – an outlying house on the edge of the Estate. Their son and heir, John Conroy, was born in Kensington in 1845.

Princess Sophia was John Conroy's godmother, and, as a small boy, he was to remember being taken to visit her, 'an old blind lady, sitting at a table, and that she gave me some tin soldiers, one of which took on and off his horse . . . I remember there were a great many clocks in the room, which all began to strike at once: at which I began to cry and was removed.'[22]

At Arborfield, it was hoped, Sir John would retire gracefully to farm in a modest way, to watch his grand-children grow, and to forget the past. It was not to be.

'From the year 1837, my poor Father was never really a happy man', Edward explained to the Duchess. 'He was restless and required occupation for a mind, which if left unemployed, preyed on itself – He lived in the Country, & suddenly turned his attention to the science of agriculture in the most energetic manner, and his talents, perseverance, and skill soon rendered his name known, as one of the successful advocates of the new style of farming.'[23]

The new style of farming had become the fashionable

plaything of the landed gentry. Controversy raged: to drain or not to drain? to make a parlour of your cow-house? to pull down the hedges? Sir James Cheetham in *Middlemarch* had been busily reading Sir Humphrey Davy's *Agricultural Chemistry* before taking one of his outlying farms in hand: 'A great mistake, Cheetham', had exclaimed Mr Brooke. '– No, no . . . your fancy-farming will not do – the most expensive sort of whistle you can buy'.

It was indeed an expensive whistle. Despite his great pensions from the Duchess and the Queen – and a salary from Princess Sophia of £5,000 a year for the management of her affairs – Sir John found the new farming a costly business. He tore down the hedges at Arborfield and drained all the fields: he built new pig sties and bought in the latest machinery. For this, in 1843, he secured a loan of £10,000 on his daughters' life insurance policies (without their consent)[24] and finally – and with much resistance from Edward (which Edward believed cost him his inheritance) – placed a £10,000 mortgage on Llanbrynmair. 'If he had settled down here as he found this beautiful place,' lamented Edward, 'farmed as others had farmed, lived on his great Pensions, & kept his daughters' insurances, instead of digging them into dreams that never can pay to anybody, he would have lived a happy contented life . . .'[25]

Sir John not unnaturally claimed his business paid: at least he did so to *The Times* newspaper in 1852 who, forgetful of the libel suits of yesteryear, ran an extensive article on his and his close neighbour's, the Duke of Wellington's, farming methods (in which the Duke would have been amused to find himself playing the subordinate role).

The changes that Conroy wrought at Arborfield were in fact permanent and far-reaching: in the late twentieth century the self-same farm became part of The Food Research Institute (thus closely associated with Reading University) with Sir John's reorganisation of the fields – and removal of hedgerows – still intact, and even the drainage system a viable feature.[26] *The Times* of 1852 was hopeful that 'other country gentlemen, now compelled by necessity to look strictly to their own business, may be tempted to take a lesson from Sir John Conroy, and to learn from him how much healthful excitement is to be obtained by personal attention to the business of farming'.[27]

If Arborfield's healthful excitement was slow to yield a financial return, Llanbrynmair had begun to show signs of recovery, and by the 1860s was to become very profitable indeed. The two lead mines owned by Conroy – Cae Conroy and Tyisaf (a lead mine of great antiquity) – rendered up to 150 tons of lead annually in the 1840s and 50s.[28] In addition Sir John owned upwards of twenty farms on the surrounding estate in which he took an active interest, establishing a local agricultural society (he was already President of the Woking-ham Agricultural Association) and introducing the idea of the 'new farming' by the use of improved implements and agricultural methods. By 1843 he had become Sherif of Montgomery and in Pennant he even established a school, run on the British and Foreign School Society's plan, which he financed almost entirely himself.[29]

Yet possibly the summit of his achievement – prompted by the fear of a French invasion – was the founding, in 1849, of the Montgomeryshire Regiment of Militia (Rifles). Sir John himself gallantly accepted the Colonelcy of the Regiment, and the District Officer, on his tour of inspection, found nothing but praise for 'this little corps, under the able & judicious management of Sir John Conroy . . .'[30]

Indeed, Sir John was gradually assuming a benign and charitable role. His grandson remembered him as 'a great big man with a very white white waistcoat. He was always very kind to me – '[31] (A photograph suggests, nevertheless, the working farmer with waistcoat far from white.) Indeed, if Sir John was thus compelled to use other people's money to forward his own destiny, it could perhaps have been worse spent than in the regeneration of Arborfield and Llanbrynmair. That it gave him a deeper satisfaction than had his years at Kensington is likely, and but for the vengeful thoughts that 'preyed' on his mind, and the perpetual anxieties about money, he might indeed have realised some kind of peace.

Certainly, Sir John's 'Model Farm' occupied almost his

entire attention during the years that followed his resignation from the Duchess. At last he had achieved due recognition. Returning home one day to Arborfield from the Birmingham and Midlands Counties Exhibition, the proud possessor of a coveted award, the bitterness of the past was temporarily assuaged. For Sir John Conroy Bart had become the triumphant winner of the Royal Agricultural Society of England's prize medal, as the 'Breeder and Exhibitor of the best pen of Fat pigs' for 1852 . . .[32]

12

THE VISCOUNT OF ELPHIN

It is fearful to speculate what might have become of the Monarchy – or indeed the country – had not Prince Albert arrived in England in October 1840, and had the Queen not fallen in love with him.

'I told Albert', confided Victoria, 'that he had come like an angel of light to save me . . . for I *alone* could not have helped myself. I was young & wilful . . .'

By an almost comic irony the reputation of the Court, under the watchful eye of Baroness Lehzen, vied in the public mind with that of Charles II. Victoria herself was deeply unpopular – criticised for her dealings with her mother; her high-handed conduct with Peel; her familiarity with Lord Melbourne and the Flora Hastings Affair. That into this appalling situation should have arrived a handsome Prince – constitutional, intelligent, and moral to a degree – was the kind of miracle that comes once in a lifetime. Victoria had the instinct to recognise her deliverer no sooner than he had arrived at Windsor, where she stood waiting for him at the top of the stairs.

Their marriage had taken place on the 10th February 1840, and heralded the end of Baroness Lehzen's domination. The Governess however was not to surrender without a struggle; for those very characteristics of which Conroy himself had accused her – jealousy and vengefulness; the possessiveness of Victoria – had not vanished with the departure of Sir John. Like a terrier, she had stood waiting to snap; and following the introduction of Prince Albert into her domain, Lehzen was to foolishly direct those old attitudes and emotions towards her new rival.

Indeed, it must be said that the education that Baroness Lehzen had provided for the future Queen of England may have equipped her young charge with strength and determination, but was entirely at odds with the creation of a docile and equable wife. Such a role for Victoria would never have crossed her Governess's mind. Her 'ideal' after all had been Elizabeth I – that Virgin Queen, whom she herself emulated, and whose strength she endeavoured to impart 'by example'. That, in fact, Queen Victoria was destined to be the mother of nine children, and to lean for support and advice in all things upon a young husband whose authority was to far outweigh that of her Governess, was a reality for which the Baroness found herself totally unprepared.

The young husband himself was in an almost impossible situation: he had no role within Victoria's Household, but was sufficiently intelligent as to see where reform was due. Yet Lehzen was immovable. Her life had belonged to the Queen's since childhood; for better for worse she had formed her. Together they had stood against Conroy and the Duchess, and at Ramsgate she had proved her worth. But Victoria had outgrown her. She had entered a world for which Lehzen could not have prepared her, and in which the Governess was neither needed nor wanted. 'A crazy, stupid intriguer, obsessed with the lust of power', raged the Prince, 'who regards herself as a demi-God, and anyone who refuses to recognise her as such is a criminal . . .'[1]

Lehzen had taken to herself the very arrogance she had combated in Conroy: she believed she could fight Prince Albert and win the battle; that her relationship with Victoria would prove transcendent. Albert was to make the discovery Sir John had made before him that Lehzen had persuaded the Queen to believe 'she was only safe in her hands'.[2] Stockmar shook his head: if the Governess had conformed to her new situation he sighed, and respected Victoria's husband, she might have stayed at the Palace for life. As it was Lehzen had to go. ('She fell by an intrigue', chuckled Conroy, 'and the Q. gave her up, to her amazement'.)[3] Lehzen left for Germany in September 1842 with a carriage and £800 a year. She did not wish the Duchess goodbye.

Both Lehzen and Melbourne were now receding into Victoria's past. 'Lord M' parted from his young Queen with greater dignity but a swifter decline. In 1841 the Conservative Party (led by Sir Robert Peel) came to power, and Melbourne, in failing health, at length retired to Brocket where financial worries agitated his mind. He died in 1849 at the age of sixty-nine.

Albert replaced both Governess and Prime Minister in the young Queen's life: Melbourne, whose conversation had so delighted her – and on whose emotional support she had so relied – became at last but a fond memory. Lehzen's faults (of which Albert was at pains to persuade her) were softened by the recollection of their shared trials; yet even Lehzen's removal could not sadden the Queen. Albert had stabilised her. Indeed his ascendance was almost complete. For with the removal of the Baroness he had reorganised the nursery, reformed the Household and eventually graduated from blotting the Queen's letters to dealing with much of her personal correspondence.

He had in fact become her Private Secretary.

Despite the rural occupations Conroy had so diligently fashioned for himself, he had still too many hours in which to brood. As promised in his letters to Edward, Sir John had cut himself off from all his old friends and former activities. Indeed, Lord Dunfermline was much hurt by Conroy's silence and by so many unanswered letters. '. . . I have not in thought word or deed done anything to offend & still less to injure him . . .' he protested, 'I fear that his mind is in an unstable state'.[4]

There is evidence to suggest that this was all too true. Behind the jovial exterior of the successful farmer, it is possible to trace in The Conroy Papers the tell-tale footsteps of a man striving to justify his past. Former events (dramatic enough in themselves) were re-drawn to portray Sir John's role as one of indispensable chivalry – vital, even, to the course of history.

One such press-cutting describing the famous 'narrow escape' from a falling mast, on board the *Emerald* in 1833, was carefully annotated by Conroy: the Captain, reported the newspaper (and later Lady Wharncliffe), 'lifted Victoria in his arms and carried her off to the forepart of the vessel'.

'Not true', thundered Sir John, in the margin. 'At the moment of collision, the Princess was in front of Sir John Conroy – who seeing that anything aloft might come down told her, to lay on the deck, but showed no hurt, she shall not, so he threw himself over her.'[5]

Victoria in her Journal, had described the Captain as carrying her little dog Dashy, but had made no mention of herself at all. It is difficult perhaps to imagine Victoria reporting any gallantry of Conroy's, but it is equally unlikely she allowed herself to be forced so dramatically to the ground by Sir John (or indeed by anyone else).

An even more celebrated incident, for which Conroy claimed responsibility, lay in a memorandum headed 'Memo on the visit of the Prince of Orange and his sons. May 1836'.[6] This event had coincided with the first visit to England of Prince Albert and his brother, whom King William in his anger had desired the Duchess to 'turn back'.

Conroy, it will be remembered, had hurried to Palmerston with a letter from the Duchess (written by himself) refusing to turn back the two Princes. Sir John, (in his memorandum) claimed that the Duchess had agreed to stop the Princes coming, but that he had 'disapproved of the way She [the Duchess] had been taken by surprise and alarmed. He saw, that to stop the Dk of Coburg and his two sons at Rotterdam, and turn them back into Germany, was indeed calculated to give to the Dchs of K. the character of having brought them over to check on the Oranges. To turn them back, was not only to make the Coburgs appear as fortune hunters – the sister and aunt [the Duchess] as pandering to those voices betraying truly the great trust reposed in her. Sir John Conroy succeeded in showing the Dchs of K. how she would be injured, how her brothers and Nephews would be insulted . . . She wrote to Lord Palmerston to whom Sir J.C. carried the letter . . .'

Prince Albert, Conroy claimed, would be indebted to him as the man who 'in the dark of the storm . . . saved them from a most painful and rascally catastrophe'.

The King – through Palmerston – had indeed written to King Leopold 'a half-official communication' that it would be 'highly desirable' that the Coburgs did not visit England that year. Following the Duchess's letter he grudgingly agreed to welcome the party if – as apparently happened – they had missed his instructions to Leopold. It can be said therefore that the Coburgs' welcome in England may have owed something to Sir John's intervention. However the King's letter to Leopold was not an out-and-out refusal, and it is likely that in any event they would have been civilly received. Neither is there any record of the Duchess's 'agreement' to 'turn back' the Princes.

'I never heard this', was Victoria's guarded observation on reading Frances Conroy's account of the affair.[7]

What was Sir John's motivation in thus so privately promoting his own cause? Such stories were doubtless spread about his family and acqaintance; but notes in the margin and 'slips' of paper would seem to be for posterity to discover. And what is posterity to make of them? Like his wife's own supposed origins, they were not true – but evidently believed by himself. Could they have been symptoms of a troubled conscience; a justification of his former behaviour? Proof against rumour unseemly in a peer of the Realm?

For Sir John's mind was perpetually dwelling upon his eventual elevation. What was his peerage to be? Where situated? Carefully, he drew up a title which could have happily adorned the most noble leprechaun: 'Viscount of Elphin Co. Roscm and Baron Llanbrynmair Co. Montgomery in the Peerage of Ireland'.[8]

*

The whole question of Victoria's promise to Conroy was now about to surface, and the royal verdict on Sir John's past behaviour and suspected crimes was to be roundly delivered by Prince Albert himself.

On the first chance of an Irish peerage, on the 29th May 1844, Conroy wrote to Sir Robert Peel, Prince Albert and Queen Victoria. To the Prime Minister he reiterated his claim and reminded him of Victoria's pledge;[9] to Albert he even touched on 'the important service, I rendered to the late much lamented Duke of Saxe Coburg Gotha in the year 1836'.[10] But to Victoria he launched straight into the attack – begging her 'most respectfully to recall to Your Majesty's recollection that after your accession, you desired Baron Stockmar to inform me, that I should receive such a promise in writing, as would be under any change of Government, binding, on the Crown'.[11]

The disturbing presence of Conroy once again fluttered alarmingly into the Queen's happy domesticity. The subject was not a new one to Albert, who, as early as 1841, had had to deal with the Duchess's renewed pleas on Sir John's behalf; while for Baron Stockmar the question of Victoria's promise had long been troubling his conscience. Indeed he took full responsibility for the matter. In 1841 the Baron had told George Anson, Prince Albert's Private Secretary, that 'the Queen would be still pledged to grant him an Irish Peerage, as he [Stockmar] told Conroy that his Letters were written to him with Her Majesty's full approbation . . .'[12] It is probably to this that Sir John referred in his letter to the Queen of the 29th May – reminding her she 'desired Baron Stockmar to inform me, that I should receive such a promise in writing, as would be under any change of Government, binding on the Crown'. In fact Stockmar described the promise as Lord Melbourne's own act, but '*with Your Majesty's concurrence*'.[13]

Lord Melbourne himself had had a long conversation with Victoria on the subject as long ago as 1839:

'I said . . .' wrote the Queen in her Journal, 'there was a thing I was afraid would give trouble, which was that promise to give J.C. the Irish Peerage.'

'Must give it him,' insisted Lord Melbourne.

'I said,' continued the Queen, 'I thought I could never consent to it.'

'You must keep your promise', warned Lord M. 'You will remember I was very much against it.'

Victoria then argued that Conroy had behaved so badly; that he had not gone away as he said he would – and besides they knew now so much more about the man.

'But', returned Melbourne, putting his finger on the crucial point, 'there's nothing you could allege; I've pledged my honour so to do it, and with the express knowledge and consent of Your Majesty.'[14]

There was indeed nothing to allege: a court of law had decided that. The critical question now was whether Victoria was bound to a promise. The feeling of the older men – those children of the eighteenth century – had been that she was so bound. The Queen had agreed to Melbourne's pledge. Nevertheless, technically, her Prime Minister's promise was binding upon himself alone. (Stockmar in a memorandum to Victoria had stated: 'The promise of the Irish Peerage will be given by Lord Melbourne.')[15] On this pretext Sir Robert Peel refused Sir John his peerage in 1844. Nevertheless it was still the Queen's prerogative to overrule her minister.

'If now . . .' Stockmar concluded, after Sir John had petitioned for the Irish peerage a second time in 1847, 'it may appear to Your Majesty *that* . . . you are in mere Regal Magnanimity bound to *make good* now, what *Lord Melbourne promised with Your Majesty's concurrence in 1837*, Baron Stockmar feels equally bound to warn Your Majesty of a dilemma from which in adopting so generous a course, *Your Majesty cannot escape.*

'That you confer the highest honors in your kingly power, which power conscienciously to exercise is your duty, *on a man whom Your Majesty knows best, to be one of the most immoral and unprincipled men in your Kingdom.*'[16]

Prince Albert was in no doubt as to what Victoria's decision should be: he was determined that Conroy, as with Lehzen before him, should be got rid of once and for all:

'The questions whether he got a promise, whether it is to be kept or not, whether he forfeited his claim by his subsequent conduct or not etc. etc. ought not to be treated with him', he wrote to the then Prime Minister Lord John Russell, 'as this would afford him an opportunity of making thousands of assertions, vindications, accusations etc. etc. and would lead to an endless and unpleasant correspondence, nor is the Queen bound to enter into her reasons with him.'[7]

Albert's sensible advice was heeded, and with what relief that decision would soon be regarded (even by the Duchess herself) the future alone would show.

'To be a Peer of the United Kingdom was my ambition,' Conroy had written to the Duchess in 1837. If he had failed in this endeavour, it had been a very close run thing. In the event, it was the earnest intention of Victoria and her ministers to supply Sir John with at least an Irish peerage. That none had become available had not been their fault. The lack, however, had bought them time. Prime Ministers changed; Prince Albert arrived – and Conroy's attempt to bring the matter from a Constitutional to a personal level, had been finally thwarted. For the defeated Viscount Elphin himself, there was no further appeal: the dream formed so long ago had vanished. The sense of injustice however was to remain beyond the grave.

'Nothing can alter Her Majesty's "promise", in a moral and an honourable point of view,' was the final and embittered comment of the Baronet, Sir John Conroy.

*

In May 1848 Princess Sophia died – and from the comfort and grandeur of Arborfield Hall Sir John was forced at last to confront reality. It was Sophia who, with her un-birthday presents, had entered so whole-heartedly into the fantasies of her *cher ami*. Almost certainly she had been convinced, when agreeing to support his plan for a peerage, that she helped – in the Conroy children – her own great nephews and nieces. Both Llanbrynmair and Arborfield were purchased to that end; indeed to Arborfield she had promised a yearly sum of money. That support – a constant and regular flow over twenty-five years – now ceased for ever.

Princess Sophia had died intestate. Less than £2,000 of her vast fortune remained. Knowing catastrophe to be near, Sir John, in July 1849, drew up his will (witnessed by the faithful Appleby) in favour of Lady Conroy.[18] At about this time, too, he burned a considerable portion of his private papers.

In 1851, he wrote a further 'Instruction' for his wife, in which – anticipating his legacy of family dissent – he explained the disposal of his property. Arborfield, he realised, must be sold, and the money used to pay his debts; Lady Conroy could live off the proceeds of Llanbrynmair. At her death the receipts of the property would be shared by his children and their descendants in trust.[19]

This arrangement was indeed to ensure the solvency of the Conroys. The sad reduction in their circumstances – circumstances that had hung so entirely on Princess Sophia's life and Sir John's own salary and pensions – Conroy himself would not live to see.

A man of considerable physical strength, Sir John had worked hard all his life with little in the way of ill health. At sixty-eight years of age however, gout and heart trouble assailed him. In February 1854 he began visibly to fail, and on the 25th February Mr Merriman and two other doctors were called to Arborfield.

Conroy's financial concerns being always uppermost in his mind, the Baronet asked the doctors to inform him if he was in any danger, for he 'had some important business to arrange before death'. The family however decided he should not be told the truth.

On the 27th February, Sir John had gone out driving with Victoire in her carriage and then dined with his family, as Edward recalled, 'for the *last time*'. He went early to bed, and was soon sound asleep.

By midnight he was very ill, and at seven o'clock the next morning he gathered the entire family around his bed. He had much on his mind, he told them, and wished to relieve it while he had the power of speech. He then explained the financial situation, and rested more easily.[20]

Sir John made some effort too to be reconciled with his eldest son; for, carefully preserved in The Conroy Papers, is the Baronet's last 'slip' – written to Edward shortly before his death: 'May all possible good occur to you – my dear Edward, this year. I still hope, after you see me . . . that you will send to say, you love me. I am safe now, I think . . . I am stronger, but I really have no energy for these sort of things.'[21]

In the early afternoon of the 2nd March 1854 Mr Merriman hurried to the Duchess of Kent who was waiting for news of Sir John.

'How is he?' she asked anxiously as the doctor entered the room.

'It is all over!' Mr Merriman replied. 'He died at 2 o'clock surrounded by his family.'

The past rose painfully before the Duchess's mind; the shock was huge. 'I pity his family,' was all she could find to say.[22]

'So gently did the lamp of life expire', Edward remembered, 'that we could not believe that he was really dead. He died with his hand in mine, and as a brave man ought!'

And perhaps in Sir John's final moments there may be seen, as from the distant past, the ghost of his father, John Conry, performing Falstaff in the little theatre in Fishamble Street, a life-time ago. For, shortly before his death, the Baronet had been moved to a larger, sunnier room, where – opposite his bed – hung a copy of Fowler's portrait of Queen Victoria as a child. Sir John raised himself, and as he gazed 'long and earnestly' at the picture, the family watched him slightly bow his head as if to say: 'Ah! there I did my duty.'[23]

As the still moment before a storm, so was the simplicity of Conroy's funeral before the grim discoveries his death would bring.

Sir John had asked that he be buried in the churchyard at Arborfield between the two services on a Sunday, and 'that no expenses be gone to for my funeral but that Christian decency requires'. On 8th March 1854, the family carried Sir John's coffin the short distance from the house to the graveside in the tiny churchyard under the yews.

'Conroy is dead,' acknowledged King Leopold to Victoria with both relief and resignation; 'what a strange character he was . . .'[24]

13

THE RECKONING

With the death of Sir John Conroy, the inevitable judgement upon his life and affairs was at hand – and Lady Conroy, Queen Victoria and the Duchess herself would have to face the consequences of Conroy's financial irresponsibility with startling brutality.

For the Duchess, however, the revelations were to be but a further corroboration of behaviour that, over the last few years, she had sorrowfully begun to accept. Indeed, if the Duchess had suffered from Sir John's ambition in the past, yet one question had never seemed to concern her: from where had he found the money to pay for his own extravagant way of life? Vague murmurs of Irish Estates and the assumption of inherited wealth had been sufficient to allay her fears. In 1850, however, Sir John's successor, Colonel Couper, had revealed astonishing evidence of apparent mismanagement of her affairs that had shaken the Duchess's faith. Could it have been the memory of these deceits that had caused Sir John's self-justifying notes and memoranda? Coded messages written in fear of this terrible evidence, so impossible to explain away . . .

Following the reading of Sir John Conroy's Will at Arborfield, the family's resentment at their father's behaviour broke forth in letters – presumably directed from room to room – which were filled with grief and anguish: '– it was not the P[rincess] S[ophia]'s death that drove him to this', insisted Edward to his mother, 'but his own unjustifiable expenditure here – I tried to check him . . . I had no-one to help me. He had not *one true* & clear sighted friend. Those who saw his mistakes, saw it was useless to check him. they withdrew from him & left him to his parasites. I alone of all the family foresaw & tried to save. I did not however contemplate such a gigantic smash. he has left us the inheritance of poverty & what is worse an inheritance of family dissention. may God grant no law suits grow out of it . . .'[1]

There can be no doubt Edward was right; Sir John had been friendless; and those who would have retained his friendship were rebuffed. Conroy, as King Leopold had observed, was incorrigible.

Lady Conroy however, remained, to the end, blind to her husband's faults: 'The very long history . . . & tirade about your poor father I had heard from you before!' she replied to Edward. 'He, poor man, when at Woolwich was anything but rich, & he thought then that he was acting for the best, for you & all his little children – & he, Rea, was really a good master to begin with . . .

'You are in fact', she pointed out, 'better off than anyone here, you have a House over your head & everything as usual – *I* have not, nor Victoire either, & at this moment I do not know where to go to, or what to do! added to which I have poor sick *Jane* who requires the greatest care & comforts & to all this the loss of your dear Father! – These dissensions & quarrels & *so soon* too after his loss are to my mind very bad and discreditable to you & all!'[2]

In fact it was not certain that Edward had 'a House over his head': Arborfield Grange was part of the Arborfield Estate and included in the mortgage of the entire property. These and many other details were soon to be discovered by Sir George Couper when the financial affairs of the Conroys finally came under his scrutiny.

Not unnaturally the Conroy family had seen both the Queen and her mother as a possible source of financial support in this their ultimate disaster. Edward had written a lengthy letter to the Duchess, detailing the events of the past years (Prince Albert didn't believe a word of it) and even asking her for a post at Court. This communication was gently fielded by Sir George Couper, whose sober uprightness the Duchess was now beginning to appreciate.

'Mr Conroy', warned Sir George, 'is of an overbearing temper, without the manners of his father.' Mr Wellesley (Conroy's neighbour) he added, had been the first to warn him that Edward was 'an immoral man' – 'a deceitful cunning man'.[3]

Indeed, Sir George Couper, being the first disinterested person to come within the Duchess's sphere, had for some time been readily making available to her the rumours and assumptions of society on the subject of Sir John and his family. Nevertheless, Sir George was, Dunfermline maintained, a 'mild, easy and sensible' man, with 'energy and decision': in all 'a safe guide'. Within weeks of his appointment as Private Secretary in 1840 he had begun to have his doubts as to the honesty of William Rea.

William Rea, it will be remembered, had been appointed accounts clerk to the Duchess of Kent in October 1826, and in the following month given sole charge of the library at Kensington Palace. Only he and the Duchess possessed a key to enter the library (Sir John, although Comptroller, does not appear to have held one).[4] Rea on his retirement in 1845 (and unknown to Sir George) packed all the accounts into two commodes at Clarence House, delivering the keys to the Duchess. She frequently spoke of the accounts to Sir George, as if they troubled her mind, and eventually on 15th February 1850, gave him the keys: 'Here is the key of the commodes in the library', wrote the Duchess from Clarence House, 'I remember now that amongst the Private Accounts are also some Household Accounts.

'Be so good as to have the Private Accounts put in a large box in your presence, and order the box to be sent here . . .'[5]

The dreadful evidence that had confronted them when the box was opened admitted of only two interpretations; the first being that Rea had obediently carried out the dishonest schemes of Sir John; the other that Rea alone had perpetrated the deception.

The most striking omission to be found was that no General Accounts had been kept since 1829. Sir George informed the Duchess that Rea had admitted reluctantly (and before his retirement) that in fact no accounts had been kept since 1834. Although the Duchess never actually signed the General Accounts she asserted that 'Sir John always submitted those Accounts for Her examination and signature . . .' previous to the Queen's accession. She insisted on this fact several times.[6]

If the Duchess's statement was correct, recorded Sir George, the account books must have been 'carried away, and Rea's assertion to me that no General Account Books had been kept from 1834, and none kept regularly for several preceding years must be untrue.'[7]

The Duchess had then opened the portmanteau containing her Private Accounts. None existed after 1830. Telling Sir George she would send him the surviving accounts – she in fact burnt them.

'Where did Rea put the others?' demanded the Duchess. 'It is very odd – what does this mean?'

'Does Y.R.H. wish that Rea should be asked about them?' enquired Sir George.

'I think not,' replied the Duchess, 'why did I not look after the papers sooner – of what use would it be now?'

It had been the personal opinion of Sir George that Sir John was the culprit; in this he was supported by King Leopold, Stockmar and Lord Melbourne. The Duchess pointed out that Leopold, Stockmar and Lord Dunfermline had all recommended Conroy to her. She knew he was vain and had made many enemies but she did not consider him dishonest. Rea, on the other hand, she had distrusted deeply.

Sir George had added that both Stockmar and King Leopold had told him that Leopold had given the Duchess £16,000 prior to his accession in 1831. This sum was not recorded in her Coutts Public Account. Conroy actually claimed the money was lent on condition of repayment, which Victoria said was a lie.[8] ('That was one of the sacrifices probably,' concluded Leopold.)[9] Nevertheless £10,000 given to the Duchess by King William IV to pay off a debt of £8,000 was in fact credited in August 1834 to her Coutts Public Account 'on Her Bond of 13th inst & security' – despite a denial by Baron Stockmar.[10]

Many of Sir George's suspicions had been founded on the fact that since Princess Sophia's death in 1848 Sir John's use of her money had been generally known amongst the Royal Family (although not apparently by the Duchess). Having found Sophia had left no Will, 'Aunt Gloucester' and 'Aunt Cambridge' (as Victoria called them) had sent for Sir John Conroy who found everything in 'the greatest order' (as well he might) but – despite having 'several times expressed the wish to make one' – Sophia had left no Will. Over the next few months however the disappearance of her money was gradually uncovered . . .

Following Sir John's own death in 1854 Sir George related at last to a bewildered Duchess of Kent the full extent of Princess Sophia's loss.

'Where that money has gone', he admitted, 'no-one can say – Sir John managed The Princess's affairs, and he declined to give any account of Her money –

'The world therefore believes that it was given, *from time to time* by The Princess to him – She drew all the cheques on the Bankers, and nothing of the disposal of the money so drawn, after She received it, is known –

'He certainly had ample means to have lived according to his position in life; and it is fearful to think on the want of principle & of heart which could have allowed him to go on for so many years gratifying his own vanity . . .

'He bore the character of being untrue, and, I am sorry to say, his family are also accused of it . . .

'I consider it a duty, & a very painful duty, to submit these remarks to Y.R.H. . . .'[11]

The natural inference was that Sir John had used the Duchess's money in the same way as he had used Princess Sophia's (but without her permission). Indeed, at the time of her discovery of the missing accounts in 1850, Sir George had put forward a number of commonly-held beliefs that proved how inaccurate was the public knowledge of Sir John's background and affairs in his own life time.

Sir John, it was said, had bought an estate in Wales for £35,000 (it was generally believed the Duchess's money had paid for it). Again, Sir George asserted, his 'brother officers, who knew all about him' believed he had no property in Ireland – or indeed any property of his own at all.

'. . . in this as in some other things, he had deceived H.R.H.', concluded Sir George.

'. . . for instance he had stated that he was an intimate friend of Lord Hastings when Master General of the Ordnance; whereas his brother officers doubted whether Lord Hastings had even spoken to him in his life.'

'He never said so to me,' objected the Duchess. 'He certainly said so to Lady Flora Hastings,' returned Sir George.

Colonel Wylde, he added, rising to his theme, 'cut him' [Sir John] saying he could not be on their former terms until he explained how he bought his Estate in Wales.

'– she had never heard Sir John mention Colonel Wylde', protested the Duchess.[12]

This wretched catalogue of rumour and misinformation does not seem to have greatly disturbed the Duchess of Kent at the time. The possibility that her own money might have been used to feather Sir John's nest never seriously worried her (the suggestion had, after all, been successfully denied in a court of law many years before). Now, however, Sir George's disturbing new evidence about Princess Sophia put more than a shadow of doubt in her mind. Everyone, it appeared, shared her Private Secretary's opinion; Sir John had deceived her. Her heart began to harden . . .

Lady Conroy, meanwhile, was writing a desperate letter to the Queen: 'The one to whom your kindness & goodness gave so much is now taken from me', it ran, '& in addition to this unlooked for, & dreadful event, all my dear children & myself are left with but very very little.'[13]

There is no doubt that both Victoria and the Duchess were shocked by the state in which Sir John had left his family: the Duchess – who did not seem to care so much for any possible deception in her own affairs – was deeply distressed by Lady Conroy's plight.

'– you have not erred', wrote Colonel Phipps on the Queen's behalf, 'in supposing that you have Her Majesty's sincere sympathy in the heavy affliction that has fallen upon you . . .'[14]

After some consultation between the Queen, Prince Albert and the Duchess, it was decided that something should be done for Lady Conroy: but not before a careful scrutiny of the Conroys' financial affairs had been undergone by Colonel Phipps and Colonel Couper. Indeed, Colonel Couper – who had originally considered a visit to Arborfield as useless – eventually arrived for an interview with Edward; ('what brought him, I wonder?' wrote Lady Conroy excitedly, '& what did he say').

By May 1854 an assessment of Sir John's assets had been drawn up and a sum of money made over to Lady Conroy. The payment, however, does not seem to have been on a regular basis. Edward complained that the Queen 'did nothing'; and indeed we find that by November Lady Conroy had evidently appealed again for money.

The Queen then replied that Sir John, having been paid more than most, should have provided for Lady Conroy and his family.[15] (Indeed, Colonel Couper's report had been firm: 'The family has £3100 amongst them', he informed the Duchess, 'they may live very well on that if they will.')[16] Nevertheless, on a further financial report being placed before the Queen, a pension of £400 per annum for life was finally bestowed on Lady Conroy[15] ('in the most unkind manner', in the opinion of Edward).

Now convinced of Sir John's guilt, the Duchess, however, was relieved; 'To return good for evil', she observed, 'brings always happiness to the giver.'[17]

Edward in fact was someone the Duchess had had to

face: within two weeks of his father's death he had brought
to her, at her request, a number of letters from Prince
Leiningen, King Leopold and the Duchess herself, including
'the Dchss's *own* private papers which would damn the
Queen'.[18]

'It affected me very much to see him', the Duchess
admitted; 'he is very much changed. The conduct of his
Father to me and Victoria has totally destroyed any
remaining feeling of friendship for him.'

By July 1854 Arborfield Hall had been sold, and Lady
Conroy and Jane had gone to live near their Fisher cousins
in Kingston; Henry had nobly sold his Army Commission of
£6,000 to repay Victoire and Edward Hanmer for their
marriage settlement (which in fact they had never received).
Edward and Alicia – who by now had separated –
continued to live in neighbouring houses on the Arborfield
estate. Desolate outposts of the once-thriving dynastic
dream.

What then is the reader to make of this accumulation of
financial evidence? The Royal Family, including the Duchess, seemed convinced of Sir John's fraudulence. Yet we are
perhaps in a stronger position than were Sir John's
contemporaries to suggest an alternative interpretation of his
affairs.

After the death of Sir John, the Conroys had never made
any secret of Princess Sophia's financial support: 'H.R.H. the
Princess Sophia whose heir was Sir John Conroy Bt, de
facto – ', stated Edward, 'for she gave him nearly all her
large income . . .'[19]

In December 1875, Edward's son John wrote a memorandum which dealt with the overriding problem of how
Princess Sophia's fortune could have vanished so completely.
Firstly, he itemised the amount of money which, to his
knowledge, had come from the Royal Family:

From P. S[ophia].

A House at K[ensington]	–	£4,000
Llanbrynmair	–	£18,000
"	–	£10,000

Arborfield	– £20,000
From 1826 to '48	
22 years at 3,000 a year	– £66,000
from '42 to '48, at 5,000 a year	– £30,000

From P.S.	£148,000

From Queen

June 1837 to June 1854

17 years at 3,000	– £51,000

From D.K. [Duchess of Kent]

From 1837 to 1854

17 years at £1,500	– £25,500
Total from Royals	£224,000 [sic]

Say nil of *Public Offices*; army pay, or Private fortune!
Sir John *ought* to have *provided* for his family.

This indeed had been the conclusion of Sir George
Couper. (However Sir John's 'private fortune' could not
have amounted to more than his Irish estate and his wife's
marriage settlement of £15,000 which had been absorbed
long ago in a mortgage.)

'When Sir John died', concluded his grandson, 'though he
had been in the receipt of large pensions, his debts amounted
to nearly £40,000 though with the exception of his farm
(which *he* said produced a profit) he had no expensive tastes
– He neither raced or played, did not shoot or hunt; and his
establishment consisted of a butler & 2 footmen, a cook,
kitchen maid, 2 housemaids and I suppose a laundry and
dairy maid. There were a pair of carriage horses – a hack
and a single outside horse in the stable, and a coachman
with a groom and helper.

'Had he helped himself to the Princess's money there
would not have been this debt.

'HRH paid (I believe) large sums to the Duke of York
(whose residuary legatee she was) and also to Mr T. Garth,
whose debts she paid.'[20]

The Duke of York had indeed owed his sister £60,000. In
part payment (regular payments of £60 were made into her

Drummond's Account in 1825)[21] he left Sophia the lease of
the Nova Scotia Mines, granted to him by the Government
in 1792 'for life and 21 years thereafter'. The mines,
purchased by him with a grant from Hamlet the London
jeweller, proved valueless. 'Loss upon loss succeeded, and in
the end bankruptcy.'[22] Princess Sophia made over this
dubious inheritance to Sir John Conroy in 1841.[23]

It is unlikely that Thomas Garth had any claim on his
mother's property, for he was the beneficiary of a settlement;
besides which Conroy had been useful in getting rid of
Garth's 'bullying importunities'. However, Sir John's grandson was probably ignorant of the enormous sums received by
Conroy in the relatively small but numerous payments from
Princess Sophia over a period of thirty years.

Bearing all this in mind, one would not have expected to
find Sir John still looking for every means of support for
Arborfield and Llanbrynmair. Yet both estates were heavily
mortgaged (£30,000 for Arborfield, and £10,000 for Wales),
additional money coming from his pensions, from the sale of
his and his daughters' life insurance – plus the non-payment
of Victoire's £6,000 marriage settlement. At his death Sir
John's debts totalled £46,035.

Which brings us to the question of the Duchess of Kent.

In a memorandum, written in April 1837,[24] Sir John
described the Duchess's financial situation up to the year
1831. Although debts for expenses were incurred at her
marriage, it was the death of the Duke of Kent that had
forced her to borrow from Coutts on a bond signed by
herself, General Wetherall and Captain Conroy to provide
£12,000 (two years' income). By 1825 she was receiving
£4,000 from Prince Leopold, plus £6,000 from the Government; and following the Regency in 1830 her gross income
totalled £22,000 a year.

It would seem to have been subsequent to this relative
affluence that the upkeep of her Private and General
Accounts had disintegrated. At the same time her expenditure soared. From 1830 Royal Tours were undertaken; lavish
concerts and other entertainments promoted; and expensive

holidays indulged. In the neglect of her affairs the Duchess –
that innocent goose – was right to have admitted that 'if
others have been *wrong*, I have also been wrong, I blame
myself severely'.[25]

At his libel trial in 1838 Sir John had stated that in the
previous year the Duchess's debts amounted to £63,195.3.0
(not £80,000 as published in *The Times*). The official sum
had been £55,000. Conroy himself had, on 30th June 1837,
produced a rough statement of the Duchess's accounts
amounting to debts of £54,491. (The greater part was in a
loan of £30,000 from Coutts, but we find 'Bills to 31 May
1837 – £18,576' – and the Duchess owed Sir John himself
£1,201 for 'Ramsgate Bills'.)[26]

'About the debts', wrote Conroy to Stockmar, with
breathtaking casualness, 'you may say, it was an invention of
the late King's. The Duchess has none, She never thought of
asking the public to pay, will that do for the Government,
She, will I hope, be able to pay what she owes. I am
responsible for that. I write this candidly – for you to act on
– at once – to bring, all to a close – '[27]

In December, Parliament voted the Duchess £30,000 with
which to gradually repay her debts.

Lord Liverpool was horrified: 'enough has transpired
about debts & C – to lead people *to know* that every farthing
of this that can be diverted will be applied to C's private
purposes. I confess to you that much as I was prepared for
Ld M's careless way of doing things I did not expect that he
would so completely have let himself be duped as he has on
this occasion.'[28]

How, one wonders, were all these financial matters
assessed? Did the General and Private Accounts slumber on
unopened? Or had they vanished long ago? And, if so, why
did no one think of finding out before the year 1850?

Sir George Couper had in fact been reluctant to study
them. In his memorandum of 3rd April 1850, Sir George
stated that in talking with Melbourne in 1840 on his not
having seen the accounts, 'nothing had passed through my
hands to justify the belief that Sir John was other than an
honourable man'. Lord Melbourne had considered Sir

George wise in having nothing to do with the accounts: 'but if you had seen them you would have formed a very different opinion of Sir John Conroy'.

Had Lord Melbourne actually seen the accounts? And if so, which ledgers had he seen if no Private or General Accounts were said to exist after 1834?

Again, is it possible that both Houses of Parliament could have voted the Duchess £30,000 a year without some form of detailed evidence being supplied? Lord Liverpool had urged Stockmar to a close investigation of the Duchess's debts so that Leopold could 'stop Conroy's mouth . . . by the proof of his dissipation of the Duchess's money . . .'[29] While Sir George Couper had assumed that, because for so many years no regular accounts were kept, this had 'cost HRH [the Duchess] very dearly. It prevented YRH ['s] debts from being paid by Parliament. Conroy had no regular – no General accounts to submit to it, and he worked to prevent that from being known.'[30] Certainly, if such investigations were carried out in 1837, no positive proof against Conroy seems to have been forthcoming.

Such questions, unanswerable though they may be, could go some way to justifying the Duchess's protestations that she had always seen the General Accounts prior to the Queen's accession. If this was so, had Rea been lying? And if so, why?

It will be remembered that in 1837 William Rea – with considerable arrogance – had declined to enter into the Queen's service at her accession. It was in the year 1837, too, that Sir John claimed Rea had intrigued with the Duchess of Kent to bring about his dismissal. The Duchess herself admitted 'she was afraid of him'.

Both with large families (and both with supposed royal connections) Rea and Conroy were similarly situated. One of Rea's daughters was a dresser to the Duchess of Kent; his son ('Edward' of course) became Principal Clerk of the General Post Office.

Could William Rea have embezzled from the Duchess of Kent without Conroy's knowledge? According to Rea himself his account books – and it was his job to keep them – were not recorded after 1834. (Or perhaps they had been kept, but with damning evidence that Sir John had not bothered to check?) Had he entered the Queen's service in 1837 these matters would have been discovered a good deal earlier than 1850. Equally, the Duchess's removal of Conroy would have given Rea the opportunity to cover up his tracks.

A second possibility remains that Sir John, unable to admit that his Estates had been paid for by Princess Sophia, had to keep the secret of his clerk's dishonesty in order to buy Rea's silence on his own affairs. Undoubtedly, an uncomfortable relationship existed between these two men. If, as seems probable, Conroy did not have full authority over Rea, he may have had to acquiesce in the misappropriation of the Duchess's funds. (If this was so, however, they did not carry Rea and his family very far; at Rea's death his son had to appeal to Queen Victoria for pensions for his five unmarried sisters.)

Much of Conroy's later reputation was to hang on the assumption that he was guilty of fraud. Indeed, it became virtually a matter of fact that he had embezzled the Duchess. Frances Conroy's doubtful statement that Sir John 'never drew his own pay from the Duchess of Kent', exacted a laconic note from Queen Victoria: 'He pocketed a gt deal of the money we have reason to believe.'[31]

In fact, it seems certain Sir John was paid a salary from 1832 onward, although the account books do not exist to verify this. (Nor is it recorded in his grandson's resumé.) A memorandum stated that the Duchess's Government Grant of 1831 enabled her to pay servants who had given their services 'gratuitously',[32] and Sir John himself confirmed that for thirteen years he received no salary (being the years 1819 to 1832) implying that he had received one thereafter.[33] Indeed, it would scarcely have been in Sir John's interest to steal from the Duchess of Kent. He had hoped for a peerage through her and she herself had rashly promised him an estate, and £5,000 a year to maintain it.[34] Furthermore, he would have had no need of her money before his retirement, for Princess Sophia 'gave him nearly all her large income'. (Even King Leopold was to admit that Sir John 'must have collected a rich harvest from Pss Sophia'.)[35] Melbourne (despite his remarks about the accounts) had insisted that 'there is nothing you can allege'; and so *The Times* newspaper had discovered when they made their attempt in 1838.

Speculation apart, concrete evidence of embezzlement of the Duchess, by either Conroy or Rea, is not available and must be assumed not to exist. Nevertheless, large sums of money were unaccounted for. If, however, either Rea or Conroy had 'pocketed' such wealth (and the figure £35,000 was mentioned) there remains the question of what they spent it on. Rea was not a rich man and lived in a grace-and-favour house at Kensington. Conroy died deeply in debt.

We know Sir John, in his own family affairs, took enormous risks – it was always his naïve hope that debts would somehow be paid – and it is certain he took the same attitude towards the Duchess's finances as to his own. Nothing – certainly not absence of money – was to stand in the way of Conroy's romantic schemes. The Duchess herself lived extravagantly, and her Royal Tours were colossally expensive. Nothing could have been easier than for whole fortunes to have silently trickled away. (Even Queen Victoria, in 1839, managed to spend £34,000 on charities alone.) Such gross irresponsibility might have verged upon the criminal but would not have been viciously dishonest.

'Her entire income', declared Conroy of the Duchess, 'has been devoted to the encouragement of british manufactureres, british tradesmen, british artists, british institutions, british charities, and in fact everything of national growth and production.'[36]

As to the money he was given by Princess Sophia, it is possible that both she and Conroy looked upon it as 'family money' and his children's rightful inheritance. Certainly this cannot be proved, but it makes better sense of the Princess's overwhelming generosity towards him. Again, money so freely given did Conroy little credit, but could not be said to be fraudulently acquired.

It was the fact, however, that he had secrets – his wife's supposed origins; Princess Sophia's money; even, perhaps, his association with Rea – that not only prevented him explaining openly the origin of such wealth (or of his true reason for acquiring it) but allowed false rumours to circulate, so contributing at last to his downfall.

*

'All Sir John's invention', Victoria had said of Conroy over the Cumberland affair and with uncanny accuracy the Queen had summed up Sir John's entire existence. The mainspring of Conroy's life had been a belief that his children were the descendants of George III, and this fantasy inspired, to an almost diabolical extent, the actions of his career. Yet service, too, was Conroy's inheritance: the presentation by his ancestors of the 'White Wand' to the Kings of Ireland curiously foreshadowed the Duke of Kent's commitment of the Duchess of Kent and her daughter into his care. That this mystical strand permeated a character within whom Falstaff and Malvolio competed for centre-stage could scarcely have been appreciated at the time.

If much may be conquered in the world by charm, then – as with his grandfather before him – rewards had floated effortlessly Conroy's way. But the young man who was the baby Victoria's 'Captain Dispery'; who went searching for writing-boxes for Feodora and who laboriously gave the Duchess her English lessons, had flaws sufficient to bring down the better part of his character.

For Kensington Palace had been run under Conroy's regimental eye with all the harsh discipline of a girls' boarding-school: no whispering on the stairs or running in the passages; the clocks to be wound at a certain moment – the coffee to be brought in at another. When, one winter's evening, the dancing mistress, Madame Bourdin, was discovered wandering the corridors with a candle in her hand, it was a matter of grave concern. To find within this tight little kingdom a militant Governess preaching defiance, had been enough to light the fuse that had led to Sir John's and the Duchess's downfall.

But what had been the long-term effect of this strange man and the curious childhood he provided upon Victoria herself?

Assuredly there had been advantages Queen Victoria

could never have acquired through a more conventional upbringing. Life with William IV would certainly not have produced the 'journeys' that had made her known to the people 'without party'. (A lesson she herself failed to learn. The Duchess's warnings before the Princess's accession that Victoria should be above Party had proved all too true: speaking of the Bedchamber Plot as late as 1897 Queen Victoria admitted: 'Yes! It was a mistake . . .')

Victoria's Tours had in fact been enormously beneficial to the Monarchy, emerging as it was into a new era of democracy. 'I wish to rally as large a portion of the British people, as is possible . . . round the existing institutions of King, Lords & Commons,' Lord Durham had declared – and with Victoria as their figurehead he and Conroy had succeeded in introducing the country to its future Queen. The attainment through Victoria of a popular Constitutional Monarchy was an achievement Prince Albert was to consolidate, but it had its beginnings in these royal progresses, the like of which had never been seen before. Furthermore, Victoria's early contact with trade and manufacture inspired an interest – begun at eleven years of age at the Boulton and Watts Manufactory in Birmingham – which she never lost, and in which she took great personal pride.

Victoria's journeys covered Wales, the North and the West Country: but for the King's obstruction she would have visited Ireland where, as Conroy rightly believed, 'in coming times, it would have been well to have left no stone unturned to draw the countries closer together . . .' As it was, Queen Victoria's visit (after the Irish Famine in 1849), though a personal success, had come too late. It was probably as much in recognition of these Tours and their particular contribution to Victoria's education that Sir John had gained his doctorate from Oxford University in 1832.

It has been long understood that Victoria was in want of a father-figure, and she played up her fatherless state with some success throughout her life. Men with whom she felt 'safe' – King Leopold, Melbourne, Disraeli, John Brown – all enacted for Victoria this protective role. Even Prince Albert, some months younger than herself, became a paternal substitute upon whom she could gratefully lean. Had Conroy endeared himself to the young Princess – as the sober Colonel Couper might have done – Victoria's psychology could well have been more stable.

For in fact Sir John was the closest Victoria came to possessing a father on a day-to-day basis. That he forbade her visits to the Opera or to attend parties with undesirable relatives (as any real parent might have done) was reason enough for his unpopularity; but Sir John did not even conduct himself with the deference she felt her high station deserved (in his eyes his own children were her actual equals). It was this inexplicable shift in attitude, that assumed an almost direct and actual paternity instead of the reverential role-play of his successors, that had so disturbed and puzzled Victoria.

But was Sir John solely to blame for the terrible atmosphere within which the Queen grew up? It would be easy enough to devise an argument that denounced Sir John, and indeed his futile ambitions and absurd dynastic beliefs might entirely condemn him were they not placed within the social context of their time. Of his work to gain the Regency, the Duchess (as Wellington shrewdly acknowledged) was an improvement on the reactionary Cumberland and the candidate Parliament preferred: if the Regency had given the Duchess a power that Leopold and Lehzen despised, it left the country in greater security. Certainly the Duchess's and Sir John's interest in Victoria came to be political whilst Lehzen's remained personal. But, although she had seen through Conroy's ambitions, the Governess did not appreciate that her hatred of him and the Duchess polarised mother and daughter with the most destructive consequences. From this ostracisation had proceeded many of the terrible events prior to the marriage of the Queen.

It is true that Sir John was a liar, a bully and a fool. Totally irresponsible over money, he was entirely unsuitable for royal service and should never have been employed: that he was retained after 1825 had been the fault of Leopold and Stockmar.

'The Baroness', wrote Victoria, 'at the risk of her health if

not of *her life* preserved the Queen from this *horrible man* . . .
The *awful* scenes in the house with her poor dear, kind
mother (who in later years grieved no doubt over it) her
being deceived by this man . . .'[37]

Lehzen's role in these vengeful confrontations was not one
Victoria could have understood, but it is clear that the
'awful scenes' were in fact the responsibility of all those
involved in her future. The Flora Hastings Affair did no
credit to anyone except the Duchess, and the Bedchamber
Plot showed the extremes to which Lehzen's unconstitutional
theories of monarchy could lead. Yet this unsatisfactory
collection of people produced a self-controlled young woman
with an authority beyond her years.

It has been said that Queen Victoria was made by
Baroness Lehzen – and it is true that the Governess gave her
discipline and a clear-sighted vision; but she was much to
blame for the conflict at Kensington, and it was this conflict
that had made Victoria. In a more lax environment it is
unlikely that her obstinacy would have found a worthwhile
focus, nor that her capacity to perceive disinterested loyalty
would have been so youthfully exercised. Adversity had
created her, and the unexpected influence of Conroy's hated
regime and presence was to be England's gain in the end.

The death of Sir John had brought the Duchess and her
daughter closer together. Swept along by the ambitions of
Conroy, the Duchess of Kent had believed her actions to
have been for Victoria's good: surrounding the young Queen
with their protective partnership had been her fondest hope.
Disillusionment when it came was the more profound
because the Duchess alone understood the real debt she had
owed Sir John: '– the death of this man', she wrote to
Victoria, 'who has been for *many*, *many*, years with me, who
was present at your birth, who was a very faithful Servant of
your Father, and who has been of great use to me, but
unfortunately has also done me great harm! has shocked me
very much, I am sure you can understand. I say no more
about it. He had many good qualities but also *very great*
faults'.[38]

The spell, 'like witchcraft', that Sir John had thrown over

the Duchess had lifted at last, but the resultant remorse and blame should not have been hers to bear alone. Stockmar and King Leopold, and indeed all those involved in the Kensington System, had been responsible for encouraging Conroy's initial policies. Even his plan to become Victoria's Private Secretary had been at one time supported by Stockmar, Lord Liverpool and Lord Dunfirmline. It is scarcely surprising that the Duchess had become so confused.

Yet of all those involved with Victoria's childhood, it was the Duchess herself who rose from the wreckage with some degree of integrity. She had been a natural victim; not especially intelligent, she had behaved (when not influenced directly by Conroy) with kindness and principle. In both the Flora Hastings Affair and the Bedchamber crisis her instinctive judgement had been correct.

By 1854, Queen Victoria, whom the years had mellowed and who could now acknowledge her own mistakes, had come at last to appreciate her mother's loving character. As the Duchess herself had admitted, it was 'the passions of those who stood between us' that had so bitterly estranged them: '. . . pray *don't ever* dwell on those sad past times', Victoria urged her mother. 'They are gone for ever & no one knows your love & affection towards me or returns it & values it *more truly* than I do. If it comes to accusing *oneself*, she acknowledged '– I fear I might do so *also* for *I* was *also* wrong in my behaviour towards you very *often* in those miserable days.'[39]

It had been the hope of Sir John Conroy that history would remember him as the maker of a great Queen, and that this achievement would be enshrined in a peerage: a peerage justified not only by his own worth but by the regal blood of his offspring. Instead, in the historical imagination, he became at best a buffoon; at worst, a monster whose evil hold over the Duchess of Kent was the stuff of Shakespearian tragedy.

If both these elements have their place in the strange amalgam that was Sir John, the accusations of fraud, immorality and ambition must now be seen in the light of

The Conroy Papers and what they have to tell. It cannot be entirely forgotten that Sir John was unjustly accused of adultery in the Flora Hastings Affair (however much he may have contributed to such suspicions). Nor that he was promised a peerage he never received – however little he may have deserved it. Furthermore, no whisper of an indiscretion with the Duchess of Kent has yet to be found among the remainder of Sir John's family papers. Again, where there might have been hope of finding concrete evidence of fraud, the Royal Archives disclose obvious deceit and negligence, but only suspicion of theft. That this suspicion finally destroyed his relationship with the Duchess of Kent, when Princess Sophia's affairs were revealed to her in 1854, was a tragedy for them both. Whether in fact it was a necessary tragedy is something that may never be known.

It is possible the Duchess herself never entirely condemned Sir John. 'Peace to his soul', she had written at his death, 'I have forgiven him. I shall always remain the friend of his family.'[40]

It was with a heavy heart, however, that she picked up the documents that Edward had brought to her from Arborfield.

'These papers will interest you to read', the Duchess told Colonel Couper. 'I found them amongst the *sad* distressing papers I had to go through. I burnt all!' she admitted. 'It was a severe punishment to read them.'[41]

One package had the following statement written in Sir John's hand on the outside: 'When the papers are delivered they will show H.R.H. how faithfully I have served her to the last.'

Carefully Colonel Couper studied the contents. All the old arguments of service and sacrifice lay once more before him, and gradually he became aware of the magnitude of Conroy's delusions. The good man's heart filled with pity as he returned the papers to the Duchess: 'Poor Sir John!' he exclaimed.

Few perhaps will summon such as Colonel Couper's compassion to bear on the case. But even if history offers an open verdict, the attraction of Sir John's story lies not simply in the discovery of facts (essential though these be) but in the unfolding drama of character . . . a character that amuses, irritates, angers and amazes. As with the Duchess, it is this we must come to accept – or make what judgement we will.

EPILOGUE

On 22nd January 1901 the great bell of Christ Church tolled across the hushed City of Oxford. No cheering crowds of students thronged the streets as they had seventy years before, to see the young Princess pass by: only aimless, silent groups wandered in the gloom. For the curtain had been drawn for ever across the Victorian Age.

Queen Victoria had survived the entire Conroy family by scarcely one month. Indeed, the last of the Conroys – the Third Baronet Sir John Conroy – had died of pneumonia the previous December, 1900, in Rome.

Oxford had been his home. The little boy who had played tin soldiers with Princess Sophia had inherited from the Rosse family scientific gifts of a high order; and it was following his mother Alicia's death in 1885, that, as a Fellow and Tutor in Natural Science, he had settled in to his rooms at Balliol College – a much-loved University man; an assiduous worker for the High Church, and an indefatigable letter-writer.

His correspondence, however, would have surprised his colleagues – for it was dominated by the unorthodox affairs of his strange Conroy inheritance. And few have been more tried by the behaviour of their father, or by the baleful inanities of relatives and in-laws, than had the Third Baronet.

In fact, Lord Wellesley had almost certainly been right

when he described Edward Conroy to Colonel Couper as an 'immoral' man. Among the boxes that the Third Baronet stored at Balliol was a bundle of letters (*c*.1847) from Edward to a certain 'Mary'. The nature of their relationship – with its clandestine meetings at Arborfield and punting trips on the river – was painfully clear.[1] Shortly afterwards Alicia left Edward and, taking her child with her, went to live on another part of the Estate, at Arborfield Cottage.

It was some years later that Edward's 'adopted' daughter Emily appeared on the scene, when she married her cousin, Augustus Ayshford Conroy, the eldest grandson of Sir John's brother, Llewellin. The marriage may have been enforced ('Augustus C. told me *she* lead him astray,' commented Henry wearily) but even at this stage her parentage was uncertain.

'Poor child', related Edward, in his deathbed confessions, 'she is no daughter of mine, but I adopted her & educated her when she was a child.'[2]

In truth, however, Emily was almost certainly the off-spring of Edward and Mary Russell, the daughter of Sir Henry Russell Bt of neighbouring Swallowfield.[3] Nevertheless, the Conroy family remained unsure: 'Surmises now are useless about Mrs E. Good [as Emily had become] – I hazarded a great many various ones to you before – ' declared Henry to his nephew, John, in 1880.[4]

Emily herself descended into a life of such pathetic dishevelment as might have been depicted in an illustration by 'Phiz'. Her marriage to Augustus having come to nothing, she married a Mr Good, who fathered too many children, and was clearly no good at all. In 1883 John was summoned to her bedside ('go for the day, don't *sleep*', warned the Duke of Northumberland) where he discovered 'a hideous little peasant girl' whom he clearly found impossible to accept as a relative (informing her she was but the daughter of a village woman).

At this, Emily rose to the full height of her tattered dignity: '*I do not believe* it', she declared, '– as I should not have been brought up as the daughter of your father if such had been the case . . . It would make your father seem and be a dreadful liar and I should think', she added darkly, 'you would rather let his memory rest with a great many other things not known in the world . . .'[5]

Undaunted, the Third Baronet continued to give Emily the £200 a year Willed to her by his father. (The eventual success and sale of the lead mines of Llanbrynmair had made the Conroys rich.) For having spent his final years 'in very hot rooms', Edward had died – a victim of the Fisher tuberculosis.

On his death-bed Edward had attempted to be reconciled with his wife, Alicia: 'Oh,' he lamented to his son, 'if your mother had only forgiven my foolish flirtation in 1847 & been kind & not driven me from her by coldness, all would have come right . . .'[6] But it was not to be. Alicia wrote kindly to him in his final illness, but the pair never met again.

Edward's sister Elizabeth Jane had not long survived her father's death; she too died of tuberculosis in 1855. Her mother, Lady Conroy – still battling with her neuralgias – lived on amongst the mementoes of the past until 1864; surviving her old friend the Duchess of Kent by only three years. Indeed, it was said that on hearing of the death of the Duchess 'she fell fainting to the ground, and was ill for many days'.[7]

But at last all the Conroys were taken to their rest under the yew trees in Arborfield church yard, and only the Third Baronet and his uncle Henry remained.

If, however, the new Sir John Conroy had hoped he would be left in peace to organise Jowett's Mastership elections, correspond with Cardinal Newman or potter about his laboratory at Balliol, he was to find that his Conroy past did not allow of such an easy escape.

Sir John's attitude to his grandfather was clearly the balanced outlook of an educated man. It is unlikely he was fooled by Conroy's behaviour, although it is certain that he took a more lenient view of his character than later evidence has admitted. 'I know but little of those events which took place in the year 1820 to 1840 but I know enough to have a very decided and [firm?] view on this point . . .' he wrote to Frances Conroy in 1893, when once again the subject of a biography of Sir John Conroy had emerged.[8]

In fact, the Conroys' royal connections had never been entirely severed. Frances Conroy, the simple-minded second wife of Henry Conroy, had remained dazzled by her splendid in-laws, but harassed by their impecuniousness. On his death in 1890 Henry had left his wife without the 'very means of *existence*'. (A plea from Frances to Edward in 1868 had met with a total rebuff.) The Queen generously granted Frances a new pension of £150 – a portion of that which she had been making to Henry. Sir John augmented this with a further £100 a year.[9] Such was Frances's gratitude that she had allowed herself a confession that certainly raised the eyebrows of the Third Baronet.

In 1875 the publication of *The Greville Memoirs*, edited by Henry Reeve, caused an anxious stir in the Conroy households ('Let us all keep diaries!' growled Henry defensively). Even the Baronet confessed he 'looked in to it with some anxiety' – but finding nothing alarming concluded 'there would have been more about Sir J had the diaries been published in full. Greville apparently wrote down all the gossip & how disagreeable to us much of that gossip would be we both know – and to feel that it was gossip and not fact, would not be much comfort!!'[10]

Henry, however, had brooded so much over Greville's spite and innuendo that his wife suggested he should write down his own version of events: '– it would be useless', sighed Henry, '– he would only receive a snub.'

It was in 1875 therefore that Frances Conroy took the bull by the horns. Having heard so much family history over the years ('especially after dinner, during dessert') she felt well-equipped to do the job herself. Down it all went in a blue leather notebook:[11] the Duke of Kent's bestowal of trust; the Cumberland poisoning; the 'turning back' of Prince Albert; the Flora Hastings Affair . . . 'for I am sure the *truth* must always prevail, if properly told'.

She then wrote to Victoria's Lady-in-Waiting, Lady Ely, to ask permission to send her account to the Queen. A 'stiff' reply directed her to Sir Theodore Martin (Prince Albert's official biographer). Sir Theodore replied that it was 'extremely "interesting" and shortly after this', related Mrs Conroy, 'I received letters from Lady E. couched in such a different strain, it was impossible not to see the papers had been read & had created a passable impression'.[12] It was because of this, so Frances claimed, that she had requested and received a pension from the Queen.

The Third Baronet was less credulous: 'I was, I own, a good deal surprised when you told me [at] Connaught St about the statements sent to Lady Ely in 1875 – I said nothing as there was obviously no use in discussing past events, when the discussion could lead to no practical conclusion.'[13]

If the Baronet had sensed with unease the probable reception of the leather note book he had been right: 'The Queen has finished Mrs H Conroy's "sketch"', announced Victoria angrily, 'but it cost her an immense *effort to* force her self to read a tissue of lies . . .'

Across the passage of forty years her thoughts had flown to Ramsgate and Lehzen; the '*awful* scenes in the house'; the '*determination* of Sir John to lock the Queen up if [s]he did *not* take Sir John as her P. Sec'.

'It is with indignation The Queen has read this . . . full of *misrepresentations utter falsehoods* Mrs C. has *raked up things* she hoped were buried for ever.'[14]

The innocent Mrs C. remained in blissful ignorance of the royal indignation. She believed her account was true and that the truth had prevailed. Alas, for Mrs Conroy the truth was more subtle, complicated and illusive than either she or Victoria could have been capable of grasping. In fact, an educated scrutiny of the notebook now reveals some verifiable truth: the rest exhibits those familiar fantasies that had enveloped Conroy's entire career.

'– The Queen knows *all*', Victoria pronounced confidently as she closed Mrs Conroy's notebook.

But even a Queen cannot claim omniscience; that is for the future alone to assume. Indeed, perhaps all any of us can know is how best to respond to others as their behaviour affects ourselves. If we judge that to be unacceptable we must take what action we can.

Today Arborfield Old Church stands a ruin. Sheep crop the grass surrounding the tombs and shelter under the yew-trees in the churchyard. Here, beneath the stones in the roofless Conroy chapel lie the unmarked graves of the Conroy family ('the only members for centuries buried out of Ireland'). No monument now survives to tell where they rest or who they were in life.

Yet as late as the early 1960s the curious passerby could find in place the armorial bearings and monumental slabs that since have disappeared.[15] Here was a tablet to Sir Edward Conroy Bt, 'the lineal representative of the chiefs of the native Irish sept of O'Malconroy. Co: Roscommon in the Province of Connaught'; another commemorated his mother, Elizabeth, 'wife of Sir John Conroy . . . born 1791 in the Government House in Quebec . . .'

A further plaque had told the beginning of an intriguing story: that in the family vault in the churchyard lay the remains of a Knight and Baronet Sir John Conroy, who was 'created a Knight Commander of Hanover by George IV and received many other distinguished honours for his long and faithful services to their Royal Highnesses the Duke and Duchess of Kent and to the Princess Victoria, who on her accession to the throne created him a baron, with a promise to create him a peer of Ireland as soon as the state of the peerage of that kingdom would permit.'

Yet one other memorial, long since carried away, bore a variation of the Conroy family motto: a declaration that perhaps any biographer might half hope to be true:

'History once written in the book cannot be destroyed by Time.'

NOTES

[See page 236 for List of Principal Sources]

Prologue (pp. *1–5*)

1 *Jackson's Oxford Journal*, Saturday 10th November 1832.
2 RA Queen Victoria's Journal, 8th November 1832.
3 *Jackson's Oxford Journal*, Saturday 10th November 1832.
4 CP 14B+ 'A Literal translation of An Oration Spoken in the Sheldonian Theatre by Joseph Phillimore Regius Professor of Civil Law on the occasion of Sir John Conroy being made an Hon. DCL.'
5 RA Queen Victoria's Journal, 8th November 1832.
6 RA M7/44 Prince Leiningen to Princess Victoria, 10th June 1837.

1: Snakes in the Grass (pp. *7–21*)

1 Hanmer Papers Charlotte Hanmer's 'Diary'.
2 CP 13 Edward Conroy's family history.
3 CP 14A 'Edward Conroy's Notes from questions to Sir J.C. in 1838'.
4 CP 7A Prologue for a play, by John Conroy.
5 RA Z 485/6 Mrs Frances Conroy's Memorandum.
6 CP Add. Mss. Princess Feodora to Captain Conroy, 18th December *c.*1825.

7 *The Journal of Mrs Arbuthnot*, Vol. 1, 6th May 1828.
8 RA Z 294 Journal of the Duchess of Kent.
9 RA Queen Victoria's Journal, 26th February 1836.
10 Coutts Archives Sir John Conroy's Account 1825.
11 Drummond's Archives Princess Sophia's Account 1825.
12 CP 3 E.C. Statement 31st December 1875, Sir John Conroy 3rd Baronet.
13 RA Queen Victoria's Journal, 21st January 1839.
14 CP 3 E.C. Statement. 31st December 1875. Sir John Conroy 3rd Baronet.
15 RA Add. 0/57c p 8 Duchess of Kent's Accounts, Ledger 1826–29.
16 CP 6B Lady Conroy to Sir Edward Conroy, 14th April 1854.
17 RA Z 484/36 Sir George Couper's Memorandum, 18th February 1854.
18 CP 14B+ Duchess of Kent to Conroy pencilled note, 26th December 1838.
19 RA Z 484/36 Sir George Couper's Memorandum, 25th February 1854.
20 RA Z 484/36 Sir George Couper's Memorandum, 25th February 1854.

21 CP 10 Sir John Conroy to Edward Conroy, 9th [March 1848].

22 RA M4/1 Captain Conroy to the Duchess of Kent, 14th July 1826.

23 Hanmer Papers Answers to a questionnaire (Conroy).

24 RA Y / 203/80.

25 Hanmer Papers Charlotte Hanmer's papers.

26 RA Y/99/9 Queen Victoria to the King of the Belgians.

27 RA Y/172 19th October 1878.

2: 'A Disgrace to the Honour' (pp. 22–37)

1 RA Y 155/1 Baron Ernest Stockmar to Queen Victoria, 20th January 1871. RA Y 155/2 Memorandum of Sir Thomas Biddulph, 24th January 1871. RA Y 155/3 Queen Victoria to the Crown Princess of Prussia, 10th July 1872.

2 CP 1 CE Sir John Conroy, 3rd Baronet to Mrs Frances Conroy, 13th June 1893.

3 Burke's Peerage.

4 CP 9A.

5 CP 13 Edward Conroy's family history.

6 Ibid.

7 Ibid.

8 *Tour in Ireland*, Arthur Young (1776–79) London 1892.

9 Land Tax Records. *See also*: Royal Commission on Historic Buildings, Caernarfonshire Inventory, Vol. 1.

10 Caerhun Parish Register.

11 *The Autobiography of Wolfe Tone* 1763–1798. Vol. 1, London 1893.

12 CP 13 Edward Conroy's family history.

13 Ibid.

14 CP 14B+ Memorandum on Fisher family; Edward Conroy.

15 CP 14A Edward Conroy's Notes. R.H.A. List of Officers, p. 32.

16 *The Royal Horse Artillery*. Shelford Bidwell, London 1973.

17 CP 3D9 John Conroy's Diary 1868/9 (Third Baronet).

18 CP 14B+ and 6F Memoranda by Edward Conroy.

19 CP 6F Edward Conroy's Memorandum.

20 Public Archives of Canada, Quebec, Que.: Holy Trinity Anglican Cathedral MG8 G70 Vol. 2, pp. 409 reel C – 2898 and original Baptismal Register, Holy Trinity Anglican Cathedral, Quebec.

21 RA Queen Victoria's Journal, 25th November 1832.

22 PRO: Adm 36/11005 Muster list of Resistance, from *The Prince and His Lady*, M. Gillen.

23 CP 2E.E Duke of Kent to the Duke of Wellington. Amorbach, 4th December 1818.

24 Sir John Conroy 3rd Baronet. Will, Somerset House.

25 CP 14B+ Edward Conroy – Memoranda on Fisher Connection.

26 CP 9A.2. F. Galton 'Record of Family Faculties' as described by Sir John Conroy, Third Baronet.

27 Ibid.

28 RA Z 484.62. The Duchess of Kent to Colonel Couper.

29 CP 7A.2. John Conroy to 'Eliza'.

3: 'An Excellent Pen and Ink Man' (pp. 38–55.)

1 'England in 1819', Percy Bysshe Shelley.

2 *Memoirs of the Court of George IV, 1820–30.* Vol. 1. Duke of Buckingham and Chandos. Mr W.H. Fremantle to the Marquis of Buckingham, 16th June 1821.

3 RA Z484/55 Colonel Couper to the Duchess of Kent.

4 RA Geo Addl. MS 51134–5/6 27th August 1824

5 CP 14A Edward Conroy's 'Notes from questions to Sir J.C. in 1838'.

6 CP 2E.E. Sir John Conroy's Military Career papers.

7 Archdeacon Fisher to John Constable. *John Constable and The*

Fishers, R.B. Beckett, Suffolk Records Society.

8 *Letters of George IV* 1812–30 Vol. I. Bishop of Salisbury to Unknown Correspondent, 10th October 1814. Letter 492.

9 CP 13 Edward Conroy's family history.

10 CP 2E.E. Lt Col Chapman Secretary to Maj. Gen. Lord Mulgrave.

11 CP 14B+ Edward Conroy's Memorandum.

12 RA 51136 Captain Conroy to Sir William Knighton, 1824.

13 CP 2E.E. Duke of Kent to Sir George Beckwith, 18th October 1816.

14 CP 2E.E. Lt. Col. Maclean to Captain Conroy, 23rd July 1818.

15 CP 2E.E. Lt. Col. Jenkinson.

16 RA Y63/47 King Leopold to Victoria, 1837.

17 CP 14B+ Edward Conroy's Memorandum.

18 RA Z484/40 Duchess of Kent to Queen Victoria, 2nd March 1854.

19 CP Duchess of Kent to Mrs Conroy, 15th October 1819.

20 Hanmer Papers The Duchess of Kent to Elizabeth Jane Conroy, 27th March 1841.

21 *Letters of George IV* 1812–30 Vol. II Duke of Cumberland to the Prince Regent. Berlin, 4th February 1820. Letter 790.

22 Ibid.

23 CP 6F.

24 RA Z485/6 Mrs Frances Conroy's Memorandum.

25 RA M7/47 Duchess of Kent to Queen Victoria.

26 RA Y/65/37 King Leopold of the Belgians to Queen Victoria, 12th March 1839.

27 BM Add. Ms. 38286 2nd Lord Liverpool, 30th June 1820.

28 RA Add. MSS 15/1127 Captain Conroy to General Wetherall, 3rd February 1820.

29 RA M3/36 18th April 1821.

30 RA M7/67 (trans Add V/II).

31 RA M3/39 Duchess of Kent to Lord Grey.

32 Wellington Papers 1/949/16 Duchess of Kent to Duke of Wellington, 28th August 1828.

33 RA Y 82/113 King Leopold of the Belgians to Queen Victoria, 12th April 1861.

34 RA M3/37 Stockmar to Captain Conroy, 20th May 1825.

4: The Kensington System (pp 56–70)

1 RA Z 482/1 Sir John Conroy to the Duchess of Kent, 15th July 1837.

2 LP Lord Durham to Conroy, 16th November 1833.

3 RA Account of the Kensington System M7/67 (trans. Add. v/11).

4 Ibid.

5 LP Sir John Conroy to Lord Durham, 27th [September 1834?].

6 Hanmer Papers Answers to questionnaire (Conroy).

7 LP Lord Durham to Sir John Conroy, no date.

8 RA Queen Victoria's Journal, 21st April 1838.

9 RA Z 294 Journal of the Duchess of Kent.

10 *The Journal of Mrs Arbuthnot* 1820–32, 29th May 1829.

11 RA Queen Victoria's Journal, 6th February 1839.

12 *The Journal of Mrs Arbuthnot* 1820–32, 6th May 1829.

13 CP 14B+ Edward Conroy 'Mem. for Memoirs of Sir J.C. respecting the Peerage'.

14 RA M7/47 Duchess of Kent to Baroness Lehzen, 13th June 1837. Transcrip. Trans Hudson and RA M7/46 The Duchess of Kent to Princess Victoria.

15 CP 14B+ Edward Conroy 'Mem. for Memoirs'.

16 CP 14B+ Duchess of Kent to Sir John Conroy, pencilled note 26th December 1838.

17 CP 14B+ Edward Conroy 'Mem. for Memoirs'.

18 RA Y54/89 Anson 24th October 1841.

19 CP 14+ Edward Conroy 'Mem. for Memoirs'.

20 Ibid.

21 CP 2A F Henry Conroy to Sir John Conroy (3rd Baronet), 29th October 1885.

22 CP 14B+ Edward Conroy 'Mem. for Memoirs'.

23 RA Z 485/6 Mrs Frances Conroy's Memorandum.

24 RA M7/47 Duchess of Kent to Baroness Lehzen, 13th June 1837. Transcrip. transl. Hudson.

25 Peel Papers BM Add. MSS 40385.238 Stephen to Hamilton. Petition.

26 Peel Papers BM Add. MSS 40380.142 Robert Peel to Captain Conroy, 19th July 1825.

27 Peel Papers BM Add. MSS 40380.144 Captain Conroy to Robert Peel, 19th July 1825.

28 Peel Papers BM Add. MSS 40385.221 Stephen to Duchess of Kent, 13th February 1826.

29 Peel Papers BM Add. MSS 40385.223 Robert Peel to Captain Conroy, 17th February 1826.

30 Peel Papers BM Add. MSS 40385.237 A. Hamilton, 16th February 1826.

31 Peel Papers BM Add. MSS 40385.235 Captain Conroy to Robert Peel, 18th February 1826.

32 RA M4/1 Captain Conroy to Duchess of Kent, 14th July 1826.

33 Letters Vol. 1, pp. 14–18, 24 RA Y 36/28 Princess Feodora to Queen Victoria, 17th March 1843.

5: 'It was one Family' (pp. 71–87)

1 RA Z485/6 Mrs Frances Conroy's Memorandum.

2 RA Queen Victoria's Journal, 24th December 1832.

3 RA Queen Victoria's Journal, 6th December 1832.

4 RA Queen Victoria's Journal, 28th November 1832.

5 CP 6. F Edward Conroy's Memorandum 'Hints and Memos'.

6 RA M7/48 Baroness Lehzen to the Duchess of Kent, 13th June 1837 (trans Hudson).

7 RA Queen Victoria's Journal, 3rd February 1838.

8 CP 14B+ Edward Conroy 'Mem. for Memoirs'.

9 RA M7/47 Duchess of Kent to Baroness Lehzen, 13th June 1837 (trans Hudson).

10 RA M4/16 Duchess of Clarence to Duchess of Kent, 12th January 1830 (trans Hudson).

11 RA Queen Victoria's Journal, 21st January 1839.

12 RA Queen Victoria's Journal, 27th February 1839.

13 CP 2E. G. Sir John Conroy to Edward Conroy, Rome, 17th December 1839.

14 LP Duchess of Kent to Lord Durham, 7th March 1832.

15 RA Z482/1 Sir John Conroy to the Duchess of Kent, 15th July 1837.

16 RA M4/20 Duchess of Kent to the Duke of Wellington, 27th June 1830.

17 RA M4/22 Duchess of Kent to the Duke of Wellington, 27th June 1830.

18 RA Z482/26 Duplicate of Vol. 481 Nos. 2 and 3. Memorandum by Sir John Conroy on the Duchess's Financial position etc. (see also Conroy Papers), April 1837. Add. Mss

19 Central Literary Magazine Vol. 15, 1901. 'Queen Victoria and Birmingham', Birmingham Public Library (Aris's Birmingham Gazette, 9th August 1830).

20 Ibid.

21 RA Add.U171/22 28th August 1830.

22 The Statutes at Large. Regency Act. I Will IV C2.

23 RA M7/44 Prince Leiningen to Princess Victoria, 10th June 1837.

24 CP 2E.C. Duchess of Kent to Sir John Conroy, 21st October 1830.

25 The Works of Sir Charles Hanbury Williams, 3 Vols. 1822. An Ode to the Honourable Henry Fox.

26 RA   Queen Victoria's Journal, 21st January 1839.

27 CP Add.Mss   Duchess of Kent to Lady Conroy, 2nd April 1829.

28 RA   Queen Victoria's Journal, 30th August 1833.

29 RA M4/19   Memorandum by Princess Sophia to Sir John Conroy, 14th October 1829.

30 CP 2E.G.   Sir John Conroy to Edward Conroy. Rome, 14th December 1839.

31 CP 2A.F.   Henry Conroy to Sir John Conroy (3rd Baronet), 29th October 1885.

32 LP   Sir John Conroy to Lord Durham, 8th September 1831.

33 RA MP Box 116/89 Memorandum by Sir John Conroy, undated.

34 CP 14B+   Edward Conroy 'Mem. for Memoirs' and Royal Archives Household Index, 'Miss Martha Wilson'.

35 RA   Queen Victoria's Journal, 16th March 1838.

36 Hanmer Papers   Answers to a questionnaire (Conroy).

37 RA   Queen Victoria's Journal, 17th June 1838.

38 Hanmer Papers   Answers to a questionnaire (Conroy).

39 CP 6B   Sir Edward Conroy to Lady Conroy, 14th April 1854.

40 CP 6.1.   Poem to Victoire and Jane by Edward Conroy, 1836.

41 RA PP1/58/56.

6: *'Victoria – Pride of our Land!'* (pp. 88–107)

1 RA M7/44   Prince Leiningen to Princess Victoria, 10th June 1837.

2 RA   Queen Victoria's Journal, 25th September 1835.

3 LP   Lord Durham to Sir John Conroy, no date.

4 RA 1837 MP Box 116/93   Sir John Conroy to Lord Melbourne, 9th August 1837.

5 Princess Lieven to Earl Grey, 3rd March 1831. Correspondence of

Princess Lieven and Earl Grey, ed Guy le Strange, 1890.

6 RA M7/47   Duchess of Kent to Baroness Lehzen, 13th June 1837.

7 LP   Sir John Conroy to Lord Durham, 20th June 1832.

8 LP   Sir John Conroy to Lord Durham, 30th May 1833.

9 LP   Sir John Conroy to Lord Durham, 21st July 1836.

10 RA M4/28   The Duchess of Kent to Lord Grey. Copied in pencil by Sir John Conroy.

11 RA M4/37   Memorandum from Sir John Conroy to the Duchess of Kent.

12 LP   Sir John Conroy to Lord Durham, 8th September 1831.

13 RA M4/40   King William IV to Lord Grey.

14 The Creevey Papers, 23rd September 1831.

15 LP   Sir John Conroy to Lord Durham, 8th September 1831.

16 LP   Sir John Conroy to Lord Durham, 13th October 1832.

17 RA Y/63/63   King of the Belgians to Queen Victoria, 19th August 1837.

18 CP 14BA (b)5 Dowager Marchioness of Hastings to Sir John Conroy, 2nd January 1839.

19 RA   Queen Victoria's Journal, 18th April 1838.

20 CP 14BA (a) 4 Lady Flora Hastings to Sir John Conroy, October 1837.

21 RA Add U72/15   Princess Feodora to the Duchess of Northumberland, 25th March 1835.

22 LP   Sir John Conroy to Lord Durham, 9th October 1833.

23 LP   Sir John Conroy to Lord Durham, no date.

24 RA Add. Mss C 17/26   Orders, accounts, etc. of Nathaniel Date.

25 LP   Sir John Conroy to Lord Durham, no date.

26 RA M5/84   Duchess of Kent to Princess Victoria, 2nd September 1835.

27 RA Y 63/41   King Leopold of the Belgians to Princess Victoria.

28 LP Sir John Conroy to Lord Durham, 11th April 1836.

29 RA M7/42 Baron Stockmar to the Duchess of Kent (trans Hudson).

30 RA Queen Victoria's Journal, 21st April 1838.

31 RA Queen Victoria's Journal, 10th July 1838.

32 LP Sir John Conroy to Lord Durham, 9th December 1835.

33 RA A11/22 Lehzen to King Leopold (n.d. trans).

34 RA Y79/35 King Leopold of the Belgians to Queen Victoria, 9th March 1854.

35 Ibid.

36 Ibid.

37 RA Queen Victoria's Journal, 4th October 1835.

38 RA Add Mss A/11/22 Baroness Lehzen to King Leopold of the Belgians.

39 RA Queen Victoria's Journal, 21st January 1839.

40 RA Queen Victoria's Journal, 26th February 1838.

41 LP Sir John Conroy to Lord Durham, 9th December 1835.

7: 'A Crowd of Princes'
(pp. 108–23)

1 Panshanger Mss Box 9 William Lamb (later Viscount Melbourne) to Caroline Lamb, 9th October 1827. From *Melbourne* by Philip Ziegler.

2 Lord Palmerston to Baron Stockmar, 18th December 1835, p. 360. From *The Memoirs of Baron Stockmar* by Baron E. von Stockmar.

3 RA M47/30 Memorandum (Sir John Conroy), 22nd January 1836.

4 RA M47/16 Duchess of Kent to Lord Melbourne, 8th January 1836.

5 RA M47/30 Memorandum (Sir John Conroy), 22nd January 1836.

6 LP Sir John Conroy to Lord Durham, 11th April 1836.

7 *The Lieven – Palmerston Correspondence* 1828–56. Princess Lieven to Lady Cowper. Paris, 14th March 1836.

8 CP Box 6 D & E Lord Palmerston to Sir John Conroy, 2nd May 1836.

9 CP Box 6E Prince Leiningen to Sir John Conroy, 13th March 1835 (?).

10 CP Box 6E Prince Leiningen to Sir John Conroy, 4th February 1835 (?).

11 CP Box 6 D & E Lord Beresford to Duchess of Kent, 29th October 1829.

12 CP Box 6 D & E Dietz to the Duchess of Kent, 8th January 1838.

13 CP Box 6 D & E.

14 RA Y/82/113 The King of the Belgians to Queen Victoria, 12th April 1861.

15 RA MP Box 116/89 Memorandum (Sir John Conroy).

16 LP Sir John Conroy to Lord Durham, 6th February 1836.

17 RA Queen Victoria's Journal, 18th April 1839.

18 CP Box 6E Prince Leiningen to Sir John Conroy, 13th March 1835 (?).

19 *The Memoirs of Baron Stockmar* by Baron E. von Stockmar, pp. 371–2.

20 RA Queen Victoria's Journal, 30–31st December 1838.

21 RA CFP M4/49 Duchess of Kent to Lord Palmerston, 12th May 1836.

22 Ibid.

23 RA M4/50 Lord Palmerston to the Duchess of Kent, 13th May 1836.

24 RA M4/50 Lord Palmerston to the Duchess of Kent, 13th May 1836.

25 RA M4/54 Lord Palmerston to Sir John Conroy, 13th May 1836.

26 *The Letters of Queen Victoria*, Vol. I. The King of the Belgians to the Princess Victoria, 13th May 1836.

27 RA Y 88/11 Princess Victoria to King Leopold, 17th May 1836.

28 BM Add Mss 41.777 Smart Papers Sir John Conroy to Sir George Smart, ff 88–104.

29 RA Queen Victoria's Journal, 8th June 1836.

30 RA 88/15 Princess Victoria to King Leopold, 7th June 1836.

31 LP Sir John Conroy to Lord Durham, 21st July 1836.

32 RA M7/67   trans 1840.

33 RA M4/41   Sir John Conroy to Master General of the Ordnance.

34 LP   Sir John Conroy to Lord Durham, 21st July 1836.

35 LP   Sir John Conroy to Lord Durham, 9th October 1833.

36 *The Greville Memoirs*, Vol III, Ch XXXI, p. 367.

37 Ibid.

38 LP   Sir John Conroy to Lord Durham, 6th February 1836.

39 BM Add. MS 37.190   Sir John Conroy to Charles Babbage, 12th June 1837.

40 CP Box 14B   Edward Conroy: 'Of a few people who distinguished themselves by either deserting or remaining steady in friendship after the manifestation of the Queen's dislike of Sir John Conroy', 1839.

41 RA M7/67   trans 1840–

42 RA Z485/6   Mrs Frances Conroy's Memorandum.

43 RA M7/67   trans 1840–

44 Ibid.

45 Ibid.

46 RA Y 63/41   King Leopold to Princess Victoria, 25th May 1837.

47 Ibid.

48 RA M7/21/23/24   Duchess of Kent to Melbourne, 20th May 1837; Melbourne to Duchess of Kent and her reply, 21st May 1837.

49 RA   Queen Victoria's Journal, 24th April 1838.

50 RA   Queen Victoria's Journal, 5th November 1838.

51 RA   Queen Victoria's Journal, 24th June 1839.

52 RA   Queen Victoria's Journal, 1st August 1838.

53 RA M7/13   6th June 1837.

54 RA M7/15   Memorandum by Lehzen n.d.

8: 'Born and Bred a Briton' (pp. 124–39)

1 Conroy Papers 10.4   Account of elopement of Edward Conroy and Lady Alicia Parsons, 1837.

2 RA PP1/80/8   Sir Charles Phipps to Sir George Grey, 27th January 1863.

3 CP 7A.2   Edward Conroy to Sir John Conroy, 8th June 1837.

4 *The Greville Memoirs* Vol III, 2nd June 1837.

5 Minutes of the Proceedings of the Court of Common Council No. 13, 2nd June 1837. Records Office, Corporation of London.

6 Ibid.

7 CP 2A-F   Henry Conroy to Sir John Conroy (Third Baronet), 29th October 1885.

8 RA   Queen Victoria's Journal, 28th February 1839.

9 RA   Queen Victoria's Journal, 24th June 1839.

10 RA Add A11/18   Memorandum Lord Liverpool, 17th June 1837.

11 RA M7/47   Duchess of Kent to Baroness Lehzen, 13th June 1837 (trans Hudson).

12 RA M7/48   Baroness Lehzen to the Duchess of Kent, 13th June 1837 (trans Hudson).

13 RA Z294   Journal of the Duchess of Kent, 20th June 1837.

14 RA MP Box 116/88   Baron Stockmar to Viscount Melbourne, 18th July 1837.

15 RA Add A 11/26   Baron Stockmar to King Leopold of the Belgians, 24th June 1837.

16 CP 14B +   Mem. for Memoirs.

17 RA MP Box 116/89   Memorandum (Sir John Conroy).

18 RA MP Box 116/88   Baron Stockmar to Viscount Melbourne.

19 RA M 7/68   Memorandum by Stockmar, 28th October 1847.

20 RA M7/60   Memorandum Queen Victoria, 20th June 1837.

21 CP 14B   Baron Stockmar to Sir John Conroy, 11th July 1837.

22 Peel Papers BM Add. MSS 40545/305   Sir John Conroy to Sir Robert Peel, 10th June 1844.

23 RA Add A 11/23   Sir John Conroy to Baron Stockmar, 23rd June 1837.

24 Union with Ireland Act 1800 Article 4.

25 RA MP Box 116/91 Viscount Melbourne to the Duchess of Kent, 20th July 1837.

26 RA Z482/1 Sir John Conroy to the Duchess of Kent, 15th July 1837.

27 RA MP Box 116/84 Sir John Conroy to Viscount Melbourne, 8th July 1837.

28 RA MP Box 116/85 Viscount Melbourne to Sir John Conroy, 9th July 1837.

29 RA Z 482/1 Sir John Conroy to the Duchess of Kent, 15th July 1837.

30 RA MP Box 116/88 Baron Stockmar to Viscount Melbourne, 18th July 1837.

31 RA Queen Victoria's Journal, 20th June 1837.

32 LP Sir John Conroy to the Earl of Durham, 19th [July] 1837.

33 CP 14B A (a) 4. Lady Flora Hastings to Sir John Conroy, October 1837.

34 RA MP Box 116/93 Sir John Conroy to Viscount Melbourne, 9th August 1837.

35 RA Y 154/29 Lord Liverpool to Baron Stockmar, 30th July 1837.

36 RA Queen Victoria's Journal, 8th July 1837.

37 RA M7/65 Pencil 'slip' from Duchess of Kent to Queen Victoria.

38 *The Times*, 22nd June 1837.

39 Additional Conroy Papers and RAZ482/26 'The Duchess of Kent's Situation', Sir John Conroy's Memorandum, April 1837.

40 King Henry VIII Act V. Sc. V. (Conroy's own quotation used).

9: *'Monster and Demon Incarnate'* (pp. 140–58)

1 RA Queen Victoria's Journal, 29th October 1837.

2 CP Box 14B 'Slip' Duchess of Kent to Sir John Conroy, 26th December 1838.

3 CP Box 14B+ Edward Conroy. 'Mem. for Memoirs – of Sir J.C.

respecting the Peerage'.

4 RA M7/65 Duchess of Kent to Queen Victoria.

5 RA Y 154/36 Lord Liverpool to Baron Stockmar, 8th June 1838.

6 RA Add U/62 Dr Allen's Journal.

7 CP 9A.10 'History of Llanbrynmair Estate' by Edward Conroy.

8 Drummond's Archives. Princess Sophia's Account 1835.

9 RA Z482/3 Duchess of Kent to Queen Victoria.

10 RA Y/64/9 King Leopold of the Belgians to Queen Victoria, 22nd October 1837.

11 RA MP Box 116/95 Lord Duncannon to Lord Melbourne, 11th December 1937.

12 RA Queen Victoria's Journal, 20th May 1839.

13 CP 2E.G. Sir John Conroy to Edward Conroy, 13th January 1840.

14 RA MP Box 116/101 The Duchess of Kent to Lord Melbourne, 22nd April 1838.

15 CP 2E.G. Sir John Conroy to Edward Conroy, 17th December 1839.

16 RA Z484/36 Sir George Couper's Memorandum.

17 RA Correspondence 18th February 1982 Mrs P. Bateman and the Registrar's reply.

18 CP 2E.G. Sir John Conroy to Edward Conroy, 15th October 1839.

19 CP Additional MS Duchess of Kent to Sir John Conroy, 25th November 1837.

20 *The Times*, 9th March 1838 – quoted from *The Times*, 10th May 1838. Court of Queen's Bench. The Queen versus Lawson.

21 RA Y 154/39 Lord Liverpool to Baron Stockmar, 16th May 1838.

22 RA Queen Victoria's Journal, 9th March 1838.

23 CP 6.

24 Hanmer Papers Answers to a questionnaire (Conroy).

25 RA Queen Victoria's Journal, 14th March 1838.

26 CP 2E.L. Affidavit of Sir John Conroy, 1838.

27 RA Queen Victoria's Journal, 22nd June 1838.

28 CP 14BA(a) 10 Basil Hall to Sir John Conroy, 1838.

29 CP 10.10 Schedule of deeds, Llanbrynmair Estate.

30 CP 14BA (b) 8. Edward Conroy to the Common Sergeant Mirehouse (copy).

31 Hanmer Papers Answers to a questionnaire (Conroy).

32 RA Queen Victoria's Journal, 22nd December 1838.

33 RA Queen Victoria's Journal, 24th April 1838.

34 CP 14BA(a) 4. Lady Flora Hastings to Sir John Conroy, October 1837.

35 Hanmer Papers Answers to a questionnaire (Conroy).

36 CP 148 A(a) 5 Dowager Marchioness of Hastings to Sir John Conroy, 2nd January 1839.

37 RA Queen Victoria's Journal, 2nd February 1839.

38 RA Queen Victoria's Journal, 18th January 1839.

39 CP 2C A–C Letter from Lady Flora Hastings to her family, 6th April 1839. From 'The Late Lady Flora Hastings. Statements of the Marquis of Hastings, Marchioness of Tavistock, Lady Portman, Lord Portman and Sir James Clark,' London 1839.

40 Hanmer Papers Answers to a questionnaire (Conroy).

41 RA Queen Victoria's Journal, 21st February 1839.

42 CP 2C A–C Statements.

43 RA Addl. /MS 81 Baron Stockmar to Lord Liverpool, 14th March 1838.

44 CP 2C A–C Statements.

45 RA Queen Victoria's Journal, 21st February 1839.

46 CP 2C A–C The Dangers of Evil Council. A voice from the grave of Lady Flora Hastings to Her Most Gracious Majesty The Queen, London 23rd September 1839.

47 Hanmer Papers Answers to a questionnaire (Conroy).

48 CP 2C – Residue A & B Letter from Lord Hastings, 21st March. Reproduced in various newspapers.

49 RA Z 486/36. Queen Victoria to Duchess of Kent, undated.

50 RA Z486/7 Queen Victoria to Duchess of Kent, 23rd February 1839.

51 RA Z486/8 Queen Victoria to Lady Portman, 23rd February 1839.

52 RA Queen Victoria's Journal, 4th April 1839.

53 CP 2C A–C Statements.

54 RA Queen Victoria's Journal, 15th April 1839.

55 RA M7/68 Baron Stockmar's Memorandum on the Flora Hastings Affair, 1847.

56 CP 2C A–C Lord Byron, Mazeppa. Stanza 10 found in vol. of *Morning Post* cuttings on the Flora Hastings Affair.

10: 'A Pont d'Or' (pp. 159–70)

1 RA MP Box 116/102 Minute of a Conversation of HRH the reigning Duke of Coburg, with HG the Duke of Wellington 1838.

2 RA Z 483/2 17th May 1839.

3 CP 14B A (a)1 J. Abercromby (Lord Dunfermline) to Sir John Conroy, 25th May 1839.

4 CP 14B A (a)1 Sir John Conroy to the Duchess of Kent, 1st June 1839. Also in RA and Hanmer MS.

5 RA Queen Victoria's Journal, 7th June 1839.

6 RA Queen Victoria's Journal, 9th June 1839.

7 CP 14B A (a)1 Duke of Wellington to Sir John Conroy, 5th June 1839.

8 CP 14B A (a)1 Sir John Conroy to the Duke of Wellington, 5th June 1839 (original in Wellington MS. Strathfield Saye).

9 RA Z483/9A Duke of Wellington to Lord Liverpool, 6th July 1839.

10 RA Queen Victoria's Journal, 2nd June 1839.

11 CP 2E.G. Sir John Conroy to Edward Conroy from Pisa, 15th October 1839.

12 CP 2E N1 Copy of an address to Sir John Conroy by a Deputation of Tradesmen, 12th April 1838.

13 CP 2 E N1 Sir John's reply to above.

14 CP 14B A (a)1 Duchess of Kent to Sir John Conroy, 10th June 1839.

15 CP 14B A (a)2 Extract (contemporary) Sir John Conroy to unknown correspondent, 12th June 1839.

16 CP 2 C John Thompson to the Duchess of Kent, 15th April 1839.

17 RA Queen Victoria's Journal, 7th May 1839.

18 RA M7/47 Duchess of Kent to Baroness Lehzen, 13th June 1837.

19 RA Queen Victoria's Journal, 2nd February 1840.

20 Poems by the Lady Flora Hastings edited by her sister, Blackwood & Sons, 1841.

21 Hastings Papers HA 4976 Henry E. Huntington Library. Lady Loudon to the Duchess of Kent, 22nd June 1839.

22 Hastings Papers HA 4978 Henry E. Huntington Library. Lady Loudon to the Duchess of Kent, 10th July 1839.

23 RA Queen Victoria's Journal, 27th June 1839.

24 RA Queen Victoria's Journal, 6th July 1839.

25 Hanmer Papers Lady Flora Hastings to Elizabeth Jane Conroy, no date.

26 Hanmer Papers Lady Flora Hastings to Elizabeth Jane Conroy, no date.

27 RA Y 54/20 Prince Albert in an interview with the Duchess of Kent, 26th April 1841.

28 RA Y 36/40 Letter from Princess Feodora to Queen Victoria 23rd June 1841.

29 RA MP Melbourne to Lord John Russell 13th October 1839.

11: *An Expensive Whistle* (pp. 171–82)

1 CP 2 E.G. Sir John Conroy to Edward Conroy. Rome, 4th January 1840.

2 Private Collection of Fisher family letters. Mary Fisher and Mary Harley to Osmond Fisher, 18th August 1836.

3 *The Lieven – Palmerston Correspondence* 1828–56. Princess Lieven to Lady Cowper. Baden, 27th July 1839.

4 CP 2 E.G. Sir John Conroy to Edward Conroy. Pisa, 20th September 1839.

5 CP 2 E.G. Sir John Conroy to Edward Conroy. Pisa, 25th September 1839.

6 Hanmer Papers Duchess of Kent to Elizabeth Jane Conroy, 1839.

7 CP 2 E.G. Sir John Conroy to Edward Conroy. Leghorn, 31st October 1839.

8 CP 2 E.G. Sir John Conroy to Edward Conroy. Leghorn, 24th November 1839.

9 CP 2 E.G. Sir John Conroy to Edward Conroy. Rome, 14th December 1839.

10 O'Neill Mss. Bernard O'Neill, a colleague of Sir John Conroy's at Dublin Castle *c*. 1810, applied to Sir John for an appointment and was installed by him as a manager in the Woolwich Arsenal in 1837. Bernard O'Neill and his fifteen children consequently emigrated to England: Bernard's son George Bernard O'Neill became a successful artist in the Victorian 'genre' style; his youngest son, Norman O'Neill, was a well-known composer and conductor. Norman O'Neill's granddaughter is the author of this book.

11 CP 9A 7 1&2 Garth family tree.

12 CP 2 E.G. Sir John Conroy to Edward Conroy. Nice, 21st February 1840.

13 CP 2 E.G. Sir John Conroy to Edward Conroy. Rome, 11th January 1840.

14 CP 2 E.G. Sir John Conroy to

Edward Conroy. Rome, 17th December 1839.

15 CP 14A   Stephen Conroy's Diary, May [1840].

16 Hanmer Papers   Duchess of Kent to Elizabeth Jane Conroy, 1840.

17 CP 3E.C. C.P. 6B / and RA Z484/44   Sir Edward Conroy to the Duchess of Kent, 6th March 1854.

18 RA P.P. 1/58.73   Particulars of the sale of Arborfield, 11th July 1854.

19 CP 2E.B.   Count Mensdorff to the Duchess of Kent, 5th June 1841.

20 CP 2E.B.   Death Certificate of Stephen Conroy, 9th September 1841.

21 Hanmer Papers   The Duchess of Kent to Jane Conroy. Gotha, 3rd August 1841.

22 CP 3E 9   The Third Baronet's Diary 1868/9. Reminiscences of Princess Sophia.

23 RA Z484/44   Sir Edward Conroy to the Duchess of Kent, 6th March 1854.

24 Coutts Archive.

25 CP 6B   Sir Edward Conroy to Lady Conroy, 14th April 1854.

26 Roy Brigden. Institute of Agricultural History and Museum of English Rural Life. Letter to the author, 15th July 1987.

27 CP 9A. 13.2   *The Times*, 14th March 1852.

28 The Old Metal Mines of Mid-Wales, Part 4. West Montgomeryshire, David E. Bick, 1977.

29 *A History of the Parish of Llanbrynmair*, Richard Williams. The Montgomeryshire Collections, Powysland Club, vols 19–23, 1886–9.

30 CP 6.

31 CP 3D. 9   The Third Baronet's Diary. 1868/9 Reminiscences of Sir John Conroy, Third Baronet.

32 CP Further material. f. (Library uncat)   The Royal Agricultural Society of England's Prize medal, 1852.

12: The Viscount of Elphin (pp. 183–93)

1 RA Add U2/2   Prince Albert to Stockmar, 16th January 1842

(translation).

2 Hanmer Papers   Answers to a questionnaire (Conroy).

3 Hanmer Papers   Answers to a questionnaire (Conroy).

4 RA Z483/38   Lord Dunfermline to the Duchess of Kent.

5 CP   Further material B (library uncat.). Albums of newspaper extracts with manuscript notes by Sir John Conroy.

6 CP 2E. C.

7 RA Z 485/6   Mrs Frances Conroy's Memorandum.

8 CP 2. 5.   Statement in Conroy's hand describing peerage.

9 CP Letter Book   Sir John Conroy to Sir Robert Peel, 29th May 1844.

10 CP Letter Book   Sir John Conroy to Prince Albert, 29th May 1844.

11 CP Letter Book   Sir John Conroy to Queen Victoria. *Also*: B. M. Add. Mss. 40545 ff. 289, Peel Papers Sir John Conroy to Queen Victoria.

12 RA Y 54/78   George Anson. Memorandum of conversation with Baron Stockmar, 21st September 1841.

13 RA M7/68   Baron Stockmar's Memorandum, 28th October 1847.

14 RA   Queen Victoria's Journal, 14th March 1839.

15 RA Y 152/1   Baron Stockmar to Queen Victoria, 24th June 1837.

16 RA M7/68   Baron Stockmar's Memorandum (Copy), 28th October 1847.

17 RA Z 484/29   Prince Albert to Lord John Russell, 25th July 1847.

18 Public Records Office. Reg. 2, Folio 271. Sir John Conroy's Will.

19 Hanmer Papers   '"Instruction" to Lady Conroy in consequence of the trust confided to her by Sir John Conroy's Will.' Copy written by Colonel Conroy, 9th March 1854.

20 RA Z484/44 Sir Edward Conroy to the Duchess of Kent, 6th March 1854.

21 CP 7B   Last 'slip' from Sir John Conroy to Edward Conroy.

22 RA Z294   Journal of the

Duchess of Kent, 3rd March 1854.

23 RA Z485/6 Mrs Frances Conroy's Memorandum.

24 RA Y 79/34 King Leopold to Queen Victoria, 5th March 1854.

13: The Reckoning (pp. 194–214)

1 CP 6B. Sir Edward Conroy to Lady Conroy, 14th April 1854.

2 CP 6B Lady Conroy to Sir Edward Conroy, 14th April 1854.

3 RA Z484 / 45 Sir George Couper to the Duchess of Kent (Memorandum).

4 RA Add C/19 Regulations of her Royal Highness's the Duchess of Kent's Household.

5 RA Z 484/ 36 Minute from the Duchess of Kent to Sir George Couper, 15th February 1850.

6 RA Z 484/36 Sir George Couper's Memorandum, 15th February 1850.

7 RA Z484/36 Sir George Couper's Memorandum, 27th February 1850.

8 RA Z485/6 Mrs Frances Conroy's memorandum; Queen Victoria's annotations.

9 RA Y/86/10 King Leopold of the Belgians to Queen Victoria, 16th February 1864.

10 Coutts Bank/ RA Z484/55.

11 RA Z 484/48 Sir George Couper to the Duchess of Kent, 9th March 1854.

12 RA Z 484/36 Sir George Couper's Memorandum, 25th February 1850.

13 RA PP/1/58/59 Lady Conroy to Queen Victoria, 9th March 1854.

14 RA PP/1/58/60 Colonel Phipps [?] to Lady Conroy. draft, no date.

15 Hanmer Papers 11th November 1854 and others.

16 RA Z484/54 Sir George Couper's Memorandum.

17 RA Z 484/62 Sir George Couper's Memorandum.

18 CP 9A Sir George Couper to Sir Edward Conroy and note by E.C.

on envelope, 9th May 1854.

19 CP 9A. 10 History of the Llanbrynmair Estate.

20 CP 3E.C Statement, 31st December 1875, Sir John Conroy Third Baronet.

21 Drummond's Bank. Princess Sophia's Account.

22 *The Letters of King George IV*, 1812–30, Vol III no's 11196, 1197, 1198.

23 CP 3c. 11&12; 3c 15.

24 RA Z 481/2 Memorandum by Sir John Conroy. Also Conroy Papers. Add. Mss.

25 RA Z 484/36 in George Couper's Memorandum, 3rd April 1850.

26 RA Add. MSS, A/11/25 Statement of Her Royal Highness the Duchess of Kent's Account to 30th June 1837. Sir John Conroy to Baron Stockmar.

27 RA Add MSS A/11/23 Sir John Conroy to Baron Stockmar, 23rd June 1837.

28 RA Y 154/36 Lord Liverpool to Baron Stockmar, 8th January 1838.

29 RA Y 154/33 Lord Liverpool to Baron Stockmar, 10th August 1837.

30 RA Z484/55 Sir George Couper to the Duchess of Kent.

31 RA Z 485/6 Mrs Frances Conroy's Memorandum.

32 RA Z 482/ 26 Memorandum.

33 RA Z 482/1 Sir John Conroy to the Duchess of Kent, 15th July 1837.

34 CP 6. H 28th April 1843.

35 RA Y 74/63 King Leopold of the Belgians to Queen Victoria, 22nd July 1848.

36 RA Z 481/2 Memorandum by Sir John Conroy.

37 RA Z 485/6 Mrs Frances Conroy's Memorandum.

38 RA Z 484/40 The Duchess of Kent to Queen Victoria, 2nd March 1854.

39 RA Z 484/43 Queen Victoria to the Duchess of Kent, 5th March 1854.

40 RA Z294 The Journal of the Duchess of Kent.

41 RA Z 484/53 The Duchess of Kent to Sir George Couper.

Notes

Epilogue (pp. 215–20)

1 CP 6C   Love letters between Edward Conroy and 'Mary', *c*. 1847.

2 CP 6A   Correspondence concerning identity of 'Emily' 1869.

3 For more on 'Emily' the reader is referred to *The Conroy Papers* by Katherine Hudson and John Jones, Balliol College Library, 1987.

4 CP 2A D   Conroy family letters to the Third Baronet.

5 CP 2A D ibid.

6 CP10.4   Letter attached to account of Edward's elopement.

7 RA Z 485/6   Mrs Frances Conroy's Memorandum.

8 CP 1C.E   Sir John Conroy to Mrs Frances Conroy, 13th June 1893.

9 CP 1C.E (?)   Mrs Frances Conroy to Sir John Conroy, 15th November 1890.

10 CP 2. AF   Sir John Conroy to Henry Conroy, 25th October 1885.

11 RA Z485/6   Mrs Frances Conroy's Memorandum.

12 CP 1C.B   Mrs Frances Conroy to Sir John Conroy, 21st November 1890.

13 CP 1C.E   Sir John Conroy to Mrs Frances Conroy, (?) 26th November 1890.

14 RA Z485/6   Mrs Frances Conroy's Memorandum.

15 Details taken from an account in the *Reading Mercury*, Saturday, 15th June 1963. Vandals have since robbed the church of its contents (1992).

APPENDIX

The Conroy Papers

The Conroy Papers constitutes the entire collection of papers concerning the three Baronets Conroy and their families, lives and interests. The papers were left to Balliol College, Oxford, by the Third Baronet, Sir John Conroy, through his executor E.J. Palmer. They consisted originally of four items – 9A (9B) 9C and 10 – and contained the genealogy of the Conroy family plus a quantity of papers relating to the First and Second Baronets (Sir John Conroy and Sir Edward Conroy) and their families. These papers (which came to the College. *c.* 1900) included a number of letters from the Duchess of Kent. Another box of scientific papers was discovered in the Balliol Science Library, Oxford, in 1968.

Around 1974 the Collection was augmented by a large quantity of papers (1A, B – 8 inclusive, and 12, 13) via descendants of the executor of the Third Baronet's Will. This deposit was further added to during the 1980s (14A,B. 14B +) and presumably completes the original material Willed to the College. Until 1974 only 9A – 10 were available for study in Balliol College Library; however the rest of the Collection was known to Miss D. M. Stuart who, with permission from E.J. Palmer, used some items in her book *The Mother of Queen Victoria*.

The material falls into two distinct groups: papers relating to the first Baronet, Sir John Conroy, his family and career – which are especially rich in papers concerning his service with the Duchess of Kent and Princess Sophia. And the life and career of the Third Baronet, which illuminates the Oxford scene of the late nineteenth century, Balliol College and scientific and High Church affairs. The papers were listed by John Jones and Katherine Hudson from 1975 to 1977. *The Conroy Papers: A Guide* was published by Balliol College in 1987.

LIST OF PRINCIPAL SOURCES

Manuscript material

Royal Archives (RA), Windsor
The Conroy Papers (CP), Balliol College, Oxford
Peel Papers (BM Add. MSS), British Library
Hanmer Papers (Private)
Hastings Papers, Henry E. Huntington Library, California
Lambton Papers (LP), Lambton Park
Fisher Collection (Private)

Published material

Victoria. R.I., Elizabeth Longford, Weidenfeld and Nicolson, 1964

Queen Victoria Her Life and Times, Vol. 1 1819–61, Cecil Woodham-Smith, Hamish Hamilton, 1972

The Letters of King George IV 1812–1830, 3 Vols. Edited by A. Aspinall, Cambridge University Press, 1938

Memoirs of the Court of George IV 1820–1830 Vol. 1, Duke of Buckingham and Chandos, London 1859

The Journal of Mrs Arbuthnot 1820–1832, Edited by Francis Bamford and the Duke of Wellington, Macmillan & Co. 1950

The Creevey Papers A selection from the Correspondence and Diaries of the late Thomas Creevey MP, Edited by Sir Herbert Maxwell, 1903

The *Lieven–Palmerston Correspondence* 1828–1856 John Murray, 1905, Translated and Edited by Lord Sudley, John Murray, 1943

The Memoirs of Baron Stockmar, Baron E. von Stockmar, Longmans, 1872

The Letters of Queen Victoria (1837–1861) Vol. 1, John Murray, 1907

The Greville Memoirs A Journal of the Reigns of George IV and King William IV, Charles C.F. Greville, Longmans 1875

Letters of Harriet Countess Granville 1810–1845, Edited by F. Leveson Gower, Longmans, 1894

John Constable and the Fishers, R.B. Beckett, Suffolk Records Society

The First Lady Wharncliffe and her Family (1779–1856), Caroline Grosvenor and Charles Beilby, 1927

Melbourne A Biography of William Lamb, 2nd Viscount Melbourne, Collins, Philip Ziegler 1976

Lord Durham, A Biography of John George Lambton, First Earl of Durham, Chester W. New, Oxford 1929

The Conroy Papers: A Guide Katherine Hudson and John Jones, Balliol College, Oxford, 1987

INDEX

Watts, Joseph, 78–9
Wellesley, Richard Colley Wellesley, Marquis of, 196, 215
Wellington, Arthur Wellesley, 1st Duke of: on JC's relations with Duchess of Kent, 16, 105; Duke of Kent recommends JC to, 34; political influence, 39; denies promotion to JC, 42, 44–6; JC first meets, 44; at Victoria's birth, 47; Duchess of Kent writes to on JC's behalf, 54; 1828 administration, 58; wishes Victoria brought up in English court, 61; supports Duchess of Kent as Regent, 63, 76–7, 210; influence on George IV, 75; and Späth, 82; and proposed Parliamentary grant for Victoria, 123; Duchess of Kent plays whist with, 141; fairmindedness, 153; urges reconciliation between Victoria and mother, 155; and JC's resignation from Duchess of Kent's service, 159–60, 162; farming, 180
Wetherall, General Sir Frederick Augustus, 41, 49, 52–3, 203
Wharncliffe, Elizabeth Caroline Mary, Lady, 56, 97, 186
Wheatley, Sir Henry, 142
Whigs: support Kensington System, 56; and Reform, 89; Victoria favours, 140–1
Wight, Isle of: Norris Castle, 97–9
William IV, King (*formerly* Duke of Clarence): and Victoria's visit to Oxford, 2; children (*bâtards*), 12, 83, 92; marriage, 40, 45; and succession, 48; influence on Duchess of Kent, 57; accession, 75; qualities, 75–6; and care of Victoria, 77; and Victoria's tours, 78, 88, 93; and status of monarchy, 80; and Lehzen, 83; animosity to Duchess of Kent, 84, 90–2, 118–20; despises Leopold, 84, 115; dislike of JC, 84–5, 118, 120; and Reform, 89; objects to Victoria's name and title, 91; refuses improvements to Kensington Palace, 91, 119; coronation, 92, 118; objects to salutes for *Emerald*, 97; failing health, 101, 120, 122, 124–6, 128; displeased at JC's Portuguese honours, 111; obstructs Coburgs' visit, 115–16, 186–7; and Victoria's marriage plans, 115; seeks Parliamentary allowance for Victoria, 122–3; death, 130; money gift to Duchess of Kent, 198
Wilson, Francis Vernon, 28
Wilson, Martha, 84
Woolwich, 44–5
Württemberg, Antoinette, Queen of (Duchess of Kent's sister), 114
Württemberg, Charlotte, Queen of (Duchess of Kent's aunt), 65
Württemberg, Ernest, Prince of, 114
Wylde, Colonel, 199

York, Frederick, Duke of, 40, 202–3